# Radical Orthodoxy: Annual Review
## Series Preface

IF WE ARE TO believe some important contemporary sociologists, today secularism is in crisis and we are currently witnessing "the return of religion" within the cracks opened up by the failures of the late modern liberal project. Even those on the political left who had once viewed Judeo-Christian religion as an "absurd break" on historical inevitability now often recognize that there is a need to keep hold of the general form of religious belief—if not its specific content—as it is this form, especially its openness to the idea of a redemptive future, that is seen as the tacit theological basis of any progressive politics conceived as both transformative and unidirectional. However, the new theological turn in contemporary thought only takes this issue so far. Although it has little problem with the phenomenological dimensions of religion (religion as a "way of worlding" and a collective mode of experiencing and so forth) it has paid little respect to the specific institutional supports for religion as a cultural-metaphysical reality. For cultural Christianity would be *nothing* without the work of Christian institutions whose historic mission has been to protect what they have perceived to be its most important metaphysical treasures.

Here we can see why the next stage in the so-called theological turn inevitably takes this discussion onto the conceptual terrain mapped out over the years by Radical Orthodoxy. Radical Orthodoxy has always attempted to move theology into the modern political sphere and the times are now ripe for an intensification of this aspect of the RO project. *Radical Orthodoxy: Annual Review* will aim to facilitate this aspect of RO and in this way, we hope, to give the theological turn a new relevance, a clearer sense of purpose, as well as a sharper critical edge. The *Annual Review* will appear in November/December of each year and it will address the themes that we believe are beginning to (re)define contemporary intellectual agendas. It will draw on the papers submitted to the journal *Radical*

*Orthodoxy: Theology, Philosophy, and Politics,* work done at the *Centre of Theology and Philosophy's* international conferences, along with specially commissioned work. As Radical Orthodoxy (RO) seeks to intensify its intellectual energies around new theologico-political concerns, the *Annual Review* will often approach these issues with an alternative philosophical eye and with a view to prizing open wider contemporary problematics. Given the radical ontological and political uncertainties that abound at the beginning of the twenty-first century, it is now important to find ways towards a new theological understanding of the contemporary and the *Radical Orthodoxy: Annual Review* will attempt to give significant impetus to such initiatives. The *Annual Review* will thus explore a much broader range of topics than those traditionally covered in standard theology and philosophy publications, and we are open to suggestions from thinkers in all academic fields, especially those whose work opens up cutting edge theological and philosophical issues, to contribute to future issues. To this end, the *Radical Orthodoxy: Annual Review* will also publish interviews with some of the most important thinkers of the day, as well as reviews of cultural events and commentaries on the theological and philosophical dimensions of public life in Western societies.

# RADICAL ORTHODOXY

Theology, Philosophy, Politics

AN ONLINE JOURNAL
www.journal.radicalorthodoxy.org

---

**Editor:**
Neil Turnbull (Nottingham Trent University)

**Editorial Board:**
Peter M Candler, Jr. (Baylor University)
Conor Cunningham (University of Nottingham)
Andrew Davison (Oxford University)
Alessandra Gerolin (Catholic University of the Sacred Heart, Milan)
Michael Hanby (Baylor University)
John Milbank (University of Nottingham)
Simon Oliver (University of Nottingham)
Adrian Pabst (University of Kent)
Catherine Pickstock (University of Cambridge)
Aaron Riches (Edith Stein Institute, Granada)
Tracey Rowland (Jean-Paul II Institute)

*Radical Orthodoxy: Theology, Philosophy, Politics* is a new online journal dedicated to the discussion of the proposition that creedally orthodox Christianity is the most transformative of all cultural phenomena and that it remains the ineliminable core of the Middle-Eastern and European-originated civilizational project. It freely invites contributions both from those who agree with this proposition—in whatever sense—and those who reject it.

The journal intends uniquely to combine the academic and the current; the intellectual and the popular. To this end it intends to publish both pieces longer and shorter than those carried by the typical academic journal, as well as some of the usual length: taking full advantage of the flexibility offered by the online format.

"Theology" is taken to include theologies of all kinds, besides a predominant concern with the implications of orthodox Christian theology in particular. "Philosophy" is intended in the most ample possible sense, to include all the various schools, Eastern and Western, ancient, medieval, and modern, continental and analytic. It is also taken to extend to all branches of aesthetics, including literary, art, and music criticism, besides the philosophy of science. "Politics" is taken to include both political theory in the past and the present, and political practice, especially in the present. More widely, it is intended to indicate the entire practical branch of philosophy, and so to cover also ethical, social, economic, and cultural theory.

The journal will normally be published four times a year in the usual mix of standard and special issues. We intend to publish a diverse range of submitted articles and reviews as well as pieces that seek to mediate between academic and media analyses of contemporary events and cultural conditions. All articles will be peer-reviewed, because a further aim of the journal is to combine relevance with rigor, as well as rigor with relevance.

# RADICAL ORTHODOXY

Annual Review I

# RADICAL ORTHODOXY

Annual Review I

EDITED BY
Neil Turnbull

CASCADE *Books* • Eugene, Oregon

RADICAL ORTHODOXY: ANNUAL REVIEW I

Radical Orthodoxy: Annual Review Series 1

Copyright © 2012 Wipf and Stock Publishers. All rights reserved. Except for brief quotations in critical publications or reviews, no part of this book may be reproduced in any manner without prior written permission from the publisher. Write: Permissions, Wipf and Stock Publishers, 199 W. 8th Ave., Suite 3, Eugene, OR 97401.

Cascade Books
A Division of Wipf and Stock Publishers
199 W. 8th Ave., Suite 3
Eugene, OR 97401

www.wipfandstock.com

ISBN 13: 978-1-62032-604-6

*Cataloging-in-Publication data:*

Radical Orthodoxy : annual review I / edited by Neil Turnbull.

Radical Orthodoxy: Annual Review Series 1

xiv + 212 p. ; 23 cm. Includes bibliographical references.

ISBN 13: 978-1-62032-604-6

1. Metaphysics. 2. Philosophical theology. 3. Postmodern theology. 4. Religion and science. I. Series. II. Title.

BT40 T894 2012

Manufactured in the U.S.A.

# Contents

*Contributors xi*

*Acknowledgments xiii*

Introduction: Metaphysics and Politics in the Age of Neo-Liberalism | 1
*Neil Turnbull*

1 On the Surface of Things: Transient Life and Beauty in Passing | 19
*William Desmond*

2 Affect: Towards a Theology of Experience | 51
*Graham Ward*

3 On the Natural Desire of Seeing God | 75
*Louis Dupré*

4 Life, or Gift and Glissando: Evolution, Vitalism, and Transcendence | 87
*John Milbank*

5 *Analogia Naturae:* What Does Inanimate Matter Contribute to the Meaning of Life? | 114
*David C. Schindler*

6 A Short Meta-Critique of Quentin Meillassoux's Divine Nihilism | 138
*Conor Cunningham*

7 Persons or Creatures? Sellars, Whitehead, and the Metaphysical Problem of Late Modernity | 152
*Neil Turnbull*

*Contents*

  **8**  Taking Life out of Nature: Jewish Messianic Vitalism and the Problem of Denaturalization | 180
*Agata Bielek Robson*

  **9**  Reason and Church Social Doctrine: Benedict XVI and the Renewal of Tradition (2005–2008) | 199
*Evandro Botto*

# Contributors

**Agata Bielik-Robson** is currently Professor of Jewish Studies at the University of Nottingham. Her publications include the book *The Saving Lie: Harold Bloom and Deconstruction*.

**Evandro Botto** is Professor of History of Philosophy at the Catholic University of the Holy Heart, Milan. He is Director of the Athenaeum Centre for the Social Doctrine of the Church.

**Conor Cunningham** is Lecturer in Theology and Religious Studies at the University of Nottingham. He is the author of *Genealogy of Nihilism* and *Darwin's Pious Idea*.

**William Desmond** is Professor of Philosophy at the Institute of Philosophy at Katholieke Universiteit (Leuven, Belgium) and the David Cook Visiting Chair in Philosophy at Villanova University (USA). He is the author of the trilogy *Being and the Between*, *Ethics and the Between*, and *God and the Between*.

**Louis Dupré** was T. Lawrason Riggs Professor in the Philosophy of Religion at Yale University. He has published fifteen original books, and four collective works, in addition to some 200 articles in professional journals, collective works, and encyclopedias.

**John Milbank** is Professor of Religion, Politics, and Ethics at the University of Nottingham. He is the author of several books of which the most well known is *Theology and Social Theory* and the most recent *Being Reconciled: Ontology and Pardon*.

**D. C. Schindler** is currently an Associate Professor of Philosophy in the Department of Humanities at Villanova University. He is the author of several books, including the forthcoming *The Perfection of Freedom: Schiller, Schelling, and Hegel between the Ancients and the Moderns*.

*Contributors*

**Neil Turnbull** is Principal Lecturer in Philosophy at Nottingham Trent University. He has published a number of academic articles and book chapters in philosophy and social theory and has a number of forthcoming books.

**Graham Ward** is the Regius Professor of Divinity at the University of Oxford and former Head of the School of Arts, Histories and Cultures at the University of Manchester. Among his books are *Cities of God* and *Cultural Transformation and Religious Practice*.

# Acknowledgements

MANY THANKS TO ALL those who helped in bringing this initiative to fruition. Thanks especially to Eric Lee for his technical skill and his wise theological eye. Thanks also to John Milbank and Conor Cunningham for their unceasing support. But most of all thanks go out to my long-suffering family whose love and patience never cease to astound me.

# Introduction

## Metaphysics and Politics in the Age of Neo-Liberalism

*Neil Turnbull*

≈

### Radical Orthodoxy: Post-Enlightenment Metaphysicians

EVERYONE INTERESTED IN THE trajectories of contemporary philosophical and theological debate should already be very familiar with the now ubiquitous thesis that the intellectual parameters of Western modernity were forged in the intellectual crucible of the European Enlightenment. In fact, this thesis has been the habitual starting point for many styles of contemporary critique, and currently amounts to something of a normative intellectual framework for the post-Marxist left. According to this view, the Enlightenment, through a thoroughgoing naturalization of the pre-modern *Weltanschauung*, put "thought in its proper place" and created a climate of suspicion against the very idea of "the metaphysical" that has continued into the present. In so doing, it is widely perceived to have brought about the conditions for the emergence of "democratizing" forces and movements that necessarily cut against and across religious cultures and institutions.[1] In fact, when viewed by these lights, the appearance of the Enlightenment is typically conceived as an "event" in the world-historical sense of the term—a radical break or rupture in world history that was to lead to the eventual emergence of the modern democratic state and the mass-industrialization of the economic, social, and cultural realms. In

---

1. Forces that continue to play themselves out historically on the world stage; even though their basis "in any adequate political philosophy" has long since evaporated.

this way, the Enlightenment is seen to have given rise to a new universal political condition where the kingdom of God—the heavenly kingdom "above," previously extolled by organized Christianity—was replaced by the secular historical "kingdom of individual conscience," a kingdom where, as Schiller recognized, history itself, rather than a transcendent good, becomes the world's judgment.[2] However, in the concluding decades of the twentieth century, spurred on by the idea that new technological innovations were bringing to an end Enlightenment ideals of individualism, democratization, and political progress, a new counter-Enlightenment ethos emerged; in philosophical terms one largely associated with the anti-rationalist, anti-foundationalism of the linguistic turn and its associated post-68 modes of French cultural criticism. As is well known, in this context a number of philosophers mounted a forceful attack on both Enlightenment universalism (typically on the ground of Nietzschean perspectivism) and on its possessive sovereign individualism (often on the ground of a post-humanist cybernetic subjectivity). However, these critiques, although supremely useful in reopening philosophical debates that had been diminished to mere antique curiosities, only succeeded in securing the pyrrhic victory of an essentially ludic philosophy that was, with the benefit of hindsight, entirely on all fours with a new informational capitalism.[3] In fact, the "post-structuralist" attack on the Enlightenment, in the end, spawned a philistine anti-intellectual culture of feeling and dandy-like modes of self-presentation that, in reality, were little more than facile posturings against a (disavowed) political reality, of capital seemingly globally triumphant.

Furthermore, the recent counter-Enlightenment era, that was also the era of the end of the great "modern ideologies," proved to be little more than one of comfort and ease for an expanded global intellectual elite increasingly unsure of its ultimate moral and political purpose. This state of affairs came at a significant cultural cost, especially at the level of the general social intellect; as for many today non-instrumental thinking—and perhaps even, more importantly, "the very capacity to philosophize"—has become truncated through a seemingly endless "propagandizing of being" within the deafeningly hegemonic market-driven cultures of perpetual self-promotion. One specific cultural consequence of all this is that, outside of a few "doggedly classicist" philosophical spaces, what might be termed

---

2. See Ridley Scott's film, *The Kingdom of Heaven*.

3. A capitalism that is completely relaxed about, often positively celebratory of, the existence of radically antinomian subjectivities.

"authentic thought," thinking about the universals that generate "belief" and that transcend the narrow of confines of disciplinary paradigms, is now widely perceived as "bizarre" and the philosophical desire to discern a "true conceptuality" from within the maelstrom of (modern) experience is increasingly rendered null and void. There are many ways to account for the emergence of this culture of *denkverboten*, some of which have already been mentioned; but one important reason is that late modern culture has disconnected thinking from being, as well as from the perennial intellectual quest to understand "the whole" and humanity's place within it—that is, from *metaphysics*. It may sound excessively nostalgic, and not little overly conservative, to claim that concepts were once "adventurous" and that metaphysical thinking once "mattered." However, whatever one thinks of this claim, it is indisputable that the many and various attacks on metaphysics that dominated Western intellectual life in the past 100 years have given real credence to the idea that thought, thoughtfulness, and a creedal understanding of the world more generally had greater potency in those eras that valued not only thoughts' efficacy but also its sanctity.

It has been the very great merit of Radical Orthodoxy (RO) over the years to be a staunch defender of authentic thought (and the metaphysical spirit more generally) in an age dominated by thoughtless pragmatism, social constructivism, and the forms of cybernetic solipsism that have been definitive of the recent counter-Enlightenment era.[4] In relation to this ongoing philosophical catastrophe, the intriguing beauty and intellectual bravery of RO has stemmed from its willingness to contest contemporary discourses on the Enlightenment in the name of another, grander, ideal of reason; that is without being led down the blind allies of relativism and aestheticism associated with the post-structuralist moment. In its attempts to provide contemporary intellectual life with "another orthodoxy"—one simultaneously more theological and more radical in its willingness to challenge the "false conventionalizations" of late modernity—RO has offered us the possibility of another *Ausgang*, an exit, but this time lit up by a broadly Catholic metaphysical vision of ethics, politics, and epistemology.[5]

4. It is difficult today to say precisely what the RO constituency is. This is because its influence now spreads way beyond theology and even beyond the confines of the academy. Clearly, the founders of the movement—John Milbank, Catherine Pickstock, and Graham Ward—are still important, as is the contribution of younger members such as Conor Cunnigham and Adrian Pabst. However, there are many more who would identify themselves with RO in terms of its overall dispensation, far too many to mention here.

5. From an Enlightenment ideal, that, as Adorno and Horkheimer recognized, seems to be radically and perpetually self-undermining.

In making this move, RO has presented an alternative account of "natural order" through an integral conception of existence that denies the historical inevitability of the Enlightenment of dream of free-standing autonomous individuals (and of scientific naturalism more generally) on precise metaphysical grounds. In so doing, it has pointed us towards an ethical and political critique of the modern metaphysical order of birth, predation, and death in the name of *another universal*—a creedally orthodox Christianity. The idea of nature as a self-contained, self-organizing, system—nature as a monad, Spinoza's God—that has no "outside" is here rejected in favor of an idea of "nature as creature" that stands in relation to a transcendent that "graces" everything as beautiful, worthy of wonder, and radically open to human forms of investigation and inquiry.[6] The philosophical question of human nature, the anthropological question, also looms large in this context, and in the context of late-modern metaphysical and political problematics RO has called for a more authentic humanism within which there can be no knowledge or self-knowledge in isolation from an idea of the good (thus beginning the long process towards a viable idea of "ethical knowing," the only epistemology that can, in the last Marxist analysis, save late modernity from itself).[7]

---

6. In RO discourse there must of necessity be an "outside" (or a beyond) to all things as there is no *quidditas* without a constitutional transcendent. Seen thus, a Leibnizian idea of worldhood is not only impossible but also radically counter-ethical. Ethics, we might say, requires a conception of being that is always something more than the philosophical articulation of "being as system."

7. As is now well known, in modern positivism the methods of experimental science were widely understood to have provided general criteria allowing for a final demarcation between authentic knowledge and what is "merely expressed or shown." As a consequence, in positivist thinking, all forms of ethical reflection and judgment were relegated to the subjective realm, and any talk of "ethical thinking"—or "ethical knowing"—were seen as "category mistakes." In the positivist's epistemological universe, where "the ethical cannot know," modern science asserted its own counter-ethics: that we should refrain from using ethical terms when making epistemological claims, as the former cannot be assimilated into a "unified science" defined as a final historical totality of scientific theory. Against this, RO takes up a familiar hermeneutic position in viewing scientific knowledge as a sub-species of "interpretation" and "understanding," and in so doing, in it opens the way to the viewing all knowledge as both infused with and guided by wider sets of values. Seen thus, modern science represents, as modern hermeneuts have always recognized, "only *one* type of knowledge' that "cannot be taken as the canonical standard for all forms of knowledge." Bernstein, "Introduction," 9. However, RO goes beyond the standard hermeneutic critique of scientific positivism in many respects. It rejects Heidegger's claim that "science does not think." In RO scientific thought (and knowledge) *is possible* via a "prior illumination," that is through a specific relation to the divine. For RO, without this prior metaphysical relation, science would be little more that a useful fiction and a blind instrumentalism.

In this way, RO has offered us an ontological redefinition of modernity; a modernity where the task of authentic social and political critique is seen as a "bringing modernity home," back to its origins in a re-instituted—*heimlich*—rational theo-ontology; to a *world created*, a world of mutual participation and belonging.[8] Thus RO recognizes that metaphysics always has implications for how we understand the nature and extent of *the political*. When politics is reconceived along these lines it can no longer be viewed as an attempt to devise a "regime" capable of a better management of an increasingly recalcitrant polity, but (re)appears as something that satisfies the deeper anthropological and ontological demand for home, community, and ontological security.[9] Modernity's Machiavellian politics—which denies the political significance of the metaphysical in its endorsement of a political naturalism—forgets this and in so doing presents us with a conception of politics that is radically pathological (only livable in terms of self-destructive drives for power and hollow forms of self-glorification). As RO has pointed out, the consequences of a politics without a supporting metaphysics are deeply nihilistic, revealing the extent to which modern forms of politics have undermined their attempts at (a manipulative) worldly self-founding—because all such attempts produce the, now universal, debilitating existential symptom that "nothing is inherently worth doing" and that there is a "terrifying emptiness lurking beneath all things."[10]

---

8. The Kantian good will—the will as informed only by duty—is thus not necessarily good and can, in its detached coldness, be seen as evil. The political implications of this conception of the good, the horrors of the 1930s, have been well documented in contemporary social thought.

9. The "Enlightenment thesis" neglected to take into account the way in which modernity's most significant organizational form—the modern state—legitimized, and continues to legitimize, itself via the re-invention and redeployment of orthodox religious values, symbols, and institutions. Thus, the modern state cannot simply be conceived as religion's functional secular replacement (as Hegel suggested). It is, in fact, more usefully conceived as founded upon what Weber would have termed "quasi-charismatic factors"—to the extent that the modern state, and *mutandis mutatis* modernity itself, must be seen as, essentially, a theological-political reality. Seen thus, the "event of modernity" did not give rise to secularizing movements *as such*, but rather to new theologico-political configurations where religious factors and forces were more subtly, but no less centrally, significant. Therefore secularization to a large extent involved the recuperation of religious values and symbols and their subtle redeployment as instruments of much wider social and political projects. In this way, Modernity often requires, and sometimes demands, its own ersatz religion as a necessary but "dangerous" supplement to its political projects.

10. See Taylor, *Sources*, 18.

For RO, then, any progressive politics, any attempt to engage with the world and transform it, presupposes a metaphysics and ultimately a *theology*. In this vein, John Milbank has asked contemporary socialists to consider taking up a Platonic vision of socialism that acknowledges, as a necessity, a conception of a "transcendent good" in all of its radical discourses and forms of political action. In his view, only a strong, "metaphysically grounded," idea of the good can provide us with a meaningful critique of capitalism today after the demise of the grand dialectical Hegelian "metanarrative" (one that, in the end, RO has revealed to be little more than a heterodox mode of Christianity anyway).[11] Through this double politicization—a politicization of theology and a theologization of politics—RO theologians have begun to transform the way we understand modernity through a rethinking of the nature of knowledge, the city, nature, technology, politics, culture, and society; thus showing why metaphysics must be part of and essential to any attempt to understand modern social reality in all its complexity and uncertainty. Unusual within the academy of today, RO *is widely noticed*; and with good reason. By way of anecdote, my experience of RO conferences and seminar events has been one of an experience of a profound non-dogmatic openness to authentic thought; one that supports a wide-raging and inclusive conversation—not grounded in fashion—founded upon an appreciation of the perennial need for serious philosophical reflection on the serious issues of the day. In a spirit of "true liberalism," for me, RO has stood for the enactment of a universalism expressed as an embodied hospitality—what might also be termed *a true cosmopolitanism*—and a *contra sec* attitude to all forms of intellectual inquiry.

RO's vision has always also been profoundly sociological—or perhaps better "counter-sociological." In fact, RO has, ever since John Milbank's groundbreaking *Theology and Social Theory*, occupied a position in between Marxist, Weberian, and Durkheimian sociologies, exposing all three of these modernist acids to the universal alkali of theological reflection. As a result, in the neutralization of orthodox sociology and in its search for a new theologically-inspired conception of the social, RO has developed a sharp critical sociological edge; exposing the orthodox sociological vision of the world as one that, in its radical *exclusivity*, is profoundly at odds with humanity's true universal vocation.[12] It may

---

11. See Milbank, "The Double Glory," 112.

12. And showing the extent to which what Whitehead was to term "the industrial freedom" of the Protestant era, the freedom that has, in many ways, been the primary object of sociological reflection, was an expression of a "bad metaphysics." Whitehead,

sound odd, to some, to view as both "radical and critical" a movement that is conservative in its theological orientation, but Western societies are changing very rapidly, and old allegiances and historic animosities are shifting at a pace[13]—and in many ways RO today now presents itself as much a cultural and political movement, occupying the space of what used to be called "the left," as it is a straightforwardly theological one.[14] Importantly, RO is now a cultural signifier for a non-reactionary, theologically informed politics within a new political imaginary where a Christian conception of the significance of worldly life is recognized as the necessary intellectual anchor required of any project of radical social change.[15] When viewed in this way, what has been (historically) important about RO has been the way in which it has recognized that theology and metaphysics are much more than academic disciplines. Especially by dint of its alternative version of the philosophical history of the West—one that, in the near future, may well emerge as paradigmatic—RO has reconstituted a uniquely Christian yet profoundly modern metaphysico-political vision that draws together a number of important—"critical"—political motifs implicit within orthodox Christian theology. Three in particular stand out in this regard: a liturgical critique of modernity via a neo-Platonic appeal to ideas of "higher causes" and the need for more "enlightened elites"; a critique of liberalism as the political form of the self-possessive, "Scotist," metaphysics of freedom that downplays the social and political dimensions of human existence; and an attack on the "univocity" of a capitalist modernity that closes down all possibility of transcendence.[16]

---

*Adventures*, 33–36.

13. Western economies and polities are currently in crisis, with no obvious long-term solution in sight other than through labor intensification and heightened forms of social control. The slow corrosion of a liberal version of modernity that began in the 1930s (with the rise modern political paganism) has now begun to affect modernity's liberal ideological core; rendering liberalism a busted historical flush without the support of techno-scientific forms of innovation. However, increasingly hollow—and often downright hypocritical—political voices within the academy have remained eerily silent on the wider significance of this "event"; an event that has already happened, but one that in, a Pauline manner, we now have to decide how to act upon and find a way to construct a viable political response.

14. See Milbank, "The Grandeur of Reason," 367.

15. What is needed today is an "innovative" realignment of intellectual and political forces, and in order to achieve this, some significant conceptual revision, perhaps even a new metaphysics, will be is needed. RO has been at the forefront of such calls.

16. See Pickstock, "Duns Scotus."

It is with great pleasure, then, that we can announce the next phase of RO; one that, in building upon these theological initiatives, is now beginning to explore in a more systematic and purposeful manner the way in which an alternative Christianized metaphysical account of the modern (and its pathologies) can provide the basis for an *alternative modernity*: one based on the "real political universals" of the *common good* and the *ennoblement of the individual*. Through the new on-line journal *Radical Orthodoxy: Theology, Philosophy, Politics*, RO is now expressing its theological voice in order to address the contemporary crisis of capitalism (and the West more generally); and this publication, *The RO Annual Review*, will publish a selection of what we believe to have been the most interesting and pertinent submissions to the journal over the last year (plus others that we feel reflect the importance of the new agenda). Thus importantly, for those, like myself, who still identify with the ideals of the "old left," RO now stands as an important resource for all those wanting to expose the philosophical errors of the neo-liberal era; an era that, in denying the reality of the social—a reality of ontological relation and relatedness, that is ultimately a reality of belonging and participation—denies the truth of the human condition.[17] In this regard, RO points out that only a Christianization of politics and society can begin to repair the damage done to the social fabric of Western modernity in the last forty years—an idea whose time has now come.

## Ethics, Politics, and the Metaphysics of Life

Politics is obviously an activity that not only takes place within life, but is also, if the term is to mean anything at all, an activity that presupposes an idea of life as good, meaningful, and significant. However, to say this is to claim that politics always presumes a metaphysics, in this context one that allows us to discern the nature of the relationship between primordial life and collective human living. However, today, the precise content of any such metaphysics is shrouded in controversy, especially since a

---

17. More specifically, as a new alliance of orthodox theology and what remains of the orthodox, pre-culturalist, and pre-individualist left, RO has emerged at the center of a new social and political agenda, one that is attempting to reclaim, for a new Christian political vision, the vacated "social-democratic" intellectual territory once occupied by Keynes, Rawls, and Habermas et al. One of the most egregious problems of the last forty years, in political terms, has been the result of a left posing as a "radicalism without a tradition" and its wrong-headed flirtation with social and political liberalism can be seen as symptomatic of this.

culturally dominant liberalism now operates in collaboration with a naturalistic metaphysics that conceives of life, reductively, as a set of causal processes within a larger, causally ordered cosmos. Liberalism, we might say, has claimed a monopoly on "the meaning of life" (or perhaps better, given its restriction of life to one of struggle and survival, "the meaninglessness of life"). Importantly, contemporary liberalism demonstrates why all metaphysical questions surrounding the nature of life today are inherently political—as contemporary Foucauldians have observed—and why the philosophical question of life takes thought beyond technically-circumscribed vistas.

The papers contained in this volume were first delivered at the *Centre of Theology and Philosophy* conference in Krakow in June 2011 and are all, some more explicitly than others, dedicated to an examination of this issue. All explore, in their own way, the issue of how an understanding of what life *is* conditions our specific claims on how it should be lived both personally and collectively in a way that points both the theologian and philosopher towards another idea of modern life. Some attempt this through a reconsideration of the theological, philosophical, and political significance of the neo-Bergsonian "new vitalist" philosophical moment in contemporary philosophy; others through a theological critique of modern naturalism and biologism; others still, by attempting to forge a break with scientific metaphysics in a way that makes human life appear more redolent with theological and, ultimately, ethical and political significance. Taken as a whole, the papers contained here address the issue of how a metaphysical conception of life impacts upon the wider social, cultural, and political conditions under which we, in the West, now live; and why a theologically informed conception of life offers us a way out of a late-modern philosophical terrain that, to many, appears to be a sterile and incapacitating intellectual landscape. The discussion is ongoing, but we hope that these offerings represent the beginnings of a new appreciation of the way in which Christian theology and philosophy can begin to contribute to a deeper and more sophisticated understanding of the ethics, politics, and metaphysics of a modernity that now, more than ever, needs a new philosophical identity and a renewed theological sense of direction.

William Desmond, in his piece, explores the philosophical dimensions of life through his now—increasingly celebrated—idea of *metaxu*, "the between." Desmond's perspective is in many ways inspired by Heidegger, in that he emphasizes the importance of the "happening of being" and the poetics of an "originary coming to be" in an openness that suggests the need for metaphysics beyond a univocal givenness. As such, he takes Heideggereanism beyond its Husserlian preoccupations with "the thing" into a genuinely innovative metaphysical vision that views things as "spaces" open to the possibility of transcendence. In the piece published here, he develops this perspective in relation to the philosophical problem of transience and surfacing. Surfaces, he argues, are an important example of a metaxological relation, as they are porous openings through which we are "given to be." Surfaces thus open onto a series of "other relations," to an order of creation that is more primordial than that of evolution. This is an order of being that is more to do with passion and relation than to the Spinozist metaphysics of self-preservation—thus showing the extent to which the modern liberal "striving to be," to preserve oneself in the face of Hobbessian liberal "war of all against all," is in fact a flight from oneself and from the true source that allows one to be. In order to appreciate the importance of "life on the surface," Desmond suggests that we require a different sense of mindfulness, one that recognizes that surfaces are in fact the depths—thresholds between "the above" and "the below." Surfaces, we might say, force us to recognize the importance of the ontology of the vertical—an ontology that the horizontal metaphysics of modernity cannot conceive of (an important theme in RO discussion over the years)—and an ethics and politics that is always open to a beyond. In this way, Desmond shows us how to bring the modern back to the surface, back from its buried forgetfulness in the modern mine; a modernity where, as Freud recognized, the truth can only be "unearthed."

In Graham Ward's piece, RO-style critiques of the errors of autonomous reason are carried over into an examination of theological significance of contemporary research in the neurosciences as well as the wider philosophical and political significance of *embodied affect* (especially the so-called "affective turn" in contemporary thought, brought to a certain fruition in many ways by the work of Gilles Deleuze). In this regard, Ward explores the importance of the meaning of "experience"—defined more broadly than "mere sensation," as the sense of something "experienced"; a connotation that implies feeling as much as it does perception—for the way in which we understand human life. For Ward, experiences are never solely "our own but singularities that exist apart from individuals"—and hence are necessarily fluid and mobile; can be given and received; owned, shared, perfected, or destroyed. Ward frames all this in terms of a wider series of reflections on the theological problem of the formation of the soul, especially the question how to understand the processes involved in its sanctification. In Ward's view, the sanctification of the soul is fundamentally an affective process that bypasses and predates both cognition and action. This process, he argues, takes place across the entire life span—a process that involves transforming "hearts of stone" to "hearts of flesh." More theologically, this shows that for Ward radical incarnation operates at the level of somatic experience, and this creates the demand for a new theology of affective life. Clearly, situating our conception of ourselves in terms of "affective life" shows the extent to which philosophy and theology can no longer begin from the assumption of the self-contained individual of modern liberalism. Such a perspective will clearly demand a radical rethinking of the liberal's economistic ideal of the "possessive individual" too.

Louis Dupré's chapter explores the historical dimensions of the idea of a natural desire for transcendence, a view that suggests that human life must be understood in relation to a goal that is naturally desired yet fundamentally unattainable. This is a desire that anticipates the attainment of a goal that surpasses human powers and shows the extent to which human nature wills itself to be "more than itself"; a notion that has profound implications for our conceptions of ethics and politics. Dupré points out that nominalist philosophy rejected this idea of a natural desire for God and deemed God's decisions to be irrelevant to our expectations—thus paving the way for the modern conception of "true desire" as one of worldly adaptation (the basis of psychoanalysis and the modern therapeutic more generally). In modernity, knowledge of God was now deemed to fall outside of philosophy—and in response philosophy attempted to define its own idea of God, "the God of the Philosophers," via an idea of divine creation grafted upon the more limited conception efficient causality (although, contra Lutheran objections, this was not the result of an Aristotelian debauchery of the theological terrain, as Dupré observes). In this way, Dupré shows not only why the idea of a natural desire for God is hard to entertain from a modern philosophical vantage point, but also why thinkers in the Middle Ages would have found it hard to conceive of nature without a transcendent warrant, suggesting a certain relativity vis-à-vis the metaphysical orientations of these two epochs. Dupré goes on to contrast the modern idea of creation with that of Aquinas. For Aquinas, creation was understood as something quite different from efficient causality because he conceived it as a quasi-formal causality (an idea that has been resurrected recently by the new Whiteheadians). Moreover, according to Aquinas, all creatures seek a similitude with their creator that corresponds to their nature—and so for intellectual creatures the highest desire is desire for the highest knowledge. In this scheme, all human spiritual activity already implies a transcendent goal and it is this that gives human life what might be termed its "intellectually adventurous quality" (another theme explored by Whitehead)—an idea that again should form part of any adequate politics of the modern. More recently, Dupré observes, the natural desire for transcendence has reappeared as an important theme in contemporary philosophical thought, and here he notes that Heidegger is the central figure. After Heidegger, the question of the natural desire for an infinite ideal, constantly pursued yet never attained, re-emerges and thus opens up a space for new articulation between the theological and the philosophical. Here, Dupré argues that contemporary philosophy has exceeded Kant in its commencement of a form of reflection no longer constrained by fixed ideas of the *a priori*. Metaphysics reappears in this context as an active inquiry into the transcendent horizon of being—something that reinstates the idea of a natural trajectory of the mind towards a transcendent terminus.

David C. Schindler, in his piece, proposes an analogical conception of nature that addresses the problems associated with purely mechanistic conceptions of the natural, as well as the failure of Schelling's "tragic experiment" that attempted to re-conceive nature in terms of a cosmic vitalism. Schindler shows how only an analogical conception of life—one that recognizes life as hierarchically differentiated in terms of a logic of similarity and difference—can do justice to the dignity and autonomy of the human person in relation to a wider understanding of the goodness of creation. In addition, according to Schindler, an analogical conception of nature reveals that the natural order is essentially cruciform, with transcendence (spirit) and externality (matter) representing the vertical dimension. When viewed in this way, inorganic matter can be viewed as much more than mere mechanism (or inert stuff) as it shares in the living properties of higher orders. In this way, an analogical conception of nature is seen as allowing for a certain ontological porosity between different kinds of thing—an idea also explored in Desmond's piece—to the extent that even "elemental" aspects of nature can be viewed as displaying analogically properties that are generally seen as authentically belonging to organisms. The idea that different orders of nature stand in an analogical relationship indicates a sense of mutual participation, what Schindler terms a "profound exchange of being"—suggesting that the cosmos is sufficed with the meaning of a gift, something that he believes is the most adequate metaphysical response to the dehumanizing metaphysics that has accompanied the scientific revolution. The political dimensions of this conception of the nature should not be lost on us, especially in relation to ecological issues.

John Milbank, in his piece, examines some metaphysical issues associated with Darwinian evolution. He notes that Darwinism is founded upon a Newtonian-Malthusian metaphysics—one that is both mechanistic and hyper-competitive—that shows that in many ways it is in strange collusion with its Christian fundamentalist enemies (even though its key idea that "life evolves" does not, strictly, imply a rejection of any orthodox metaphysics of creation). Thus Milbank tries to sidestep what he terms "the fight between two fundamentalisms" and searches for an alternative vitalist (neo-Bergsonian) conception of evolution that rejects as "mystification" the idea, central to all forms mechanistic metaphysics, that life is epiphenomenal. In this vein, Milbank points out that to date Darwinism has effectively begged the question of the ontological status of the living agent—for what is it, exactly, asks Milbank, that "seeks to survive in the survival of the fittest?" More generally, he asks why should there be unities in nature at all (rather than just a meaningless *glissando* of perpetually organismic fluidity). This may suggest that a conception of evolution in line with a Bergsonian *élan vital* would be sufficient in this regard. However, Milbank rejects any immanentist conception of vitalism in that for him all such conceptions are secretly dualistic. Milbank also draws out the political consequences of all forms of unreconstructed Bergsonianism and shows how in their radical non-relationality they reduce the position of the creature to one of passive subservience in the vital flow, where the only salvation is a Stoic *amor fati* and ultimately a final self-abolition (a critique of the modern Stoic conception of ethics and politics that has been central to RO over the years).

Conor Cunningham's piece explores the wider ethical, political, and theological implications of the speculative materialist moment in contemporary philosophy with particular emphasis given to the work of Quentin Meillassoux, for whom nihilism is viewed, in a celebratory tone, as simply a reflection of an absolutely contingent facticity (and thus resides beyond the "old" theism/atheism divide). In so doing, Cunningham develops a thesis that he has helped to position at the core of RO agendas—that nihilism implodes upon itself because, from its own metaphysical presuppositions, it simply cannot be thought (it is we might term species of "the impossible"). As Cunningham points out, if reason is itself the product of radical contingency, then it remains unclear how this contingency, as an absolute without reason, could ever be amenable to a rational apprehension. Nihilism is thus barred from itself in intellectual terms; it is cognitively inert—dead. However, Cunningham is alert to the threat this position poses to theological orthodoxy and he recognizes that this philosophical tradition stands as an attempt to colonize theology for the purposes of "political radicalism" (nowhere is this more evident than in the work of Meillassoux's master Alain Badiou, for whom an immanent infinity and an idea of radical nihilistic "possibilism" are seen to provide the basis for a philosophically reconfigured political program from the left). In this scheme, if *anything* is possible, then, it seems, there are grounds for political hope in the appearance of some kind of "socio-political novelty" from within neo-liberalism's technologically authorized routines (some consolation, given the dearth of philosophical input from the mainstream left these days). One immediately thinks here of the recent slogan of the anti-globalization movement "another world is possible." But what world? Cunningham explores the ethical and political problems buried within this metaphysics. He shows how nihilistic possibilism is in many ways the suppressed metaphysics of neo-liberal capitalism and, more damningly, only makes sense if we assume the vantage point of the "normal actor/observer"—a normative vantage point that in fact presumes a metaphysics very different from that espoused by the speculative materialists (for the "normal observer" is nothing if not *ethical*). For another world may be possible, but it may also be "radically evil"—unless, that is, we can incorporate within it a metaphysical account of how people should act and react; that is, defend and espouse a world grounded in a metaphysics of the good.

In my (Neil Turnbull's) piece, I explore the way in which late-modern forms of everyday life seem to generate a very specific metaphysical problem; the problem of what Wilfred Sellars famously termed "the clash of the images"—a deep conceptual antinomy between the particulate metaphysics of science and the personalist metaphysics of quotidian life. This, I suggest, shows the extent to which "the everyday" has now become imbued with metaphysical significance, suggesting a new promiscuity of metaphysical concerns outside and beyond the confines of the academy. I then go onto to explore two possible metaphysical resolutions to this clash—one broadly Kantian (advocated by Sellars), that aims to retain a degree of "personalism" in its synoptic metaphysical vision; and the other, broadly Platonic, advocated by A. N. Whitehead, that views the person as "creature," an effect of deeper creative processes and thus possessing no special ontological status. The former represents—against Sellars' eliminativist acolytes in the speculative materialist camp—an attempt to preserve key aspects of the metaphysics of the everyday within an expanded version on the scientific image; the latter an attempt to reform everyday metaphysics in terms of an alternative metaphysics of biological (creaturely) life. In the end, I suggest that, ethically and politically, the former may prove to have the edge over the latter, in that it allows us to retain an idea of the special dignity of the person in a conception of the human as both politically agentive and a locus of "aspirational" (developmental) significance.

Agata Bielik-Robson, in her piece, examines the claim that "denaturalization" is the main point of demarcation between Greek and Jewish thought, in that the latter stands as the signifier of an exodus from humanity out of its bondage to the natural order. However, she points out that the relationship here is more complex, "dialectical" even, as can be seen in Nietzsche's quasi-messianic conception of nature, which views the natural order as one of perpetual self-overcoming. Robson points out that for contemporary Jewish philosophers—from Benjamin to Harold Bloom—this cyclical, self-enclosed, idea of nature is "simply boring," and in response they offer a "messianic vitalism" that goes beyond mere life "for the sake of life"—what Derrida termed "life beyond life." In this way, in contemporary Jewish thought denaturalization is not, contra Nietzsche, the basis for a vengeful hatred of life, but rather the very possibility for life's enhancement—an agonistic eros within which one recovers a more authentic idea of the natural (and one's spontaneous needs) for the purposes of a higher will and an experience of life as a series of "tender yeses." In this way, the Freudian "sadistic superego," although fundamentally a site of a historic, ontological trauma, is not merely destructive or degrading but fundamentally ontologically productive—empowering and creative in relation to the blind and inhuman repetition of natural life. In viewing life as more than "mere nature," this piece shows that another life, beyond that of mechanistic repetition is possible.

In the final chapter, Evandro Botto, addresses the relationship between metaphysics and politics directly through a discussion of Pope Benedict XVI's recent interpretation of Catholic Social Teaching. Botto points out that in Benedict's vision, Catholic Social Teaching positions itself in the interstices between faith and the political arenas shaped by the modern state, in order to find a justification for Catholic social philosophy outside of, and beyond, ecclesiastical space. In his view, this offers the possibility for the re-articulation of church teaching into the political arena as such—something to that amounts to a re-valorization of contemporary modernity, albeit one articulated from a different metaphysical starting point. Moreover, according to Botto, Benedict offers us a conception of politics that recognizes the need for truth and, more importantly, a need to preserve a "sensitivity to the truth" in an age where truth is often caricatured as the enemy of liberal tolerance. Against this, Botto informs us that for Pope Benedict, politics should be founded on the truth of human nature, and rights understood as more than "merely natural"; as an expression of a conception of universal personhood (a conception that is nothing if not metaphysical)—showing again the need for a deeper intertwining of metaphysics and politics.

In the round, what all these papers show is the extent to which questions surrounding the nature and significance of life (and lived experience) are reframing both modern philosophy and modern politics in terms of a new metaphysical vision delivered by a new theologically-inspired *Lebensphilosophie*—one that recognizes the extent to which any adequate conception of personal and political life today needs to transcend the raw and self-defeating scientism of modern philosophy. Each, in its own way, recognizes that life cannot be understood in the terms "flat naturalistic ontologies," because philosophical reflection on the status of the human and purposes will always upset any crudely naturalistic metaphysical applecart. In this way, they begin to move philosophical reflection, and reflection on the nature of the modern, away from a constituting subject/language/culture onto the terrain of a metaphysical idea of life that the modern world presupposes (yet forgets). This recovery of the metaphysical dimensions of modern life, not only begins the process of inaugurating a new dialogue between theology, philosophy, and theoretical science—one of RO's trademark contributions to contemporary intellectual debate—but also allows for a new conception of the modern to emerge; one that recognizes the importance of protecting and enhancing life in an age of risk, that respects that life's rhythms and not those of the mass-productivist ethic, and that in conceiving of human life as essentially social, as a participating together in the one universal and eternal life, endorses an "alternatively modern" idea of the human.

## Bibliography

Bernstein, Richard J. "Introduction." In *Habermas and Modernity*, edited by Richard Bernstein, 9–11. Cambridge: Polity, 1985.

Milbank, John. "The Double Glory, or Paradox versus Dialectics: On Not Quite Agreeing with Slavoj Zizek." In *The Monstrosity of Christ: Paradox or Dialectic*, edited by Creston Davis, 110–233. Cambridge: MIT, 2009.

———. "The Grandeur of Reason and the Perversity of Rationalism: Radical Orthodoxy's First Decade." In *The Radical Orthodoxy Reader*, edited by Simon Oliver, 367–404. London: Routledge, 2009.

Pickstock, Catherine. "Duns Scotus: His Historical and Contemporary Significance." *Modern Theology* 21.4 (2005) 543–74.

Taylor, Charles. *Sources of the Self: The Making of the Modern Identity*. Cambridge: Harvard University Press, 1989.

Whitehead, Alfred, N. *Adventures in Ideas*. New York: Free, 1934.

# 1

# On the Surface of Things
## Transient Life and Beauty in Passing

*William Desmond*

≈

### Philosophy on the Surface

DIFFERENT CONCEPTIONS OF LIFE might be said to fall between two extremes. On one extreme, we find more objectifying, indeed reductive conceptions: here life itself seems to disappear in the very claim to account for it. On the other extreme, we find more subjectifying conceptions: here the sense of immanent self-relation and its dynamic enjoyment is held to make intimate contact with life as lived. A purely objective account seems difficult to endorse finally, if life *disappears* in its being accounted for. An entirely immanent orientation raises for us questions about the passing of life *beyond* self-relating enjoyment. By contrast to these two, one might suggest that life as *transient* (*trans-ire*: to go across) communicates more in the *passage* between these extremes. Our question then: How do we relate this transience, neither objective nor subjective, to the passing of life, to passing as passing?

In addressing this question, we need to recall that part of philosophy's vocation is to be true to the surface of things, in the transience of life on earth. Surfaces intermediate transient life. Beauty is crucially relevant as an intermediate happening, to be true to which, I will suggest, we have to be mindful of the *saturated surfaces* of things. In beauty the surface of life and the depth enigmatically communicate. Beauty is an intermediary of transient life that communicates what cannot be completely objectified and what exceeds every self-relation of the human subject. In beauty the surface and the depth communicate because beauty is the depth communicating itself. Life as transient is also an intermediate happening, and passes between being at all and not being. Beauty is intimately related to this transience of the interim of life, showing something of surplus significance on the surface of things. Beyond the excessively objectifying approach and the excessively subjectifying, it communicates an affirming sense of the excess of life itself, even in its fugitive passing. Fugitive beauty calls on our mindful attention.

But one might ask: Is it, in fact, part of philosophy's vocation to allow us to live on the surface of the earth? Have not philosophers repeatedly pointed beyond the surface and away from the earth? Do not Nietzscheans, reactionary to this pointing beyond, now point back and chant about remaining true to the earth? But surely we can only be true to the earth, behold what is on it, by attaining to the surface of things, a surface in no way exclusive of something above the earth? Not being able to be on the surface of the earth can be induced by various causes, some intellectual, some spiritual, some due to aesthetic and religious viewpoints that denigrate the surface, some due to lies in the soul which hinder us from seeing what is before us, some due to philosophical strategies that look only with suspicion on the surface.

Restoring what it means to stand on the earth, and resurrect the surface of things puts one in mind, paradoxically, of the Platonic analogy of the cave. We live underground, and when freed we undertake a painful and blinding ascent to the surface of the earth, there to be able to behold a light only equivocally present under the surface. Platonic ascent is often now said to be treasonous to the surface of the earth, but we could read this ascent differently. Is it not the sun that enables the earth to be the dynamic, becoming, intelligible, indeed worthy and good reality it is? Without it, not only the underground but also the surface would be plunged into darkness. To live in the light of the sun we need to be on the surface and behold the shine on things. Indeed is not *eidos* intimately connected with the "look" of things? The "look" of things cannot be separated from the surface that shows itself to our attentive mindfulness. The *eidos* shines on the surface of things to the looking that is mindful of the "look." Part of the ancient vocation of philosophy was said to be "saving the appearances."

Such saving knowing would be a matter of *doing justice* to what is shown on the surface. If on the surface there is surplus rather than defect, the justice of saving knowing might well have to draw on reserves of agapeic mindfulness.

Of course, the analogy of the cave recalls the ancient theme of Hades. One must ask: Is there not also a kind of hell with which we have to come to terms? In Hades beauty is under the shadow of darkness and the shades below seem to lack living beauty. But notice here how moving in the dark, whether coming to the surface or sinking deeper into darkness, allows *different directionalities* for our underground motion. We can move up, we can stay where we are, we can also move down. Some movements in the dark in modernity have taken to heart the power of Hades, but rather than ascend to the surface, their motion is *descending*, into another darkness below the floor of the cave. We seem seized by the notion that our motion is not to come again to the surface of things but rather to descend below all surfaces where there is a truer darkness that the surface hides, even as the surface also shows some foreboding of it.

It is obvious that significant currents of contemporary thought have wanted to invert Plato, but what is the meaning of that inversion? Does it, in fact, allow us to live on the surface of the earth? I think the answer has to be qualified in the opposite direction. A true inversion of Platonism would less allow us to have peace on the surface, as complete the disturbing descent, not only back into the cave, but below the ground of the cave into even more infernal darknesses.

This is what we have often found after Hegel. Hegel sublates the surface of things into self-mediating spirit in a philosophy of immanence where rational thought is consummated in absolute self-knowing. After him his ascent to absolute self-knowing is reversed, and the negative power of the dialectic produces what I would call a de-sublation. Instead of us being sublated to the highest standpoint of the identity of human and divine power, divine power is de-sublated to human power. Initially, the fruits of that de-sublation are harvested in a claim that ingests the otherness of the divine into human power, sublates (that is, de-sublates) the transcendent otherness of the divine into human power. This is well known in Feuerbach, Marx, and others. But thereafter there follows a second de-sublation: human power is itself a surface, fronting for inhuman power or powers (however defined). It now appears that Hegelian reason is fated to front for some non-rational other; say, the machinations of will to power. The first de-sublation promises the ultimate power of the divine to us humans. The second de-sublation that follows now descends into what is below reason. The divinity of the human is a god that fails, and the subject becomes less object than abject.

Again there is the theme of depth here, but it reverses the Platonic analogy of the sun, which draws us beyond the cave towards the transcendence of the good. In the cave we are underground men, but now the analogy suggests a de-sublating directionality, pointing down and down into original darkness. We are digging below the cave to pits where the sun seems not to penetrate. Of course, on this view, even on the surface of the earth, the sun does not shine either, for there is no sun, and in the end all is dark. This turn away from higher transcendence and the penetration of our transcending into the lower underground is something we find with Schopenhauer, Dostoevsky, and Nietzsche and many others right into our own time, for instance, Bataille. There is dissimilitude here but it emerges from below. It is the abyss, the dark origin; it is the inhuman. The fate of reason is to be revealed to itself as not reasonable. The inhuman is the immanent other of the human. All of this has implications for our understanding of life also, as we shall see.

Relevantly, in the Platonic directionality, beauty is the intermediate happening where the sensuous and supersensuous are in communication, and eros is not merely impelled beyond itself by its own negative self-determining energy but is drawn beyond by the loving lure of the beautiful or good.[1] Coming to the surface is an ecstasis that participates in that love of the beautiful. By contrast, in the scenario of inverted Platonism, below the underground, where could we find a comparable role to play for the beautiful? My suspicion is: nowhere. Rather, under the underground we are more likely to find more dirt, rather than tunnels of darkness that, were they to lead us back to the surface, would bring us to encounter again the glory of beauty. This would be a joyful occasion of renewing our love on the surface—rejoicing after the darkness that an abundance of beauty is there for us to behold on the surface. This return to the surface does not always happen. More likely, it is a certain fixation on the ugly that will engage our obsessions and anxieties. Here we find more the deformation than the form, more the repulsive than the attractive, more the disgusting than the serene. Even when the fluidity of life is noticed, it is the disgusting

---

1. While Plato is generally said to stress the *eidos* as beyond, its transcendence to appearance, a certain understanding of the "look" of things suggests also a non-disjunctive sense where surface and beyond communicate, as is acknowledged to be the case with beauty in the *Phaedrus*, 250d, for instance: "For the beautiful alone has this fate (*moira*), to be the most showing (*ekphanéstaton*) and most lovely (*erasmiótaton*)."

fluids, or the fluids of life as disgusting, that contaminate us. We drown Christ in piss.

Has beauty restorative power? Returning to Schopenhauer, it is remarkable that for him beauty can save us, if only episodically, from the devouring darkness of the will. But how it can do so, is a good question. Despite the darkness under the underground, the beautiful frees us into a more serene comportment. Equally, Nietzsche preaches that it is art that saves from the truth. The truth is the dark horror underneath, but art gives us the surfaces that protect us from that horror. The *"as if"* truths (that is, "lies") of art save us from *the* truth of horror. Nietzsche knew he was between a rock and a hard place. The Greeks were superficial out of profundity, he said—profoundly, in perhaps a tone of superficiality. I mention Schopenhauer and Nietzsche since with them there is some desire to recover, or at least come to terms with, the surface. To be truly on the surface of things need not be inimical to the gift of beauty and its restorative power. Whether their approaches are adequate to what restoration requires is another question and I doubt they are.

Some forms of post-Nietzschean thought practice what one might call *agenda philosophizing*, and of course the agenda here is to push through relentlessly the project of inverting Platonism. (Is it fair to say that Deleuze almost obsessively pursues this agenda?) If this is the agenda, why at all seek to come to the surface of things, to behold there things of astonishing beauty? If there is no sun, should not the "true" inversion take us below the cave into even more dismal darkness? But does not the desire to drive through this agenda of reversal show the logic of the reviled "Platonism"—now as inverted logocentrism, where everything is re-viewed according to the *idée fixe* of what is to be avoided? It would be better not to try to make any sense. And yet some "project" to make sense is still at work. The studied production of the senseless makes sense as the result of an agenda, but thus it finds itself contradicting itself, not quite senselessly, but in a manner that pays unacknowledged homage to what it would invert. Being dragged back down into hell as the true inversion of Platonic heaven is evident in the production of the ugly according to the agenda of a certain aesthetic philosophy. Beauty comes to meet one, but one immediately crosses to the other side of the road; but to cross the road to escape means one has not escaped what one wants to avoid. Love of the ugly, hatred of the beautiful—are these Siamese twins? Are love of the beautiful, hatred of the ugly also twins? But suppose one truly were to love the ugly, would there not be something lovely about the ugly? To love the ugly—would this not be the love of a god? The god who looks on the lovely where we only recoil in disgust? If we were to follow this thought through ethically and religiously, would we ourselves not have to love those who are hateful? Would we have to affirm a God who loves even the evil, forgives it because there is more in the evil than evil?

## On the Surface and the Objectivizing Reduction

The sciences have diversely tried to define life,[2] but without decrying science, one could ask about certain *scientific* temptations that recurrently emerge in reflections on its characteristic approaches. Important considerations include the following. What is given is rendered in terms of the theoretical neutrality of an objectified thereness. We are supposed to put out of play our own more subjective involvements, assume a more spectatorial rather than participatory orientation. This is all very well in relation to close attention to what shows itself from itself, and not in terms of what we might impute to it in the likeness to ourselves. The injunction is that there is to be no anthropomorphism. We are not to project ourselves and our desires onto the otherwise neutral thereness, and all this in the light of knowing what is as it is. The greatness of this orientation can be an epistemic respect for the otherness of what shows itself as such, now truthfully granted its being for itself, outside the anthropomorphic projections we might otherwise impose on things. Similarly a scientific understanding of life is to be objective in that sense. We cannot project on it our own life, for then we would meet only ourselves again and not what is living as other to us.

Of course, putting ourselves entirely in suspension is impossible. For the objective orientation is itself one of our *valued* orientations, and while its directionality is said to regard the neutral thereness as other, it still is *our* orientation, and we cannot so escape ourselves that we are entirely removed from the picture. If we were entirely removed from the picture, there would be no picture, and hence no objective understanding of life in its non-anthropomorphic otherness. The project of objectification turns out to be a project of the subject—though its primal focus on the objective as other often disguises this from the subject so oriented.

It is also the case that reflection on the project of objectivity casts in doubt the merely spectatorial orientation. I mean the orientation that claims no involvement with what is beheld, no participation in the given

2. See Morange, *Life Explained*.

reality under investigation. The more we wake up to what is at play in the scientific orientation, I would suggest, the more we see that it concerns the determination of *a certain kind of between*: between us and what is there, with concern to give an account of what is there, as precise, determinate, and univocal as possible. Determinability itself is inseparable from objectification, but determining is an engagement we undertake in a middle space between ourselves and what shows itself for this univocalizing consideration. Part of that determination is the effort to fix precisely the character of life, the precise enabling conditions that allow its emergence, conditions to which what happens on the surface can be reduced and rendered in exact mathematical formulations to the highest degree possible. In some quarters the point will be to determine the emergence of the living from the non-living. Thus is a certain extreme reached that mirrors the initial prohibition on anthropomorphisms. Remember that the prohibition barred the attribution of human characteristics to what is other than the human, in the interests of, at best, allowing the non-human to show itself as other to us. Here with a more reductionist view of life, the point is not to project life into the enabling conditions that are necessary for the emergence of life. Rather, the non-living is that relative to which the living is to be understood. But to what extent then is this the claim to derive the living from the dead, a claim that surreptitiously projects a dead condition as the base ground, or the necessary enabler, of what emerges as not dead but living?

We are dealing here with *thresholds*. On one side of the threshold is the non-living; on the other side of the threshold is the living. How is the threshold crossed? We cannot but approach the non-living side of the threshold from some position *within* life. Hence, inevitably what we know of what is on the other side of the threshold is not entirely separable from our necessarily presupposed emplacement *within* life itself. How possible is it then entirely to neutralize a kind of projection of life on non-life? Do we not risk a kind of *inverted* anthropomorphism—that is, a projection guided by just the agenda *not* to find on the other side of the threshold anything that is redolent of the living side of the divide? Is not such a project of inverted anthropomorphism still a kind of anthropomorphic projection? A threshold is always a between space, and if the threshold is of crucial importance, can we ever, in fact, approach the happening of life without in some way presupposing our necessary emplacement in life itself? If we were to give an "absolute" account of life in terms of the non-living, would we have no account at all? Indeed, would the very project as such show its impossibility in its hypothetical realization?

Thresholds are very much related to surfaces. For a surface is also a between space—on one side, one reality, on the other side, another, and the between is the space of possible communication between those two sides. If there is radical heterogeneity between the two sides, would one have a surface at all? For on or in or through such a "surface" of heterogeneity, there would be no interface. Radical heterogeneity would allow no communication between the two sides, and hence no threshold could be crossed. For what is crossing but communication in and across a between? Must one not have rather a relation that mixes the like and the unlike? A threshold, like all betweens, requires an intermediation of sameness and difference, an interplay of likeness and unlikeness. A surface is the *metaxu* of this interplay. Hence, how we relate to surfaces is all important. There is no approach to what is hidden in the surface, or beyond it, or its depth, without genuine cognitive and ontological respect for the surface as such, that is, for the surface as a *metaxu*, and hence as an interface.

The issue then is whether there is any approach to life that does not necessarily presuppose life. If we seek to reduce the living to the non-living, or to show the conditions needful for the emergence of the living from the non-living, one still has to ask if this approach, indeed any approach, can entirely escape being already emplaced in the sphere of the living as such? Even if we try in the depths of life to discover the non-living as source of the living, can we do this without indebtedness to given life precisely as given—and given on the surface? The point I make is not to deny non-living conditions enabling life but to ask whether the univocal determination of these conditions can ever be entirely true to the happening of life as such. Life is presupposed as "more," even in the approach that would reduce it to the "less" than living. This self-confirming emplacement in the between of life, of course, is taken to be a limitation to be overcome by more reductionistic approaches to life. But the between of life is itself a presupposition of these reductionistic approaches themselves. There is something we cannot escape here, and we ought to ask if it has immense significance for the understanding of life.

A science of life that ends up with no life is in a fugue state relative to this inescapability. It has not remained true to the surface of things. In its plumbing of the depths it brings us death rather than life. One thinks of Wordsworth's famous words: "We murder to dissect." We take apart, we kill, we take the life from something to understand it. We do understand something, but life dies in this anatomy of life. If this is all there is to knowing life, knowledge is an invasion of, an assault on, what it seeks to know. Even then an assault is an act that *lives* from hostility. Would a knowing that does not kill have to be a loving of what it knows? One might ask if even the most extreme reductionism is in the debt of this love. Affirming something as true reveals a love of truth, and a love of the reality as so affirmed. But loving itself is always a living—a new living of the life known, and in a sense, a living augmented in coming to know in love.

Beauty, I would say, brings us closer to this loving knowing. It brings us closer to the erotics of knowing, perhaps even the agapeics, but I cannot dwell on this right now. In the main I now want to attend to the stress on univocal determinability that is worthy of note when the scientific orientation will express itself in determining certain structures as necessary for a living being to be alive at all. Suppose we consider the integrity of a living organism. The project of objectification might be satisfied with the determination of structures in so far as they can be expressed in the precisions of mathematical formulations. Well and good: without structure we seem left with a mere formless indeterminacy. But the issue of life is not a matter of structure as such but of what *passes* in the structuring. If we only stress structure, then structure and what is passing in the structure are disjoined from each other. We have to ask if rather here with the living organism structure indicates a *structuring* that itself cannot be simply determined in the language of structure—here now taken as an order that is fixed and determinate. One recalls Bergson's famous *élan vital*. I take this as a suggestion in the face of the tendency to a more fixed spatialization in the event of structure itself. Structure as such is not adequate to the temporalization, the becoming evident in life as life, in life as passing in the structuring and not just formulated in the fixed structure. The *élan vital* is rejected, of course, by scientists, because it resists precise univocalization. But perhaps the issue of life is not just one of scientific determinability and precise univocalization but rather a question of *passing qua passing*.

We do speak of life as passing. Structure is not a passing, though it may enable passage. Passing qua passing exceeds structure. There is no necessary life in structure qua structure. Is structure itself self-explicatory? You might say that it is immanently determining, indeed self-determining in the case of *organic structure*. There is obviously something to this: here is dynamic structure, since it unfolds in an active formation, proceeding from an immanent principle. If this is so, there is an *energy* of structure that reveals a (self) structuring that just as passing cannot be just a structure.

There is structure perhaps, but the life that passes in the structure and as structure is not *just* a structure. Should we call these structures a matter of infrastructure—and then refer to what passes in and through the infrastructure? But if so, the point cannot be a dualism of infrastructure and what passes through it. This is a case where the great question of Yeats is apposite: how can we tell the dancer from the dance? Here we cannot tell—in an absolutely univocal way. In life, we cannot make an absolute division between infrastructure and what passes along it. This is especially so if we are dealing with an immanent becoming of life. This passing of life is a determining beyond determination. It is not beyond all determination but beyond absolutely univocal determination, which insists it is simply this and not that. For what is at issue is the transition *between* this and that—a transition that is not itself this or that. And so once again we are confronted with thresholds. These are not fixed boundaries, but moving thresholds, so to say. This is so, since the transitions here insinuate themselves into the determination of both this and that. And this means once again the "this" and the "that" cannot be univocally fixed in an absolute way. They too are what they are in becoming, in transition.

In sum, to identify any structure of life there must be presupposed something other than structure. The question is whether a purely objective account of any structure of life can be adequate to the passing of life qua passing.[3] It is not that determinate objectivities are to be slighted. The becoming of an organism, say, reveals a highly complex structure and a true investigation of its being tries to do justice to the amazingly intricate determinacy of its unfolding. Still to identify life in terms of structure presupposes life as living and lived in a non-structural sense. Structures as such, like mathematical formulations, even of life, do not themselves live. The recognition of life passes beyond structure.

Take the case of something beautiful, important for my chosen theme, for instance, that of the live song of a bird. Its music can be sometimes strikingly beautiful. It can also be measured, the determinacies of

---

3. A rose flowers out of the earth. The rose is beautiful though the earth is dirty. Something shimmers in the appearance of the rose though the earth from which it blooms is heavy and dull. The earth is a surface as well as a ground, and what shows itself on the surface is intimately related to what is in the ground, but it is more than its own enabling conditions. What passes from the earth and into the seed that shoots up into the earth as the blooming rose? It is not just the earth, not just the seed, but the fertile life that must be buried in the earth to rise to the surface of the earth and above the earth. The laws of material nature are not themselves material. The law of gravity is not heavy, for instance—it does not fall, for it cannot be dropped or thrown, or leap. Flowers are beautiful but we do not (tend to) eat them.

sounds studied, the connection with environment, and communication between mates explored, and so on. But none of this exhausts the living happening of the singing qua singing. What passes in and through the bird, what passes between this bird and other birds, what joy of being at all is sung out under the embracing sky, what is communicated in the song: to grant that all this is not so easy to objectively measure does not entail one derides objective measure. Suppose the music has something to do with the living subjectivity of the bird—the selving of its transient being? The singing is the living integrity of the being in communication with what is other to itself and with itself too as other. There is no derogation from determinacy but rather the granting of an *overdeterminacy* in the happening as such. There is something more in communication in the happening of song. While determinate it is more than determinate, it is overdeterminate.

The making of music connects us with the long tradition stretching back to the Pythagoreans which connect mathematics with harmonies, and well expressed by Leibniz who highlights the connection with determinability when, for example, he says: "Music is a hidden arithmetic exercise of the soul, which does not know that it is counting" (*Musica est exercitium arithmeticae occultum nescientis se numerare animi*. Letter to Christian Goldbach, April 17, 1712).[4] Music is unknowing mathematics. Singing does not know that secretly it is arithmetical determination. From the view I am suggesting, one wonders if it is the opposite that is more truly the case: not that music is secretly mathematics, but that *mathematics is a music the intellect does not know it is singing*. It is worth asking if song is more in communication with the overdeterminate, in which structure determinately participates but which it does not and can never exhaust. If we were to use the terms of another great mathematician and scientist, and connect music with the *esprit de finesse* and arithmetic with the *esprit de géométrie*, Leibniz's God comes across more as a God of geometry than a God of finesse.[5] The God of finesse is a God of music—a God of living beauty. One thinks of the justly famous jubilation of Augustine: *Sero te amavi! pulchritudo tam antiqua, et tam nova, sero te amavi!* . . . Living beauty, older than all age and younger than all youth. The God of finesse is one who sings the world into being and continues to sing it in being,

---

4. Schopenhauer cleverly reformulated this in the first book of *Die Welt als Wille und Vorstellung*: *Musica est exercitium metaphysicis occultum nescientis se philosophari animi*. Music is a hidden metaphysical exercise of the soul, which does not know that it is philosophizing.

5. See Desmond, *God and the Between*, chapter 3.

in and through and with the cooing coaxing dovebird Spirit. This God is living not dead, this God is singing before calculating. For singing structuring is more than and before mathematical structure. The music of the spheres is not due to the geometry of the heavens; the geometry of the heavens is due to the music.

## Interlude I

### *On Objectivistic Non-Recognition of the Living*

I offer two pictures of a revealing *disconnection* between the objectivistic reduction and the saturated surface of things. *First:* Descartes, it has been claimed, conducted vivisection experiments on animals. Animals are automata; they have no souls. The automaton reveals a mechanical autonomy in the sense of being entirely determined by the soul-less self-law (*auto-nomos*) inscribed in it. We stick a knife in the animal and it seems to scream in pain but animals, who have no anima, feel no pain. They mimic our behavior but they are soulless machines. So the pigs squeal when we cut into their living flesh. The squeal of the flesh is the surface of the thing. The reality is no pain. The pigs have no soul. Why then do we want to stop our ears to these screams? (Recall Galileo speaking of science and the "rape" of the senses.) The pigs have no pain, and if you say, "listen, they squeal," or "look they twist and kick," it is a mimicry, a counterfeit of a squeal or a shudder. The surface of things is not the thing.[6] We superior knowers scientifically do not hear the scream of non-human beings. The surface says "life"; the scientist says "lifeless." The surface is nothing.

*Second:* the Dead Parrot sketch performed by Monty Python. There is a *comedy* of the surface and its denial. A customer buys a parrot, only to return to the shop to demand satisfaction, since the parrot is dead. The surface says "dead" but the seller says "alive." The surface screams a dead parrot, but no, the seller says obdurately, it is only sleeping. The seller pokes the parrot and, of course, it moves, and the seller pounces, there it is alive! He's not dead; he was only "stunned." A Norwegian Blue, he's "pinin' for the fjords." The cheated buyer explodes:

> 'E's not pinin'! 'E's passed on! This parrot is no more! He has ceased to be! 'E's expired and gone to meet 'is maker! 'E's a stiff! Bereft of life, 'e rests in peace! If you hadn't nailed 'im to the perch 'e'd be pushing up the daisies! 'Is metabolic processes are

---

6. See Jonas, *Phenomenon of Life*, 55.

now 'istory! 'E's off the twig! 'E's kicked the bucket, 'e's shuffled off 'is mortal coil, run down the curtain and joined the bleedin' choir invisible!! THIS IS AN EX-PARROT!!

The seller finally relents. The truth of the surface triumphs.[7]

What does our laughter tell us? That there is a living recognition of a living being, the denial of which generates the nonsense of cutting off our noses to spite our faces. The laughter reveals the living recognition of the living, prior to all theories and more than our forced or false descriptions.

## On the Surface and the Subjectivizing Reduction

The above argument is that all approaches to life presuppose life as already able to relate to life, even if the preferred relation is one of reducing the living to the non-living. This is more than a logical trick to critique the more objectivist orientation by invoking a necessary self-implication in the search for life itself, its intelligibility and truth. In fact, one of the major characteristics of the living being is some power of self-motion. It is already in passage, living itself is a passing, and in the passing the living being in some sense or other moves itself. Self-motion was one of the major characteristics that the ancients ascribed to *psyche* or *anima*, and hence to living beings. This moving is not just a matter of locomotion, the spatial displacement of an otherwise inert being from one location to another. There is the self-movement that is the becoming of the being—its self-becoming. There is an integrity at work, but it is one in process. This integrity cannot be univocally fixed simply as this or that. In its becoming of itself, it is now this and now that but this and that cannot be frozen as too univocalized snapshots of instantaneity. It is both this and that, and moreover it is the transition between them. Its integrity in process is a nisus to be and become itself. It is an anticipation of a fuller realization of itself, and as more fully realized, it is as *a spanning of its own timing*— a spanning that is its being gathered into a new living and more or less poised integrity of being.

The integrity in self-becoming of the living being is the basis of its ability to move itself in relation to other such integrities and through between spaces, all diversely qualified. There is a certain rootedness and

---

7. One thinks here of the bird that brings forth the analytic anxiety of epistemological uncertainty: the goldfinch—real or stuffed or whatnot—at the end of the garden, in Stanley Cavell's discussion of J. L. Austin in Cavell, *Claim of Reason*, for instance, 50ff., 58, 73, 132–33, 160, 163, 194.

spread of ontological power in the living being. Here it is as this, and in a sense rooted in itself, but what it is entails a spread of itself to the space defining the parameters of its power to be. Some forms of life are more rooted—the plant. Some are more moving in this spread—witness the freer power of animals to range over their environment. All this is recognized by Aristotle in *De Anima*. But the living animated being resists reduction to more rudimentary matters in so far as the integrity in process answers to a unity that cannot be univocalized in a purely determinate way. Something of the powers of its own self-determination is at work in its self-becoming, as well as its interplay with what is other than itself. This interplay is no less essential to defining the dynamic integrity that is itself in its process of becoming itself. The living being is transient in the double sense of being in self-becoming and in its passage between itself and other beings, living and non-living. Transience means a being's going from here to there, but its being there is itself again, so that while it moves from here, it does not just move from here, and thus comes to itself again there. Transience also means that it moves beyond itself in relation to what is other to itself. In some forms of transience, the point is not recuperation of itself—the living being is given over, or gives itself over to what is other. Transience means that the timing of the being in becoming is not only a growing and a maturing, it is also an aging. Transience means that the interim of its time is temporary.

Here once again what shows itself on the surface is very important and it testifies there to the recognition of the living by the living. An objective science is not needed for this recognition. Rather there would be no science of life without this pre-scientific, extra-scientific recognition of life. A simple example: an animal sees an object lying there, seemingly inert. If it is willing to approach it, then the important distinction for it concerns that between "living" or "dead." Is it alive or is it not? Is it friend or foe? It knows it is alive if it moves. To test it, the thing is gingerly poked or prodded. If there is no reaction, no movement, a certain equivocity is settled in the direction of the diminution of danger. Recognition of the motion of life is communicated in the signs of an inward vitality on the part of the thing seen as alive, and the thing seeing what is alive, for self-motion and the animation of life are bound up with each other. There is some univocity to the outcome of recognition. Not moving, the thing is not dangerous. If it is alive, it might be either an enemy or it might be food. It might be a form of life one might eat or one that might eat one. Surfaces and the interaction of the animal with them will help it tell the difference.

The testing animal is alive and in the lack or not of movement in the other thing, the recognition of life by the animal is elemental. Animals love life—even in killing—the killing that comes with eating. Humans alone are able to hate life, killing in hate, even for no purpose—though the hatred is a mutation of the love of life.

Of course, it happens that some animals in danger play being dead—they do not move, they play possum, and the lack of movement either makes it invisible to the perceptual powers of the attacker, or its "deadness" deceives with the impression that there is nothing of interest there. Only the living can play being dead. The dead animal does not play being dead. An animal also could play being dead to induce a prey to come closer, only then to pounce at the unexpected moment. There is a certain asymmetry here in that life can in a living way relate to death and the surface of death—but the dead cannot do this. Does this mean there is a certain priority of the living then also? It does mean that the recognition of life is something primitive. This is not to underestimate the way the recognition is entangled in many possibilities of equivocity. The surface is not a matter of univocal clarity. It is an equivocal showing that hides as much as shows: in showing it also hides, even as in hiding it also shows.

From this I would stress a sense of the living that is prior to objectivizing reason. In objective life living is beyond the fully objectifiable. One might speak of the energy of the "to be," which, in certain formations, flowers into dynamic integrities of being that appear as self-affirming. Life is affirming itself, and one of the notable things about life, and lost in the more objectifying account, is this entirely *intimate self-relation*. I think one could speak of a certain intimacy of life that cannot be entirely exhausted with determinable accounts that approach it from the outside. This intimacy of life is also known intimately from within in the form of a certain self-affection. When Schopenhauer, for one, talked about the will as beyond sufficient reason, he could be seen to point to this character of life that exceeds the more objective fixation by determinate reason, determining reason. This more primordial life is lived from within, and in fact all of us know something of it in our own bodies. In our being embodied, there is no absolute dualistic disjunction between awareness and being alive in a bodily sense. I speak of a certain idiocy of being. Life has this idiocy in the sense of never being entirely reducible to the more determinable generalities or universals of neutrally available reason. Reason itself participates in this idiocy, which is not something absurd but something irreducible in the relation of the being to itself—a self-relation presupposed by reason itself, if reason is to know what it knows as known by me. I know—knowing as a neutral happening does not know. This is not to decry the universal, but to say that there is an intimacy that cannot be rendered in the neutral language of abstract universals. There is a kind of *intimate universality to life* in that the living recognizes the living, the living knows itself as living and recognizes other living being as living with a kind of overdeterminate innerness that exceeds both the determinacy and self-determination of any particular being. (The power of beauty is very much bound up with this intimate universality.)

This self-relation has often been the basis for emphasizing something more "subjective" about life—and this is not wrong. But just as objectification does not always do justice to the overdeterminacy of given otherness, subjectification does not always do justice to the overdeterminacy of this intimate life. Subjectification fastens on the self-relation, and rightly, but does not go rightly into this and rediscover the threshold spoken of above in relation to external otherness. There is also the threshold of an inward otherness that marks a between, across which the transitions are between the given life and its more ultimate giving source. I will come to this next when I talk about a more metaxological understanding of living.

It is important to grant that there is a plurivocity possible to selving. I would speak of selving(s) rather than subjectivity, since again the integrity in process is evident in this. In idiotic selving it is not a matter of autistic particularity but of a living and affectionate relation to oneself. We feel ourselves prior to thinking ourselves, or even thinking as ourselves—the intimacy, the idiocy reveals a pre-objective and pre-subjective self-relation—and this is the living relation of the living being to itself. Example: We sense something of it in the morning; we have this taste of self—before the day's determinations take over. We awake to ourselves and savor ourselves, brimming with new zest perhaps or dragging with weary disgust. This is not a determinate self-consciousness but a more floating indeterminate self-feeling—but it communicates how we are in relation to ourselves in the world we are shortly about to engage again more determinately. This is intimate life in its transience returning to the day of its self-relation and its relation to what is beyond it. It happens at a threshold, and hence most often it is not objectified, or not yet channeled into a more determinate or self-determining subjectification.

All forms of life might be said to be marked by a more or less relatively undeveloped senses of inwardness—of selving. All things selve in that respect. To selve is not the privilege of the human being alone. I think of Hopkins' great poem "As Kingfishers Catch Fire":[8]

> Each mortal thing does one and the same:
> Deals out that being indoors each one dwells;
> Selves—goes itself; *myself* it speaks and spells,
> Crying *What I do is me: for that I came.*

The surface of the thing as selving is the face of the thing. A face is the (micro)cosmos of facets that is the living surface of the selving being. Facets are surfaces and the higher integrities of being have faces that selve more and more intensively. In the sublunary world the human being is the acme of this facing. We are a surface that faces the world, but we are our faces—the show of the intimate selving communicating itself. Is this why our faces are, in a sense, more intimate to us than even our intimate parts?

We can have many faces, and equivocity increases with surfaces like the human face. We have the ability to seem other than we are, to show half-truly and to lie, to smile and hide hate in the smile. The power of equivocal surfacing is not confined to us. In *Being and the Between*, I pointed out the equivocity of the beautiful orchid, or the being other than what one is by being what one is, in the power of camouflage that surfaces in the selvings of animals, like the chameleon. In this equivocity we find some of the reasons we often distrust surfaces. But the distrust of surfaces follows from what we learn from surfaces, not in isolation from what surfaces. The equivocity eludes complete univocal determinability, for showing is also always hiding, there are forms of showing which simultaneously are forms of keeping secret.

In any event, the self-relation of life to itself is very important and exceeds the terms of every objective determination of it. A living being is not subjective simply, it has its own objectivities, but as a living integrity of being it holds itself in a self-relation that comes to feel and know itself as

---

8. The poem is in the public domain. The kingfisher is not the dead parrot of Monty Python, not the stuffed/real goldfinch of Austin/Cavell and has something of the spirit of the dovebird alive in it. There are other birds of life; for instance, the windhover of Hopkins. And birds pointing beyond death: Keats's Nightingale—"thou wast not born for death, immortal bird"; or beyond death, such as the golden birds of those great poems of Yeats's old age, "Byzantium" and "Sailing to Byzantium," birds that are "set upon a golden bough to sing / To lords and ladies of Byzantium / Of what is past, or passing, or to come." The bird may be beyond life and death, but beyond as living and not just imaged as the deathlessness of death. Only the golden sings. We do not want a base metallic metaphysics; we want a metaphysics of resurrected incarnation.

such. I think of this as a very elemental opening or porosity to the intimate universal—not as entailing a rejection of the universal as such. It demands a rethinking of the universal, in fact, not its repudiation. All living beings participate in this intimate universal, and each is the singular surfacing of the energies of its "to be" but none exhausts it. One of the signs of this participation is its generation of the intimacy of life beyond its own self-relation, beyond its own possession of its own life. (The erotics of being is the passion of life.) The being knows it does not possess its own life—but knows that in its flesh, not in its head. This is why an erotics of life surfaces—the singular participation in the intimate universal is in passage beyond itself, passage sensing itself but not possessed in the flesh. This is something beyond determination, beyond self-determination, given that the living being is a nisus to generate beyond itself. This is more explicitly metaxological and again I will come to this. (The example of equivocity I cited above, the orchid, is intimately related to the erotics of naturing, and indeed without equivocity the happening of human erotics would hardly be possible at all. In the erotics of life the surfaces of flesh are flushed, even engorged, with ambiguous significance.)

It is especially evident in humans that we have life coming to know itself as living. This self-knowing is not objective reason—it is living participation. The knowing of life is also the knowing of the transience of life. This is again not the knowing of a structure but of the passage qua passage. It is the knowing of life as in the passing of life itself as passing, and knowing ourselves as participant in the passage as such. In connection with the equivocity of the erotics of life, I will here just briefly note how this self-relation can be taken in certain directions. The self-affirmation is evident in the Schopenhauerian will. What life reveals is the will to live—and this is a dark, voracious energy in which we all participate and of which more often than not we find ourselves the victim. The matter at issue here is not only the nature of this "more" of life but the nature of love, and the love of this more primordial life. With Schopenhauer it has all the characteristics of a heedless *eros turannos*. The will is an erotic absolute but without anything of the *eros ouranios* (heavenly eros) of Plato. In Schopenhauer it is voraciously self-insistent without end. It victimizes us when we think we can be agents of its or our own self-determination. Its greedy self-insistence makes it something vile rather than good for Schopenhauer. We cannot truly love a life whose aimless aim is to controvert every claim to autonomous self-determination. Life is in an original guilt: it is not good to be, better not to be. We dip below the ground of the cave again.

We are still below the ground of the cave when Nietzsche tries to reverse the "yes" and "no" of Schopenhauer. The basic description of life persists. We live in foreboding of the Medusa below the surface—the horror that turns us to stone. Better to stay on the surface like the Greeks out of profundity. We are again dealing with the negotiation of thresholds, but here the threshold into the darkness goes down into an abyss of horror. Elemental life is this horror. It is reminiscent of the alien into which Žižek and others like to rub our faces. Of course, *the face has gone at this depth of darkness*. But the question of the surface does not dissolve. Is the surface the mask of horror or the face of something overdeterminate with an ontological good in which we participate and can never master? And perhaps not being its master has more to do with the giftedness of its good than the ruse by which the horrifying energy makes use of us for its own self-persistence and self-perpetuation.

In our time we find in Michel Henry a notable stress on life just as self-affection. He offers a remarkable development of the self-affection. Henry seems very insistent in setting the world (objectifications) over again life. This is too dualistic perhaps, but I see in what he is doing a certain rightness in drawing attention to something crucial about the incontrovertibility of the life at issue. He transforms the transcendental subject in the direction of a remarkable transcendental trinitarianism, so it strikes me, and which for me is closer to Hegel than Henry might like.[9] I note Henry had lots of respect for Schopenhauer and Nietzsche, and is right to remind us that they have seen something on the other side of objective representation, something in which we are and participate.[10] I think he does not see in both cases that the ontology of the "to be" is still defined by the modern evacuation of all the traces of qualitative value from the given being. The "to be" is without the good of the "to be." Better not to be, in fact. This is nihilism, even when it protests against nihilism, as in the case of Nietzsche. In them the resort to this other path, of the "subject" beyond the "subject" is in an ethos of devalued thereness. In Schopenhauer it leads to the evil of being, in Nietzsche to the dream of a creative self-imposing of value on the valueless flux, and eventually to the dissolving of "self" in the same flux.

---

9. See Henry, *I am the Truth*.

10. In the company of Schopenhauer, Nietzsche, and Henry, one might think of *Lebensphilosophie* more generally as seeing the irreducibility of life qua lived to the objectifications of science. One thinks again of Bergson, and also of William James's efforts to draw attention to "pure experience."

These strategies are not fully true to the self-affirming of life to which Henry perhaps is more true. But this self-affection, this self-affirmation, what is it? It is life loving itself—but what is this love? It is beyond reduction and objectification, but is it also more than every subjectification. Does it require more metaxological terms, in which there is always an opening beyond the self-affirmation of life? The affirmation of life is always between self and other—always in passing in the between, the passing in which we participate. It is very difficult to give an account of it, either in determinate terms or in terms of our self-determination. For all that, it is not a mere indetermination. There is something overdeterminate at work in its life. The interim of living passage is metaxological.[11] On the threshold, the between is worded; the between is sung.

## Surfacing on the Metaxological Threshold

By contrast with the objectivizing and subjectivizing reductions, these are now the considerations on which we must reflect. First, there is more to life than the neutral objectivities whose otherness entails no participatory involvement, since there is an ineluctable self-affirming of life even in its denial. Second, this self-affirmation, while undeniable, points to something more than a subjective self-involvement primarily circling around itself alone. As the otherness passes to self-affirmation, self-affirmation passes to the affirmation of otherness. Life is in the passage between these, and to do justice to the passage a different view of the self-affirming and the otherness is required. Living is a between process and a metaxological passage in the between.

Life is self-affirming, but there is more at play in this affirmation than just self. Self-affirmation is not the full affirmation. One way to indicate this is to look at the way in modernity the self-insistence of the living being has been called its *conatus essendi*, its endeavor to be. We find this in Hobbes and Spinoza, for instance, and also in Levinas, though criticized there. I would say there is more to the *conatus* than self-insistence. *Self-affirming endeavor*, so described, does not pay attention to the weight of both the *natus* and the *co* of *conatus*: a being born, a being born with. There is always a relation to coming to be, a being born, from an other "with" which the being is from the beginning. This opens a doubleness in the *conatus* itself. The living being endeavoring to be is received into

---

11. This metaxological view is systematically developed in Desmond, *Being and the Between*; Desmond, *Ethics and the Between*, as well as Desmond, *God and the Between*.

being itself before it comes to affirm itself as for itself. The self-affirmation of the living being risks hiding from "self" the fact that this self-affirming is always "with" what is other. It hides the truth that to be self-affirming, it must be received from an affirming that is more than itself alone, and in which it always participates. In other words, the living being as self-affirming is not the bedrock reality, since the self-affirming comes to itself as "yes" to itself because already it is "yessed" in a "being born with." In the self-affirmation, life in a more full sense affirms itself. The overdeterminacy of life affirms itself in the self-affirmation, for self-affirmation is always more than self alone.

The *co-natus*, as a *being born with*, refers to what I call a *passio essendi* more primal than this endeavor to be. This passion of being is more primal because life opens us before we open to life. We are given to be as living before we give ourselves to be as determined, or self-determining, in accord with the particular form of life we are. The patience of life—in this sense of its being received from sources beyond self-affirmation—is often hidden from sight when the *conatus essendi* is wrongly claimed to be the essence of life itself. We are then prevented from looking deeper into the ontological sources at work in the incontrovertible self-affirmation. Put differently, there is a love (of life) more original than self-love, in which self-love itself participates, and which self-love distorts when it thinks itself to be the true form of love of life as such. In so loving our own life we do not love as we are lived and do not love ourselves truly.

Thus self-affirmation, in coming to itself out of being received, opens to an otherness of life that is not this or that determinate affirmation, not our own self-determination, but communicates of an enabling power in which all living beings participate. The *passio essendi* points back to the ultimate endowing source(s) of life. Suppose we start with the surface of things, start with our being in the midst of things. But we find ourselves open to things. We are open because we are already opened. Before we come to ourselves as more reflectively thoughtful, we already are in a porosity of being, and are ourselves as this porosity of being become mindful of itself. This is one reason I would speak of living "in the between" in terms of an *original porosity of being*, that is neither objective nor subjective, but that nevertheless is enabling of both, while being more than both, and indeed enabling passing between both. The porosity is a between space where there is no fixation of the difference of minding and things, where our mindfulness wakes to itself by being woken up by the communication of being in its emphatic otherness. Living as non-objectifiable and as exceeding subjectification reveals the transient flow of the "to be" in this porous between. More objective and self-reflective orientations come later. Already before we more reflectively come to ourselves, in the original porosity of being there is the more primal participation, and indeed we open mindfully to it in the mode of a certain astonishment.

To be is to be surprised by life—even if with later determinations and our claim to be self-determining we dull the surprise with the overdeterminacy of being. In the living porosity, there is no fixed boundary between there and here, between outside and inside, between below and above. There is the coming to be of life; there is the becoming of determinate life in transient passage in the between; there is a relative self-determination with certain forms of self-becoming; but there is always the overdeterminacy, the "too muchness" of what gives itself to enable the coming to be and becoming of life. We find it again in our sometimes renewed astonishment at the surprise of life itself. There is a passage from what is into the awakening of mindfulness as, before its own self-determination, opened to what communicates to it from beyond itself. We do not open ourselves; being opened, we are as an opening. Living astonishment is not the neutral knowledge of objective structure, nor is it subjectivity simply in relation to itself. Rather it awakens the porosity of mindfulness to being, in the communication of being to mindfulness, before mind comes to itself in more determinate form(s). This living astonishment correlates with a more original "coming to be" prior to the formation of different processes of determinate becoming, and prior to the more settled arrival of relatively determinate beings and processes. Beauty is one of the happenings on the surface of things that can take our breath away and arouse wonder, that is to say, renew astonishment at the marvelous gift of life itself.[12]

The *passio essendi* and *conatus essendi* are always twinned; nevertheless a certain priority to the *passio* means always that life gives us to be before we come to ourselves as living. The passion of life is not originally of our willing, though the endeavor becomes our willing of life. Because of its source in the porosity of being the willing of life is always mingled with the possibility of nulling. My general sense is that the endeavor is always tempted to take over the passion of being. The active self-assertion

---

12. Important here are differences between wonder in the modalities of astonishment, perplexity, and curiosity. Curiosity is more tied to objectifiable determinations of life; perplexity to an indeterminacy, especially bearing on the immanent life of selving; astonishment is ontological resurrection to the wonderful overdeterminacy of the *metaxu*, and beauty is its incarnational companion. On these three see Desmond, *The Intimate Strangeness*, chapter 10.

of life overtakes the receiving of being, and to a degree tries even to null the receiving. Nevertheless, the receiving is more primordial. Truth to life entails more than endeavor on the surface of life, but openness to this patience of being. To live in the *metaxu* is to be charged with remaining true to the original porosity. The *conatus* is to be given its full significance as a being "born with"—"*co-natus*"—against its contraction into just self-affirming of life. The endeavor to be is self-affirming but self-affirming itself is witness to the double condition, in the *co-natus* itself, of twinned self-relation and relation to the other. One is with oneself because one is "born with." Selving is not just self, but is a being endowed by virtue of a constitutive relativity to an other enabling source that is not oneself alone. When our selving loses any porosity to the more primal patience, its seeming self-affirmation mutates really into a kind of self-hatred. For this endeavor to be is in flight from itself, from what it is, from the patience of being that gives it to be at all in the first instance. The conditions that make possible its being at all are refused.

The *metaxu* as immanence is a given porosity of being, already in relation to what is beyond itself in being in relation to itself. If "the between" is porous it means that it is impossible to fixate univocally a "this side" and a "that side." What is most important is the happening of passage between—of passing. And this in an ontological sense—coming to be, passing into being, passing, passing out of being. All the pathos of life and death are contained in passing, passage in and through the between. Passing itself suggests a between since it cannot be fixed to any one moment or phase. Passing is as passing—just as a between is nothing without the enabling milieu of relatedness that sustains and goes beyond the beings upheld as existents in the relatively stabilized middle.

I suggest that this difference just indicated between *coming to be* and *becoming* has some relevance to the discussion of creation and evolution, though the relevance occurs on a level that is not customary in the reigning terms of the debate. Evolution is a becoming but every becoming presupposes a coming to be. This coming to be is not an item in a process of becoming; it is not even the process of becoming as a whole. It is more in the givenness of becoming as such—in the "that it is at all." This is hiddenly presupposed in every becoming and in all of our approaches to becoming, the scientific theory of evolution included. To get some sense of the coming to be means being struck by the metaphysical astonishment that is amazed at the sheer "being there" of being. This metaphysical astonishment is not a matter of scientific curiosity and is closer to aesthetic marveling and religious adoration.

Coming to be is a more original passage than becoming and the thought might be applied to life also. The question of the origin of life is often tied to the level of evolution as a becoming—and the effort is to articulate its scientifically warranted determination. But suppose there is an approach on the level of coming to be rather than becoming. Then there is no scientific explanation for the origin of life. It is always already presupposed by every explanation, and so in a certain sense the truer approach to life can never be the scientific one. Not only is this scientific approach a contraction of our participation in life but it can only see what is on the level of a determinate becoming. It does not metaphysically see surfaces as threshold of a coming to be—more truly a creation than a becoming. In that sense, creation is more primordial than becoming, but it is not another becoming. Hence, it is more primordial than evolution also, and is not this either in terms of the big bang theory. We have to move in a different space of mindfulness. We have to see the surfaces of things differently. Rather than simply repudiate surfaces as superficial, the surfaces *are* the depths, if they are the thresholds of what is hyperbolic *in* immanent being, allowing and enabling passage of and to what is hyperbolic *to* immanent finite life.

This distinction of coming to be and becoming is also applicable to our tendency in modernity to put an emphasis on *self-becoming*. Recall that there is no self-affection of life without living in relation with others. The *co-natus* is itself between self-relation and other-relation, pointing back to a more original passion of living, itself emergent in a more primal porosity that enables passing between one being and another in the plurivocal relativity of the *metaxu*. The self-affirming of life is second—out of more original porosity. If I am not mistaken the modern subjective view is witness to a certain contraction of the *conatus* to self-affirmation alone, though with this contraction there goes a kind of *expansion* of "selving," as the self-contracted self-affirmation of the *conatus* essays to overtake the *passio essendi* entirely. And then there is no patience of being, no receptivity of life from an enigmatic endowing source. Self-generating life is misunderstood as simply for itself alone. Its self-becoming circles around itself in an entirely immanent enclosure—life is all between it and itself— there is no opening of the porous between to an endowing source of life beyond all enclosed immanence. The circle of life closes on itself, even though its life is endowed, and even though without the source it would not be, or be for itself, at all.

Oddly enough, the scientistic objectivism is implicated in a related overtaking of the *passio*. For the project of objectification, while seeming to free from anthropomorphism, is another imposition on the givenness of life as such. There is no givenness, there is no received patience of being. The given conditions of life, on the surface of things, are to be reconfigured in terms of the secret *scientistic anthropomorphism*. Not surprisingly, this scientistic objectivism passes from the self-affirmation of life to a kind of mutation of love of life into hatred of the given conditions of life as other to us. A tyrannical autonomy (*autonomia turannos*) would impose on the neutralized conditions of life what it takes to be worthy of affirmation, and what is worthy of affirmation must serve it and it alone.[13] The de-humanization strangely serves a different project of the human. There is no patience for any givenness of life as such, except the waiting game that is needed to allow the day to come when we will be its masters and possessors. The anti-anthropomorphic project secretly serves us once again, and there is no true between. Between us and the otherness of life, the entire project is, in the final reckoning, a matter between us and ourselves. Even the inhuman, the non-human, is a mirror in which we see only ourselves. We see horror, but the horror mirrors our own hatred of life as given.

## Interlude II

### Life Granted on Metaxological Thresholds

I offer now four saturated surfaces that illuminate living on a metaxological threshold.

*First surface at the beginning of life*: The scream of the newly born infant on entry into life. Some will think of the scream in terms of horror at life. Lear: "When we are born, we cry that we are come to this great stage of fools." The scream is Munch's face before the horror of being. But is it quite so? For when the infant bawls there is relief and delight. The infant is alive and its scream communicates the self-affirmation of life. Were all quiet, we would worry something was wrong, something amiss. When there is no noise, we fear death. The infant affirms its own life, it communicates beyond its own life. This is being born as *co-natus*: from another, self-affirming, crying out, reaching out. We come to be from another, we are as reaching to another. What do we need to recognize the scream as the sign of life? Not science, certainly. And there is nothing neutrally objective about this recognition. Even in the self-affirming of the infant's life, there

---

13. See Desmond, "Autonomia." This is a recurrent theme in *Ethics and the Between*.

is also a communication beyond itself, though it knows it not, and thus there is more to the self-affirmation of life than self.

*Second surface from the middle of life*: I cite an interesting observation of Wittgenstein:

> Today I saw a poster saying: "'Dead' Undergraduate speaks." The inverted commas mean: "He isn't really 'dead.'" He isn't what people call dead. They call it "dead" not quite correctly.... It suddenly struck me: If someone said "He isn't dead, although by the ordinary criteria he is dead"—couldn't I say: "He is not only dead by the ordinary criteria; he is what we call 'dead.'" "If you now call him, 'alive,' you're using language in a queer way, because you are almost deliberately preparing misunderstandings. Why don't you use some other word, and let 'dead' have the meaning it already has?"[14] In general, if you say: "He is dead" and I say "He is not dead" no one would say: "Do they mean the same by 'dead'? In the case where a man has visions I wouldn't offhand say: "He means something different."[15]

I take these remarks to be striking reminders of the strange ways we sometimes use words. Yet Wittgenstein's remarks settle no issue, since what we mean by "dead" and "alive" still are shrouded in mystery. What are the meanings "death" and "life" we already have? Even though we know, in one sense, what we are talking about, in another sense, we do not know. Ordinary usage will only get us so far—as far as the threshold of mystery: the surplus surface of too much, or almost nothing. Wittgenstein's dedication is to the "ordinary" meaning—but what is "ordinary"? It is on the surface of things, you might say, but what does it mean to take something at "face value"? It is not at all clear what "face value" is. And what if one were to think of resurrection? How ordinary can this be, or how extraordinary? How we use words will take us so far, but yet there will be something stunning about what surfaces—resurrects itself, from the grave of ordinariness, and faces us. Should we say that the Misfit in Flannery O'Connor's, "A Good Man is Hard to Find," is closer to the mystery of surfacing when he growls: Jesus was the only one that ever raised the dead... and he shouldn't have done it? Or is the Misfit a kind of ordinary-language philosopher? He murders—though not to dissect.[16]

---

14. Wittgenstein, *Lectures and Conversations*, 65.

15. Ibid., 62.

16. See also Shakespeare's *The Winter's Tale*, with the statue of Hermione coming back to life at the end in the final scene. See Cavell, *Disowning Knowledge*.

*Third surface from later in life*: The process of *aging* as revealing, in the passing between of life, something neither objective nor subjective but both. Aging is important for the time of our life, for the time of living. In the timed body, aging makes finiteness evident on the surface. True, often now we try to refigure that surface—with cosmetic surgery, for instance. We struggle to keep time at bay by means of the youth of the surface. The struggle is always finally lost. In this respect also aging is very much connected with beauty. Beauty blooms but it is also fugitive and transient. It passes and it passes away. We more easily find beauty in youth than in age. We console ourselves by saying that the former is a surface physical thing, while in the latter we may find beauty of spirit or soul, which is not tied to the beauty of the surface. All this may be quite true, and yet the importance of the surface of things is not to be denied. Aging is a surfacing of time in our embodied being, and none can evade this surfacing, even if we can postpone it provisionally.

The between character of aging is instructive. Aging is not objective, is not subjective. It is both. It happens to us; but it is something sensed intimately. The time of the body is a living time, but it is transient and mortal. The loss of beauty on the surface goes with the time of our embodiment. Something is passing, neither subjective nor objective, and yet both. What is it that passes? It is life that passes, but as passing it still is life, and hence in another sense, it does not pass. It is what it is in passing, and yet still is life. And so the old do not always intimately know their own time as old. Lived from within, as lived, it still is young for itself, even if is for others it shows the signs of decrepitude.

When we think of aging we think of old age, but why should not analogous considerations apply to youth, being young. I mean the between condition of being neither objective nor subjective, of being a threshold of passing life. For surely the sense of the passing as passing applies as much to the process of growing as to that of declining, to becoming as to undoing, to passing to blooming as to passing the zenith and falling away from it. What is passing is held in a more pleasing poise on the surface of things with a younger beauty. The surface poise of old age yields to slackness in the tuning of the surface of things. What passes in the slackness is as enigmatic in its passing away as what passes more vigorously in the younger bloom. It is not a structure, not a form. It is a forming, an animating, an enlivening—but it is also a deforming, an anaesthetizing, a deadening. The sere, the yellow leaf was once lush with green.

*Fourth surface close to the end*: I am thinking of a last illumination of life on the surface in *King Lear*, from almost beyond life and death, from life and its last breath. By comparison with the comic farce of Monty-Python, this last surface thresholds on a tragic extreme. The pig squeals, the dead parrot does not scream, the new born infant bawls, but Lear howls at the death of Cordelia: "Howl, howl, howl, howl."[17] King Lear is trying to ascertain if his beloved daughter is alive or dead. It is the surface that is attended to: Is there a breath in a mirror, does a feather stir with her breath? How delicate the images of life are: a breath that will mist a mirror—so fragile its being there is almost not there at all, even when life is thriving—an evanescent-almost-nothing that in death is indeed now nothing; a breath that will move a feather, but this is a mortal breath. It is an endowed breath that had its time. It is not quite the spirit of God that will be more than a feather floating, though it descends like a dove to brood on the earth, or ascend to the sky, also like a bird that for a while one can still follow and see, and then, almost instant-like, where before it was it now no longer is, and it seems it has as if become nothing. A person has breathed their last. Why do we stand on the earth looking up? There is huge extremity in Lear's outcry when he realizes that the life is irrevocably gone:

> And my poor fool is hang'd! No, no, no life!
> Why should a dog, a horse, a rat, have life,
> And thou no breath at all? Thou'lt come no more,
> Never, never, never, never, never!
> Pray you, undo this button: thank you, sir.
> Do you see this? Look on her, look, her lips,
> Look there, look there!

---

17. KING LEAR (5, 3):
Howl, howl, howl, howl! O, you are men of stones:
Had I your tongues and eyes, I'd use them so
That heaven's vault should crack. She's gone for ever!
I know when one is dead, and when one lives;
She's dead as earth. Lend me a looking-glass;
If that her breath will mist or stain the stone,
Why, then she lives.
KENT: Is this the promised end?
EDGAR: Or image of that horror?
ALBANY: Fall, and cease!
KING LEAR: This feather stirs; she lives! if it be so,
It is a chance which does redeem all sorrows
That ever I have felt . . .

Perhaps never has this word "never" been uttered with such agony. Of course, "never" is the negative counterpart to the word "once." The "once" of life—there in its mortal preciousness, its beloved beauty. Think how far we are from the neutralized thereness of the objectivizing reduction and how far too from the self-involvement of the subjectivizing reduction. The "once" is a gift of received beauty that gathers something ontologically good and unique to singular incarnation. The "never" is the return of the given to the enigma of the nothing from which it was given to be.

Cordelia is dead. Will there be more? Life beyond life . . . and death? If one were then to speak of saturated surfaces it would be so in a paradoxical sense. The surface is as much a place of surplus as an opening into emptiness. It is the threshold between the plenitude of life and the emptying of its gift into death. It is at once both the surplus and the emptying. The surface is a little like eros: a double creation of a poverty and resource. Is the resource a *poros*, a porosity, beyond all mortal *penia*, within whose between-space opens a threshold between humans and divinity, mortals and immortals—a threshold which can only be crossed in death?

### Coming to the Saturated Surface: Hell and Transient Beauty

In these four saturated surfaces we have passed from birth into life, and through life to death, and perhaps beyond life and death to life. What then of philosophizing on the surface of things? In this last reflection I would like to return briefly to the connection between beauty and the porosity of being, with reference to transience on an extreme threshold, putting the accent on our being as suffering, as exposed to what is other to ourselves. Beauty opens and reopens the porosity of our being; but there is a vulnerability in being porous. Just as there can be transcending upwards there can be transcending downward, and the latter can mean a descent into hell, though there are different ways of descending.

I recur to the theme with which I opened, that is, a kind of "transcending" downward, below the ground of the underground—into hell. I recount the story of the Bull of Phalaris. As a sacrifice to Apollo, Phalaris the tyrant sent to the oracle at Delphi the statue of a magnificent bronze bull. In his communication with the priests at Delphi, Phalaris recounts how he was given the bull by Perilaus. Perilaus was an architect/sculptor and constructed the bull as a kind of torture machine. A person could be put into the bronze bull and a fire lit beneath it, and as the heat spread and was communicated the person imprisoned would "feel the heat" and scream. The fiendish part of the construction had to do with the fact that reed pipes could be placed in the nostrils of the bull and they would transform the screams of the tortured prisoners into sweet music. The screams of the tortured are turned into "the sweetest possible music by the auloi, piping dolefully and lowing piteously."[18]

"A thing of beauty is a joy forever," so sang John Keats, but qua contraption, this work of art transmogrifies the excruciating pain experienced by those being burned alive into exquisite music designed to delight the tyrant. The shrieks of mortal despair serve as the source of aesthetic pleasure, but those who hear the music do not hear the shrieks. The artwork can serve, on the one hand, to reveal hell, on the other hand, to conceal hell. The perplexity this story poses for us: Is this then what beauty is—music wrung from hell, concealing hell as it is, and making it look like a heaven? The pipes bring forth lovely sounds, but what surfaces disguises the shrieks of the tormented. Is this beauty: a delicate gloss on dismal darkness? The surface of the beautiful hides the working of hell.

Remember, however, the equivocity of saturated surfaces as thresholds of transition. Think doubly of the night: night can be the time of nightmares, of blindness, of crying out from abysses of desolation and sorrow, of being overcome by monsters, of helpless struggle to escape, of dreadful quasi-movement, when one moves and one cannot move, lives but does not live. If one can be devastated by night, the night is also the time of rest and refreshment. It brings sleep that knits up the raveled sleeve of care, the balm of the darkness, the tenderness of love, the softness of the shining moon and the healing nocturnal quiet when the longing for eternity wakes. In the dark divine dreams are given and messengers from beyond this life come to visit. Remember also that equivocity when, standing on the surface of the earth, an intrusive light so assaults us that we are victim of "light-pollution." Too much of the garish light of the metallic metaphysics, and we can no longer see. We lose the mystery of things. Life is night as well as day. We need the dreams of the night for the health of the day. These dreams might mingle horror and beauty, and yet without sleep and dreaming we go mad in the noonday glare. Beauty too is a seductive night of the soul that wakes its erotic porosity.

The equivocity surfaces here in relation to hell. For there might be a different sense in which the artist turns hell into song—there may be a redemptive sense. One is reminded of Orpheus, and his music in Hades.

---

18. See Harmon, *Lucian*, 17–19. Some versions of the story downplay the cruel tyranny of Phalaris, in others it is foregrounded.

There are different ways of being in the underworld. His music could bring tears even in the underworld, and melt hard hearts. Enchanting song reopens even in hell the primal porosity. There is another way of being in hell, and communicating a power that is more than hell. Going below the surface can take us into chambers of horror, and we must spend our season in hell, but if this were the end of the matter, and there was no golden night of the agapeic heart, we would have no standing anew on the surface of the earth.

One of the most beautiful songs of the surface might be found in the final few lines of the *Inferno* of Dante. Vigil and Dante descend into the hell hole, but at a certain central point their descent turns into its opposite, namely, ascent out of hell, and upwards once again to the surface of the earth. They climb up over the fixed Lucifer and climb beyond hell. The frozen Lucifer is beyond all porosity, all permeability: fixed eternally in himself as himself—a parody of divine eternity. The center of hell is the closure of the porosity onto itself, and instead of the opening of the soul to what is beyond it, we find the frozen Lucifer who weeps eternally, as in his mouth he masticates the great traitors: Judas, Brutus, and Cassius. Virgil and Dante ascend beyond the frozen Lucifer and into an opening upwards. The journey through the Inferno has been long and replete in many scenes of horror and depravity. But this ascent now, once having passed through the heart of darkness, takes places quickly. The brevity of these last lines is notable, by comparison with the previous sojourn in hell and journey through it. But one feels there is a new invigoration of life palpable in the lines as they come to the surface and the two behold again the stars. These lines, ending on the threshold of a fresh beginning, are beautiful and worth recall:

> My guide and I entered that hidden road
> To make our way back up to the bright world.
> We never thought of resting while we climbed.
> We climbed, he first and I behind, until,
> Through a small round opening ahead of us
> I saw the lovely things the heavens hold,
> And we came out once more to see the stars.[19]

---

19. Dante, *Divine Comedy*, 133–39. Lo duca e io per quel cammino ascoso / intrammo a retornar nel chiaro mondo; / e sanza cura aver d'alcun riposo, / salimmo sù, el primo e io secondo, / tanto ch'i' vidi de le cose belle / che porta 'l ciel, per un pertugio tondo. / E quindi uscimmo a riveder le stelle.

It is night over the world when the poets come to the surface. But there is a light that shines on things, and in the night it is the borrowed light of the stars. Still more, there is a source of light above the sublunary world, beyond the stars. In the beauty of the night we do not directly see the sun, but we are not entirely cut off from its light. To come thus to the surface of things, after hell, we begin again to open to the marvel of things. We even begin to wonder if the saturated surface of things is the place of consecration where God gives himself for praise.

## Bibliography

Cavell, Stanley. *The Claim of Reason: Wittgenstein, Morality, Skepticism and Tragedy.* 2nd ed. Oxford: Oxford University Press, 1999.

———. *Disowning Knowledge: In Seven Plays of Shakespeare.* Cambridge: Cambridge University Press, 2003.

Dante, Alighieri. *The Divine Comedy: Vol. I—Inferno.* Translated by Mark Musa. New York: Penguin Classics, 1984.

Desmond, William. "*Autonomia Turranos*: On Some Dialectical Equivocities of Self-Determination." *Ethical Perspectives* 5.4 (1998) 233–52.

———. *Being and the Between.* Albany, NY: State University of New York Press, 1995.

———. *Ethics and the Between.* Albany, NY: State University of New York Press, 2001.

———. *God and the Between.* Oxford: Blackwell, 2008.

———. *The Intimate Strangeness of Being: Metaphysics after Dialectic.* Washington, DC: Catholic University of America Press, 2012.

Harmon, A. M. *Lucian*, Vol. 1. New York: Macmillan, 1913.

Henry, Michel. *I Am the Truth: Towards a Philosophy of Christianity.* Translated by Susan Emanuel. Stanford: Stanford University Press, 2003.

Jonas, Hans. *The Phenomenon of Life: Toward a Philosophical Biology.* Foreword by L. Vogel. Evanston, IL: Northwestern University Press, 2001.

Morange, Michel. *Life Explained.* Translated by M. Cobb and M. DeBevoise. New Haven: Yale University Press, 2008.

Schopenhauer, Arthur. *The World as Will and Representation.* 2 vols. Translated by E. F. J. Payne. New York: Dover, 1966.

Wittgenstein, Ludwig. *Lectures and Conversations on Aesthetics, Psychology and Religious Belief.* Edited by Cyril Barrett. Oxford: Blackwell, 1966.

# 2

# Affect

Towards a Theology of Experience

*Graham Ward*

### A Change of Heart

IN TURN I'M GOING to be biblical, philosophical (though theological in orientation), and biological, or more specifically neurophysiological. This is not a polished piece of research but an improvisation and a gamble that may not amount to anything. But let me try something and then get your response. In the time I have I can't go into all the details of the conjunctions I want to make, but the methodology is one that might be called an engaged systematic theology. And I can say more about that project later. In this paper I'm concerned primarily with two interrelated theological issues: sanctification and the formation of the soul—that is, the soul's embodiment, its sentient life, its inner reflective life and the environment in which it dwells. For the formation or rather transformation or even transubstantiation of the soul is what salvation and discipleship is all about. With every encounter with the world in which it dwells, the embodied soul is continually undergoing some process or another, some dilation or contraction, some inflexion or hardening, some present learning that will fashion its future. I'm going to switch from Greek to Hebrew now, because if I continue with the Greek "soul" (*psuchē*) then I will always have adjectivally to predicate "embodied" in order to avoid any possibility of dualism. The Hebrew "heart" (*lev*) bears no such difficulty.[1] It is the seat of the emotions and as such it is sentient; it is a name of one of the most important of our corporeal organs or viscera; and it is also the place where thinking, believing, imagining, and memory takes place. It faces both the external and the internal worlds of the body; it both embraces the conscious and the unconscious, for there are things hidden in the heart that only God can draw forth. And so with the "heart" we turn to two scriptures. I'm going to use the Authorized Version for its resonance and in honor of its four hundredth anniversary this year (2011).

The first is from Ezekiel: "A new heart also I will give you and a new spirit will I put within you; and I will take away the stony heart out of your flesh, and I will give you a heart of flesh. And I will put my spirit within you, and cause you to walk in my statutes, and ye shall keep my judgements, and do them."[2] This is the great promise of God's redemption. The spirit is *ruach*—breath, life—and it animates the heart in ways that lead from feelings and thoughts to acts: walking in God's statutes, keeping God's judgments. The promise here is the acknowledgement of a divine desire understood in Psalm 51:5: "thou desirest truth in the inward parts; and in the hidden part thou shalt make me to know wisdom." But even in this acknowledgement there lies a recognition that what God desires so God will perform: "thou shalt make me to know." How are we made to know? And how are we given a new heart of flesh? It is not, I contend, by divine fiat; rather it is by a divine working within us that discipleship inaugurates; that transformation or even transubstantiation of the heart of stone.

My second scripture is from Matthew's Gospel, and Jesus is speaking: "whatsoever entereth in at the mouth goeth into the belly, and is cast out into the draught? But those things which proceed out of the mouth come forth from the heart; and they defile a man. For out of the heart proceed evil thoughts, murders, adulteries, fornications, thefts, false witness, and blasphemies: these are the things which defile a man."[3] Here is a portrait

---

1. There has been much debate since the end of the Second World War about the virtues of the Hebrew *nephesh*, which the LXX translates as *psuchē*. *Nephesh*, it is said, is holistic rather than dualistic. For advocates of this understanding of *nephesh*, see Johnson, *The One and the Many*, 4, 7, 33. But not all biblical scholars are convinced. For the counter argument see Barr, *The Garden of Eden*, 32–44. Barr also gives an interesting contextualization for a shift in biblical hermeneutics away from Hellenistic readings to Jewish readings.

2. Ezek 36:26–27.

3. Matt 15:17–20.

of the stony heart: whose thinking, speaking, doing, and feeling are all ordered towards what Augustine, creating two (im)moral categories, calls the *libido dominandi* and the *amor sui*. It is not the heart as such which is evil, for as Jesus says elsewhere in Matthew, it is the source of what is most valuable to you—"where your treasure is there will your heart be also"[4]— and from it may also flow forgiveness:[5] "Blessed are the pure in heart, for they shall see God."[6] If it is not the heart as such that is wrong then it is the *disposition* of the heart; that is, the ordering of its feeling, knowing, and doing. So if redemption is the work of grace that transforms or transubstantiates the heart then we should expect, as the law of God is written upon our inner parts, that our sentient and emotional life, our cognitive life and the involvement of both in our behavior (and that behavior again upon our sentient and cognitive life) will be changed.

## Sanctification and Theologies of Experience

To be transformed into his likeness—to be transubstantiated—requires an inner working of his Spirit: our sanctification.[7] This inner working cannot just take place at the level of knowing and doing. There are those who may know, intellectually, an awful lot about God, what has been transcribed of his work in the Scriptures, the history of the interpretation of those Scriptures, and the traditions of those who worship him; there are people who can speak words of eloquent piety; and there are those who can act in accordance with the teachings of the tradition, its ritual laws of purity, for example. But such people may not know, intimately, as in marriage a man knows his wife—in the inner working of sanctification. Jesus himself draws attention to the hypocrisies of the Pharisees, the Sadducees, and the Temple Scribes in his own day; and any one of us who preaches

---

4. Matt 6:21.
5. Matt 18:35.
6. Matt 5:8.
7. What I am not treating here is what one might call the "other side" of the operation—that treated in a doctrine of the atonement. In a purely heuristic fashion (because the relationship between the two economies are profoundly intertwined), we could call the sanctification process the human and ecclesial side of the atonement, which is a more objective operation between God the Father and God the Son. We enter into the effects of the reconciliation Christ's death and resurrection performs. Because of the intra-divine nature of this second economy, we cannot approach this phenomenologically. We can only treat the outworking in and through the Spirit in terms of personal and collective sanctification.

recognizes that pious words are cheap and altruistic acts can often be done out of duty or fear of social stigma or a sense of moral righteousness. To be transformed then, to be turned into imitators of Christ and embody his real presence, hence our transubstantiation, is a more profound work that goes on at the level of the affections not just knowledge; affections which can never be disassociated from our corporeality, our cognitions and our embodied acts. At the basis of the "murders, adulteries, fornications, thefts, false witness, [and] blasphemies" of which Jesus speaks lies a set of emotions—hatred, anger, lust, covetousness, jealousy—emotions which are prior to acts and prior sometimes even to what theories of the emotions call the "appreciation" of the emotion, that turns them into conscious feelings.[8] More of that anon. It is then not just what proceeds from the heart but *the heart itself* that needs to be transformed. It is in the realms of our pre- or unconscious, it is in the spheres that are prior to our will to act, that the labor of sanctification must work. And this labor is not accomplished in a moment, even a moment of conversion or revelation; it has to be accomplished over a lifetime of attunement and turning. Discipleship is a learning process, a venture into an ongoing *metanoia*, repentance, and confession. Such discipleship will not just impact our ethics, and the *ethoi* that such an ethics creates; nor will it just impact our understanding. To impact our affections it has to penetrate our emotional life; and our emotional life, as we will see, is intimately connected with our biologies and physiologies. It is a "heart of flesh" that is to be formed from a "heart of stone." And if we take these phrases, and the additional description of the "hardening of the heart" that comes from unrepentance and stubborn persistence in doing things one's own way and for one's own gratification, as only metaphors then we miss the profundity of what incarnation means. The change of disposition that sanctification performs is a work of the Spirit exploring the hidden depths of the human heart. Such an exploration awakens us to our own inner motivations, revealing to us inmost secrets and emotional stirrings (perhaps aspects of ourselves and our experience we repress the acknowledgement of or psychologically forget). In this way the Spirit sanctifies the heart. It is a work of grace to which we have to give access and acceptance, from which we have to take heed and learn. Things hidden have to be brought to confession. This is

---

8. So-named "seven deadly sins" are, as Augustine understood, disorders of love. They—envy, vainglory, sloth, avarice, anger, gluttony, lust—also name profoundly affective states.

the learning that discipleship inaugurates. It is learning about ourselves, the human condition and the world around us.

"[I]nteriority does not close off the world but allows the world to penetrate us more deeply."[9] For in exploring the hidden depths of our being the Spirit is at work in and through and beyond us—in the churches to which we belong and the world in which we dwell. But we can hinder the work of the Spirit—if only for a time—through that self-assertion which "hardens" the heart and turns it to stone. The hardening is literal. We know how our emotional and intellectual life impacts the autonomic nervous system that governs our heartbeat, blood pressure, muscle tone, breathing, bowel movements, perspiration, and adrenalin glands releasing stress hormones into the bloodstream. Stress—which "hardening" indicates—has physiological affects; just as the release from stress (experiencing that peace which the world cannot give) also has physiological affects. Radical incarnation—which involves the Spirit of Christ living in us and bringing about our sanctification and the sanctification of the world—operates at the level of our somatic, emotional, and cognitive experience. "Hearts of stone," "hearts of flesh," and "hardening of the heart" are then as much physiological descriptions as accounts of moral dispositions. In his laconic notes for a lecture course on the phenomenology of Christian mediaeval mysticism of 1918–19 (a course he never actually gave), Heidegger makes some astute observations about Christianity and experience. He begins by pointing out that the "power," "grace," and "wrath" of God are all "experiential effects."[10] With mysticism we perceive the "emergence of a new motivational complex in the experiencing subject."[11] In fact, it is not simply that Christians, like all other human beings, are experiential creatures; there is also that in Christianity that motivates the Christian to seek experience—an experience of God in a relationship of love and worship towards him. The "[r]eligious longing for experience and giving effort towards the presence of Jesus is possible as genuine only as a growing out of a basic experience. Such experiences are not freely and deliberately at one's disposal in the observance of the rules of church law. 'Knowledge' about these experiences and their essence rises only in actual having-experienced."[12] As such, there needs to be then, in a way that does justice to the "full facticity" of the concrete historical context, a theology of

---

9. Wright, "Edith Stein," 139.
10. Heidegger, *Phenomenology of Religious Life*, 233.
11. Ibid., 238.
12. Ibid., 252.

experience quite at odds with any suprahistorical and universalist account of religious experience *per se*.[13]

Now a much shortened theological section: in sanctification, we are not talking about some abstract ethereal process but a concrete operation of affect: something we experience even if it is something we cannot, ourselves, calculate and measure. So let us turn to two quite similar and specifically Christian accounts of experience, the first by Schleiermacher and the second by Hegel.

Both Schleiermacher and Hegel understood that the origins of the theological and the ethical lay with "feeling" and "intuition." By feeling and its relation to intuition neither of these thinkers, from whom we have much to learn and much to appreciate, are primarily referring to something occult, paranormal, or clairvoyant. Although there are moments in Schleiermacher's early, more Romantic work, when his living "intuition of the universe"[14] is related to a certain, and idiosyncratically understood, mysticism. But primarily, Schleiermacher and Hegel speak of feeling (*Gefühl*) and intuition (*Anschauung*) from their deep, if eventually highly critical, reading of Kant. It must be emphasized that while there might be some debates about the term's meaning in Hegel, for Schleiermacher *Gefühl* is not reducible to *Sinneseindruck* (sense impression) or *Empfindung* (sentience). Together with *Anschauung* it bears a close resemblance to *Stimmung* or attunement.[15] For Kant, *Gefühl* and *Anschauung* are terms related to the primary reception of the manifold (what he calls the *Ding an sich*), which for him is ultimately unknowable.[16] It is unknowable because all our immediate perceptions of it are mediated through our consciousness: first, our faculty of the imagination, then our faculty of understanding,

---

13. Ibid., 183.

14. Schleiermacher, *On Religion*, 104. In the two subsequent editions of 1806 and 1821 the language of the "universe" is toned down because of contemporary critics reading pantheism into such a view.

15. Recognizing the affinity of "feeling" and "intuition" with "attunement" fits with a twofold emphasis in Schleiermacher's thought, over against Kant's. First, Schleiermacher's concern with ontological participation and not just epistemology that goes as far back as his 1789 essay "Über das höchste Gut," which ends on the observation that the "moral sense" (*moralisches Sinnes*) or "moral feeling" (*moralischen Gefühl*) derives from (*abgeleitet*) and is related to (*bezieht sich auf*) the moral law (all instances of which constitute the highest good). Secondly, Schleiermacher's use of the term "Gemüth," which means "soul" or the "heart" or one's disposition—a term that unities the cognitive and the sentient, the mental and the corporeal.

16. Famously in *Critique of Pure Reason*, A19: "In whatever manner and by whatever means a mode of knowledge may relate to objects, *intuition* is that through which it is in immediate relation to them and to which all thought as a means is directed."

and finally our faculty of reasoning. We only know the *Ding an sich* as it becomes conceptualized, spatialized, and temporalized; that is, as it enters the realm of phenomena. In and of itself, for Kant, it belongs to the realm of the noumenal. Both Schleiermacher and Hegel were famously skeptical, indeed scathing, about Kant's bifurcation of human existence between the noumenal and the phenomenological.[17] Nevertheless, they took the concept of intuition from him, and what was most important about intuition for both of them was Kant's claim that "intuition takes place only in the object so far as it is given to us."[18] This understanding of perception as reception is the basis for Schleiermacher's concept of religion and later piety: "what you thus intuit and perceive is not the nature of things, but their action upon you."[19] Let us also note that *Anschauung* can also mean "contemplation." This meaning is more justifiable when treating Schleiermacher because Schleiermacher was profoundly influenced by Plato (who he spent most of his working life translating). "Intuition" then would relate not to just immediate (or better a primordial preconsciousness) perception, but also to that to which the perception gives rise: *theoria* or contemplation. For Hegel intuition is the "perceptible particular," but as Georg Lasson, who edited Hegel's manuscript *System der Sittlichkeit* in 1913, wrote in his Introduction, this was part of Hegel's understanding of actuality as "the totality of life which brings all moments of life together. . . . This actuality . . . is a givenness."[20] Both Schleiermacher and Hegel are concerned with the sheer givenness of life that feeling and intuition access and from it, for both, issues ethical life. Both thinkers frame their thoughts within a Christian theology and are treating here our situatedness within this givenness of all things, which for Schleiermacher is infinite, and for Hegel (who doesn't care for the language of the early Romantics) is absolute.[21] Hegel: "Thus . . . ethical life is also an unveiling, an emergence of the universal in the face of the particular. . . . This intuition, wholly immersed

---

17. For Schleiermacher, see his 1793–94, long, unpublished essay "Über die Freiheit." For Hegel, see his 1802-3, published, long essay "Gluten und Wisent."

18. Kant, *Critique of Pure Reason*, A19.

19. Schleiermacher, *On Religion*, 104–5.

20. Quoted in Hegel, *Ethical Life*, 100.

21. The exception to this is in his 1802 *System der Sittlichkeit*, where he employs many of the terms Schleiermacher himself used, terms that later he avoided. Perhaps we should read this early text as answering Schleiermacher's 1799 *On Religion*, which was very popular at the time—although there is no mention of Schleiermacher in the text. There is a critique of Schleiermacher's book in his important 1802 publication "Faith and Knowledge."

in the singular, is *feeling*."²² We are then "wholly immersed." Schleiermacher is more effusive:

> The universe exists is uninterrupted activity and reveals itself at every moment. Every form that it brings forth, every being to which it gives a separate existence according to the fullness of life, every occurrence that spills forth from its rich, ever-fruitful womb, is an action of the same upon us. . . . [T]he drive to intuit, if it is oriented to the infinite, places the mind in unlimited freedom. . . . [E]very intuition is, by its nature, connected with feeling. Your senses mediate the connection between the object and yourselves; the same influence of the object, which reveals its existence to you, must stimulate them in various ways and produce a change in your inner consciousness. This feeling, of which you are frequently scarcely aware, can in other cases grow to such intensity . . . your whole nervous system can be so permeated by it that for a long time that sensation alone dominates and resounds and resists the effect of other impressions.²³

Schleiermacher engages the mystical when he approaches his notion of "unlimited freedom." What is evident though from what I have already presented is that for both Hegel and Schleiermacher, the body is the source whereby we create our personal world, which generates much of the meaning we make out of our experience of the world that is worlded (by others, past and present, as well as ourselves). Both expressly affirmed the inseparability of the body and the soul in a more or less Aristotelian manner. If the soul is the form of the body for Aristotle then Hegel speaks of the soul framing the body directly so that one can "neither be supposed nor conceived without the other"²⁴ and Schleiermacher admits we cannot really attain an "idea of finite spiritual life apart from that of a bodily organism."²⁵ But prior to the worlding of the world that takes place through the mental representation and communication of which human beings are capable there is that nakedness of immersion or permeation itself in the face of the given. If Schleiermacher finds the origin of religion in this primordial feeling—which later he will define in terms of the feeling of absolute dependence and Hegel, in 1802, will describe as "a universal physical dependence on one another"²⁶—I want to maintain the sense of

---

22. Hegel, *Ethical Life*, 103.
23. Schleiermacher, *On Religion*, 105–9.
24. Hegel, *Ethical Life*, 159.
25. Schleiermacher, *On Religion*, 709.
26. Hegel, *Ethical Life*, 167.

exposure it brings before it produces a change in our inner consciousness, moving our minds to think and our mouths to speak. For there is a silence in this unmediated moment; a silence can only be thought when it has been mediated and we do have words, and in being thought is broken. It is a silence of accord and attunement—that we have been created in such a way that we can become aware that the "wide earth" is where we belong; as a beating part of an overwhelming extension. And we do belong, because we are part of the givenness of all things, part of the intricate organization and balances that orders and maintains what is given. There is also then a peace insofar as this is what feeling does and this is what life does, and one accords with and supports the other. I say peace and I do not intend quietism. The peace is not ours in ourselves, it is *given* to us and we *receive* the impress of that gift. The peace is from elsewhere and we enter it, actively, as we receive. For this is a primordial encounter between what Schleiermacher would describe as the intuited and the intuiter and what we find is that our givenness recognizes the fore-givenness of all things and that we dwell here. There are two interrelated but different understandings of the suffix "for." In "forethought" the suffix means "ahead" or "in front"—to think in advance in this case. But in Old English, where we get our verbs to give (*griefan*) and to forgive (*forgriefan*) from, the suffix "for" means "completely"—that which is *completely given*, given without either qualification or constraint;[27] an absolute givenness that is both prior to and in advance of our intuiting it. We find ourselves immersed in the "wide earth," in its sheer gratuitousness, the wealth of its provision, and the effulgence of its grace.

This is what I mean by "the feeling I belong here"—that I too am given in this givenness. Given but not dissolved. I remain, as Hegel insisted, as that which is singular, particular. This feeling is always *my* feeling. In his early work, Schleiermacher comes close, if he does not fall into, a mystic fusion: "a Promethean deification of humankind and a Spinozistic deification of the universe."[28] And even Hegel points to a moment of union or rather, for him, unity; a primordial "indifference" that he equates with "enjoyment": "This enjoyment in which the object is determined purely ideally, and entirely annihilated, is purely sensuous enjoyment, i.e., the satiation which is the restoration of the indifference and emptiness of the

---

27. *Forgriefan* means to grant, allow, or to give in marriage. The same affiliation, from the same Anglo-Saxon root, between to give and to forgive is found in German, with *geben* and *vergeben*

28. Blackwell, *Schleiermacher's Early Philosophy*, 207.

individual or of his bare possibility of being ethical and rational."²⁹ But, in an early fragment reported on and perhaps in the possession of Karl Rosenkranz, Hegel, perhaps in response to Schleiermacher, observes: "it is the essence of religion that the spirit is not ashamed of any of its individuals. . . . The supercession of subjectivity is not the sheer nullification of it, but just the nullification of its empirical individuality, and by this means it is a purification for the absolute enjoyment of its [i.e., the spirit's] absolute essence."³⁰ In another fragment dated around 1803–4, Hegel speaks of "absolute self-enjoyment" and seems to be suggesting, as in the quote found in Rosenkranz, that this is the divine trinitarian condition.³¹ Our own enjoyments (even the sensuous ones) are then glimpses and distant analogical participations in divine and absolute self-enjoyment or blessedness. If Hegel then, as he increasingly understands his own dialectical method, maintains separateness and defers union, Schleiermacher expresses a unifying moment in the original intuition that relates to his "mysticism": "I lie on the bosom of the infinite world. I am in this moment its soul, for I feel its powers and its infinite life as I feel my own. In this moment it is my body, for I permeate its muscles and limbs as I do my own, and its innermost nerves, like my own, move in accordance with my sense and my presentiment."³² Nevertheless, for Schleiermacher, unlike the later development of his thought in Rudolph Otto, the self remains; even in its immersion. There is no union. It is this that Otto critiques in his own exposition of religious experience before that which is "holy." For Otto, Schleiermacher articulates a consciousness of *createdness*, but he does not articulate what Otto views as prior to that—a consciousness of *creaturehood*. The consciousness of that creaturehood issues from an "annihilation of the self" and a consciousness of "its nullity."³³ For Otto there is first an overwhelming, ineffable, non-rational encounter in which the self is dissolved and only then recovers itself in a notion of the "wholly other." This is not Schleiermacher's position. And this is perhaps why Schleiermacher pays so much more attention to the body and its senses while, for all the talk of feeling and affect, Otto's emphasis is upon the mind.³⁴

29. Hegel, *Ethical Life*, 105.
30. Rosenkrantz, *Georg Wilhelm Friedrich Hegels Leben*, 133.
31. Hegel, *Ethical Life*, 253.
32. Schleiermacher, *On Religion*, 78–79.
33. Otto, *Idea of the Holy*, 20–22.
34. It is difficult to see, in Otto, who wishes to retain the notion of dependence but articulate an experience more primordial to it, why an encounter with what is overpowering and absolutely "unapproachable" (Otto, *Idea of the Holy*, 19) could ever give

We can take something from each of these accounts. Hegel's recognition of a fundamental "enjoyment" can be understood in terms of the body's response to the divine reflection upon the conclusion of creation: "God saw everything that he had made and indeed it was very good."[35] In enjoyment the object as such is "annihilated." In a later account of such sensuous enjoyment, Hegel pays attention to that which precedes enjoyment: that is, desire. In the context of a phenomenology of sexual relations, he writes that "desire passes over into enjoyment."[36] But, at this point, where intuition is pre-conceptual and the other person has not yet entered the phenomenological frame, the enjoyment is not preceded by a conscious desire. Even so, in the annihilation that takes place, desire must be the dynamic. What is intuited in the givenness of all things is then attractive. Employing a more Platonic vocabulary, what is good is also what is beautiful, and to be desired. It is the same dynamic evident in what we can take from Schleiermacher's erotics. In German, his description of lying on the bosom of the world is more evidently erotic because the world is *die Welt*, feminine. The origin intuition from which consciousness arises can be understood in terms of the primordial encounter in feeling and intuition as a marriage and a conjugal rite, a making of one flesh. But I am more hesitant to speak of union or fusion. I want to speak instead of "rest" as in Psalm 95:11—entering into his rest: God's Sabbath satisfaction; a stillness that we must forever return to in which God is known. Or we might also speak of a condition like Mary's in her conception: "full of

---

rise to the notion of dependence at all. In fact, the encounter with the *mysterium* as described by Otto is more likely to issue in an account of the absolutely transcendent as the point of Indifference—much like Schelling's notion of God. It is with this "wholly other" that liberal theology begins, ironically. Ironically, insofar as Karl Barth thought he was recovering the "wholly other" as a descriptor for God in order to save theology from liberalism. But it is because, for Otto, God is "wholly other" that "nothing can be predicated, but that which is absolutely and intrinsically other than and opposite of everything that is and can be thought" (Otto, *Idea of the Holy*, 29). And so Otto is led towards a nominalism that, for all his commitment to Christianity and its superiority to other religions, establishes the cult and Scriptures of a particular religion as so many sets of "ideograms" naming the root and ultimate experience. So we find descriptions of the way the numinous attract and appropriates "meanings derived from social and individual ideals of obligation, justice, and goodness" (ibid., 110) so that in this way this numinous is "filled with rational and ethical meaning" (ibid., 109) but in and of itself the ineffability and total otherness of the numinous indicates its transcendent indifference to the creaturely. It is, as Otto remarks, "formally absolute" (ibid., 145). Tillich, of course, takes this line of liberal theology much further.

35. Gen 1:31.
36. Hegel, *Ethical Life*, 231.

grace." "Rest" is the concomitant of the "peace" I mentioned earlier. They are both eschatological concepts, but in the primordial intuition, which as Schleiermacher reminds us, tells us nothing about the things in themselves; we experience an intimation of the realization of the eschaton. In that rest and that peace lies this "feeling that I belong," that I dwell, of both accordance and distinction that makes possible both worship and ethical life. Again, "rest" illustrates how far we are from quietism; for quietism is not rest but resignation, an *amor fati* that we find announced in Spinoza and exalted in Nietzsche. In his early work, Schleiermacher sidles close to *amor fati* at times, but by the time we reach his mature work the feeling of absolute dependence is "devotional" in tone, developed more out of an examination of "piety" than "religion"; for "religion" is far too nebulous a term. "Piety" is expressive of the submission involved in this moment; a submission in awe, reverence, and wonder. I take this is be what the Psalms describe as the "fear" of the Lord, which is the source of wisdom. It is from this rest—which is not ours and a piety that is ours because it is our response to it—that dwelling comes, and it is from that dwelling that worship arises. Worship because the final mediation of this feeling is an opening of the lips and the showing forth of praise. As the *Book of Common Prayer* has it in both the morning and the evening liturgy:

> *Priest*: O Lord, open thou our lips.
>
> *Congregation*: And our mouths shall shew forth they praise.

Prayer is born.

I'm going to have to leave the theological as a sketch—and I'm aware this leaves begging all sorts of questions about the relationship between these accounts of feeling and intuition and Christian theology and the way Schleiermacher and Hegel develop those accounts in quite distinctive ways. But we need to proceed to the neurobiology and neuropsychology of affect, the science of emotion as it has developed over the last fifteen years through the pioneering work of researchers like Antonio Damasio and Joseph LeDoux, among many others. It is through them we can understand more about the two theological emphases found in Schleiermacher and Hegel and approach what I would call a theology of experience rather than an account of "religious" experience. In fact, there is no such thing as "religious" experience, as we shall see in engaging the work of neurobiologists and understanding more profoundly what is at stake in "feeling" and "intuition": how, since emotion is always an urge to action, this feeling/intuition is related to both doing and knowing in a highly specific context;

how what is involved in a theological emotion which, because the operations of God in the world are concerned with redemption, furthers the process of sanctification (and therefore treats sin and guilt). Now I have to be extremely brief here and considerably reductive, but allow me to make a few important observations based on the science of emotions and the importance of the concrete environments in which emotion is invoked and responds.

## Emotional Intelligence

Both Schleiermacher and Hegel recognize the preconscious character of the feeling of absolute dependence in piety and the intuition of God as himself in his creation. We are treating here what has come to be known, after Daniel Goleman, as "emotional intelligence," much of which is pre- or even un-conscious. The registration of emotion begins with sensations that are communicated to the hypothalamus handling those sensations. This is seated deep in what is called the neocortex. I'll explain why we call it "neo" in a moment. But the neocortex handles our rationalizing operations. So the information is registered and analyzed such that the objects sensed are perceived and understood, or in the case of feelings, appraised and responded to appropriately. The neocortex orchestrates our control of emotional situations. Feeling delivered from the senses, at this point, is fairly low level and arrives as judgments like "the water's hot," "that's tastes bitter," "that's soft and gentle." Such feelings are conscious ones, on the whole; though the brain processes far more sensations than consciousness is aware of. Consciousness accounts for only a small fraction of what is going on as our bodies respond to their environments and the social communities to which they belong. Such feelings demand little or nothing in terms of an emotional response. But the feeling of absolute dependence in piety and the intuition of God in his creation is not such a low-level feeling or even a feeling among other feelings. For this feeling must have a profound emotional impact, which also means a profound somatic impact, since the emotions are completely integrated into other brain features that regulate the body (muscle tone, heartbeat, blood pressure, perspiration, etc.), the hormone system (releasing chemicals like adrenaline, adrenal steroids, and peptides into the bloodstream) and various behavioral actions (freezing, running, crying, facial expressions, etc.). As I said, this is *Gefühl* not *Eindruck* or *Empfindung*. This is *An-schauung*, an inner vision or display, "inscape," as the poet Gerard Manley Hopkins would probably call it. It has a life-changing impact that energizes conversion, repentance (*metanoia*), perhaps the apprehensions of fear, guilt, and shame; it has the force of a profound and overwhelming revelation. There is an element also of surprise involved: surprised by joy. It has the power of a passion that floods the rational mind with emotion that cannot be controlled. More anatomically: Schleiermacher's *Gefühl* and Hegel's *Anschauung* "sabotage[e] the ability of the prefrontal lobe [in the neocortex] to maintain working memory."[37] The working memory is a prefrontal system that enables us to attend to and recall all that is necessary for a task in hand. Some neuropsychologists believe the contents of our working memory are what we more generally understand as "consciousness."[38] Such emotions, which override the capacity of the prefrontal lobe (on the left side) to regulate, are related to a region of the brain known as the amygdala and the limbic realm.[39] This is a much older part of the brain in terms of evolution, the root of the neocortex (neo because it is a "new" development in the brain power of mammals). The amygdala is the seat of the passions, what neuroscientists concerned with the emotions have called the "basic emotions"—emotions learnt and stored in order to survive.

To be immersed in is to be vulnerable to the world; but to be vulnerable is also to be transformable. Neurobiological and neuropsychological scientists, who treat the passions and the processes of emotion, inform us that we are continually responding to the stimulations provided by our environments, though consciousness focuses its attention on certain stimuli and others are processed subconsciously (in the subcortical regions of the brain) or unconsciously. These responses can become emotional prior to being cognitions in the sense of conscious feelings and as such trigger somatic and endocrine activities through the autonomic nervous system. Not all sensations necessarily become emotions. What is actively picked up, even searched for, by the senses has to trigger an arousal for there to be an emotional experience. Environmental psychologist, J. J. Gibson, among others, regards the senses as aggressive mechanisms that actively detect and track down (not just receive), again without necessarily engaging the intellectual process.[40] When these sensations trigger arousal systems in the brain, since each system has a different chemical identity, then different

37. Goleman, *Emotional Intelligence*, 30

38. See LeDoux, *The Emotional Brain*, 278–82.

39. There has been much research conducted as to whether there is a limbic *system*, but the current position seems to be that operations in the limbic realm do not constitute a system as such, but a series of independent relations.

40. See Gibson, *The Senses*, 97–98.

neurotransmitters are released: acetylcholine, noradrenalin, dopamine, and serotonin. All these chemicals are fundamental to establishing people's moods. Acetylcholine is a chemical associated with the amygdala area of the brain—one of the oldest, in evolutionary terms, parts of the brain below the neocortex (which mediates our thinking and rational decision making). We will return to the amygdala in a moment, for now it is important to understand that the "informational content provided by arousal systems is weak. . . . Arousal systems simply say that something important is going on."[41] Our most intense emotions, such as trauma, are related to acetylcholine and the amygdala system, which contains our innate and implicit memories. Activation of the amygdala by the sensory thalamus can connect with the neocortex region through the hippocampus (associated with long-term, explicit memory and cognition) and become conscious emotions, but can also take a much faster route by communicating directly. This "results in the automatic activation of networks that control the expression of responses . . . (freezing, fighting, facial expressions), the autonomic nervous system (ANS) responses (changes in blood pressure and heart rate, piloerection, sweating), and the hormonal responses (release of hormones, like adrenaline, adrenal steroids, as well as a host of peptides, into the bloodstream)."[42] We literally have a "gut-reaction." The different emotions can be associated, to some extent, with the different autonomic nervous system responses. Because this reaction by-passes the hippocampus and neocortex systems, which controls thinking, or only arrives at those systems later, then "we can attribute the arousal and bodily feelings to stimuli that are present in working memory. However, because the stimuli in working memory did not trigger the amygdala, the situation will be misdiagnosed."[43] In ways that cross-pollinate within psychoanalysis, neuroscientists like Joseph LeDoux, point to the unconscious as a repository for our basic emotional life and our emotional memories. Only a fraction of what goes on emotionally within us ever gets filtered through to conscious feeling in which we can identify "I am experiencing this or that." "Feelings do involve conscious content, but we don't necessarily have conscious access to the processes that produce that content. And even when we do have introspective access, the conscious content is not likely to be what triggered the emotional responses in the first place."[44] We can,

---

41. LeDoux, *The Emotional Brain*, 290–91.
42. Ibid., 291.
43. Ibid., 299.
44. Ibid.

of course, reflect upon some of these emotional processes and, to some extent, "appraise" these phenomena and name these feelings.[45] To some extent we can also trace the causes for certain feelings, usually after the event. But not always: because the emotional processing is unconscious and has somatic affects prior to rational appreciation, then our "appraisals" can be distorted—I think (cognitively) that I am angry, but on deeper reflection become aware that my anger is a reaction to a more primal fear. As to understanding their cause: because there is an emotional memory that is also mainly unconscious, and a somatic memory associated with the physiological affects of emotions, a present emotion can be associated with a forgotten or repressed stimulation. This was evidently a rich source for Freudian investigation, although more recently the psychophysiology of trauma had drawn attention to what Babette Rothschild has called "expressions of trauma not yet remembered." As she observes: "Every emotion is characterized by a discrete pattern of skeletal muscle contraction visible on the face and in body posture (somatic nervous system). Each emotion also *feels* different on the inside of the body. Different patterns of visceral muscle contractions are discernible as body sensation (the internal sense); . . . each emotion is the result of interplay between the sensory, autonomic, and somatic nervous systems interpreted within the brain's cortex."[46] Memory is needed to create emotion; it builds up a repository but it also temporalizes emotions—this is a past feeling, this is a present feeling.[47] But some emotions, traumatic ones, can generate dissociation between the stimuli, the sensory, autonomic,[48] and somatic nervous systems. In the dissociation the processing of the emotion is stalled and can then resurface as a "flashback" or somatic symptoms that Freud associated with various forms of hysteria. And some emotional triggers are so deep there is never going to be a human possibility of accessing them. For unlike the Freudian unconsciousness—from which certain things can

---

45. "Appraise" here is a technical term—see Arnold, *Emotion and Personality*. The appraisal theorists, after Arnold, see that feelings involve a mediating "appraisal" of the stimuli presented. Neuroscientists like LeDoux do not reject appraisal theorists but believe "appraisals occur unconsciously." See ibid., 52.

46. Rothschild, *Psychophysiology of Trauma*, 56

47. See Nathanson, *Shame and Pride*.

48. We have no control over the "automatic" nervous system (often abbreviated in the literature to ANS). Its operations, with respect to muscle tone (relaxed, stressed) and visceral responses (for example, sexual arousal) is involuntary. It is regulated by the limbic realm wherein our most protective instincts and reflexes abide. The two other limbic realms are called the hippocampus and the amygdale, and these process information between the body and the cerebral cortex.

be retrieved and brought to consciousness; hence therapy is through the "speaking-cure"—the emotional memory of the amygdala, since is it not directly approachable through the cortex and is a separate system from the hippocampus, cannot be plumbed at all. LeDoux sums up: "Contrary to the primary supposition of cognitive appraisal theories, the core of an emotion is not introspectively accessible to conscious representation."[49]

These cognitive scientists researching emotions and investigations into affect enable us to understand what is involved in an immersion in the world and the vulnerability of the self with respect to such an immersion. For emotions are always and only embodied. In ways more profound and more complex than thinking: "The body is crucial to emotional experience, either because it provides sensations that make an emotion feel a certain way right now or because it once provided the sensations that created memories of what specific emotions felt like in the past."[50] It involves not simply an openness to what is around us materially, socially, culturally, political, and economically—and all the complex experiences generated by such an openness—it also involves coming to terms with our own responses to all this stimulation. This "coming to terms" includes somatic and cognitive processing, understanding and managing our responses. And this goes on at the emotional level in much more complex ways than the rational. The task of processing, understanding, and management in the face of those older primitive emotions, the so-called basic emotions, even if they were all open access to our ruminations, can be overwhelming, and would be overwhelming were it not for the grace of God. But what is evident is that such affections are not abstract and generic in the way "religion" is abstract and generic. They are embodied and contextual engagements of embodiment. And there is no transcending that embodiment and contextuality. If these emotions are experienced within a tradition of piety, then they can only be theological experiences, not "religious" experiences. Lawrence Durrell ends the first part of his *The Alexandria Quartet* ("Justine") with the observation: "Does not everything depend on our interpretation of the silence around us?"[51] And he is right, but the silence is not some universal *nihil*; it is the silence of a material moment and a material place and a material circumstance.

There is still much debate concerning which emotions are primary and basic. Paul Eckman, whose research underpinned much of Daniel

---

49. LeDoux, *The Emotional Brain*, 299
50. Ibid., 298.
51. Durrell, *The Alexandria Quartet*, 195.

Goleman's influential study, *Emotional Intelligence*, lists six based upon the universal recognition of facial expressions: surprise, happiness, anger, fear, disgust, and sadness.[52] An earlier study by Jaak Panskepp, on the basis of findings from stimulating areas in the brains of rats, came up with four: panic, rage, expectancy, fear.[53] LeDoux concludes: "many if not most of the lists include some version of fear, anger, disgust, and joy. Most of the remaining disagreement is over the fringe cases, like interest, desire, and surprise."[54] It is not that with the development of the neocortex there is acquisition of certain control management for these emotions, but as I said above, these emotions can by-pass the hippocampus and its relation of cognition and memory: "the connections from the cortical areas to the amygdala are far weaker than the connections from the amygdala to the cortex. This may explain why it is so easy for emotional information to invade our conscious thoughts, but so hard for us to gain conscious control over our emotions."[55] But, as I said, theologically we understand that we are not alone in such a situation. Our immersion in the world is unavoidable, but it is a participation in Christ's immersion in the world. Only as such is the immersion bearable; only insofar as Christ as the pioneer of our faith has borne all things and brought all things in submission to him, can we possible bear the suffering of this immersion. And "suffering" here bears its older sense of "allowing things to be"; for the immersion need not be an entry into what is painful—joy, happiness, and pleasure are among our basic emotions. Augustine puts in succinctly: "*molestias et difficultates . . . tolerari iubes ea*" (You command [that we] endure troubles and difficulties).[56] In an interesting commentary, which opens up a profound meditation on being human before God, Heidegger writes: "The *tolerare* circumscribes a peculiar complex of enactment which is not operative in isolation, but which moves in a characteristic and fundamental direction of factical life."[57] Not the avoidance, but the entry more deeply into, the maintenance of an openness to allow, tolerate, endure, is the direction not only of Augustine's mediation in Book X of *Confessions*, but it is also the direction of an immersion into the glorification of all things in Christ. We may suffer sorely the complexity of human affairs, their consequences in

---

52. See Ekman, "Facial Expression."
53. Panskepp, "Theory of Emotions."
54. LeDoux, *The Emotional Brain*, 121.
55. Ibid., 265.
56. Augustine, *Confessiones*, 148–49.
57. Heidegger, *Phenomenology of Religious Life*, 152.

terms of structural sin, and their affects in terms of violence, addiction, the aggressive pursuit of self-interest, indifference, jealousy, etc. We may also suffer the world as lit up by the grace of God, his love for us, his mercy towards us, his eternal offer of forgiveness, his work of reconciliation and salvation. But, in all things, to be immersed in the world, to be vulnerable in such an immersion, is to be open to suffer in this older sense. To follow in the wake of the incarnate one is to participate in the radical nature of that incarnation, which took upon itself both our flesh, blood, passions, and experience and the sins of the whole world. But we cannot "bear all things" in the way Christ "bore all things" without a spiritual pedagogy—where spiritual engages both the corporeal and the intellectual.[58] This is a discipleship in his love. We cannot "bear all things" without having learned how to pray without ceasing. To pray without ceasing is to recognize prayer at the level of the body as well as the mind. Because, in any stretch of time the mind is preoccupied with the activities with which it is involved, and not conscious of a ceaseless interceding. To pray without ceasing is to recognize that the body too has its own knowledge and intentionality, that may or may not be attuned with what the mind, the body, and the "guts" are thinking. As Daniel Goleman points out, evolution has given emotions an important and central role in the human condition; "our deepest feelings, passions, and longing are essential guides."[59] To pray without ceasing then is not to eschew the corporeal and emotional, but to embrace them and discipline them, to cultivate the right passions, which inform and transform the soul and are informed and transformed by the soul. Only in prayer can there be that attention to the world concomitant with an immersion that is sensory, somatic, cognitive, and spiritual. This praying requires a discipline, a work, a laboring in love that opens us to an infinite responsibility. It necessitates learning how not to be defensive, how not to be fearful, and how to let go. It requires the development of what Heidegger saw as a fundamental aspect of Dasein, *Sorge* or care. But it is "care" without the worry, fear, and anxiety that is often associated with that passion. This learning in the way of love—a love in which there is no fear, no defensiveness, no self-protective reaction to what is given—is, to some

---

58. I would distinguish our contemporary understanding of mind, which from Descartes onwards has become synonymous with consciousness, from soul which embraces corporeal sense, emotional memory and processing and intellectual endeavour. The soul is both consciousness and pre-consciousness. It is a field of operations that are cognitive, somatic and spiritual—where spirit is both the life within and given to us as a gift and the life of God operating in and through Christ in creation.

59. Goleman, *Emotional Intelligence*, 4.

extent, an undoing of our evolutionary biologies. As we have evolved, we have adapted to conditions in ways that ensure our survival as a species. In this adaptation is instilled a fear of death and a need to protect ourselves. Food, shelter, and procreation will ensure that survival.

## Conclusion

What I am suggesting here is that learning the way of Christian love—which is always learned under the guidance of the Holy Spirit—physiologically will and must affect the operation of the limbic realm, that oldest part of the brain associated with the amygdala. This learning will and must engender a biological transformation in our survival instincts and reflexes, even if, for us human subjects, there is no conscious access to such areas of our emotional memory, unless things are revealed to us in prayer. For in the limbic system lies our *libido dominandi* and our *amor sui*. The two (im)moral dispositions that Augustine emphasizes are at the root of evil. Both emotional drives, rooted in the urge to self-protection, are related to the same illusion: our invulnerability. As Goleman observes, for most of us "our mental well-being is based in part on the illusion of invulnerability."[60] It is an illusion that has to be shattered; it is an illusion at the antipodes of Schleiermacher's recognition that piety rests upon the feeling of absolute dependence. As Schleiermacher recognized, and developed in his ethics, this feeling of absolute dependence in worship, as piety, is an intimation of our primordial relational condition, which constitutes the given, the gift. In the limbic realm lie the primeval and early childhood emotional memories that reinforce the innate and preconditioned fear and anger that makes us fight for our lives at all costs—rather than lay them down. Self-sacrifice, kenosis, and martyrdom as acts of love all evidence structural transformations to these survivor instincts in the limbic realm; they evidence a distinction that has been and can be made between emotional reactions, which are always an impulse to act, and deliberative actions; and they evidence degrees of conscious control of the emotional. We may never know (how could we?) whether there is a purging of the emotional memories in the amygdala that takes place in and through sanctification, but there will certainly be what Daniel Goleman describes as "an inhibition of the limbic signals to the motor cortex."[61]

---

60. Goleman, *Emotional Intelligence*, 189.
61. Ibid., 91.

If we take the core commandment cited by Jesus to the rich young Pharisee, then we observe that we "should love the Lord your God with all [our] heart and with all [our] soul and with all [our] strength and with all [our] mind."[62] It is, of course, an injunction laid down in Deuteronomy; it has an ancient provenance and encapsulates an ancient wisdom. All we have examined above concerns love as an affect, an emotion registered in and issuing from deep within the heart and the soul. It concerns the body, its energies and musculature—"strength" is an emotional, psychological, and physiological phenomenon. Strength also relates to the will and that faculty is inseparable from the "mind." Cognition plays an important function in the fulfilling of this commandment. But cognition cannot operate alone, and its deeper currents lie within the body and its affections and the soul. The grace to fulfill his core injunction affects the totality of who we are as human beings, and in keeping this commandment lies our salvation. And not only our salvation, but also the salvation of the communities to which we belong. Ethical life begins with this change of heart and its orientation towards loving God fully. To be obedient to a set of rules we recognize as a civil or even a religious code is only to be obedient to what is in our minds. It is head rather than heart knowledge. Heart knowledge knows the rules are only a guide; the following is the most important aspect—and following is an affective, corporeal response and therefore a matter of the soul and the spirit.

In conclusion, let me be clear on two issues here: first, the limbic system is not evil or the seat of evil. I am no advocate of that now outdated method of dealing with aggressive forms of emotional instability, lobotomy. The limbic system is also the home all other communications between the body and the cerebral cortex—it enables us to love with all our heart, mind, and strength. It is also the source of guilt, shame, compassion, and mercy. Two lobes, one on the right side of the brain, the hippocampus, the other on the left, the amygdala, are processing information that enables us to feel, know, and act. But consider that founding story of sin in the book of Genesis: Adam and Eve eat of the Tree of the Knowledge of Good and Evil. Before this they had existed, according to the story, in a state of freedom and joy prior to fear, to anger, and to jealousy. With all things they had been provided—food, water, companionship, work to do—in harmony with the rest of creation, they were given the task of governing. It is a fairly limited range of emotions the thin details of the story give us, and I am not trying to integrate the poetic imagination concerning the

---

62. Luke 10:27.

beginning of things with contemporary evolutionary psychology. But, it is interesting that, following the eating of the fruit from the forbidden tree, strong emotions surface that neuroscientists associate with the amygdala and primitive emotional memory. The first is fear: when the voice of God calls Adam in the garden Adam ran, hid, and froze (the fundamental somatic actions associated with fear). "I heard your voice in the garden and I was afraid," Adam tells God. He is afraid, he says, because he realizes his nakedness—his utter vulnerability before what is now a threatening other. The second emotion is shame—so God provides them with clothes to cover their nakedness. Shame is a primitive emotion associated with guilt. The third emotion is sorrow and pain: "I will greatly multiply your sorrow and your conception; in sorrow shall you bring forth children." And the final emotion is the *libido dominandi*: "your desire shall be to your husband, and he shall rule over you." All these emotions are also accompanied by now by death; for Adam and Eve will now live and labor until they return to the ground from where they were taken. The rest one might say is history—human history. But what is it we pray for when we recite the words of the prayer Jesus taught his disciples: "deliver us from evil"? Is our redemption and sanctification associated with the excision of those negative basic emotions? In the resurrection of the body will we find we have a new emotional life freed from the fear, shame, sorrow, and lust because disciplined in and by love?

The second point on which I wish to be clear concerns prayer: prayer as the condition in which our sanctification is established, our vulnerability extended, and our attunement to being absolutely dependent apprehended (felt and intuited in Schleiermacher's and early Hegel's understanding of these terms). In this advocacy for the role of prayer I am not acquiescing to quietism. It is actually thinking *with* the material world, the material world given to us, a world in which God operates in Christ, through the Spirit. This prayer is obedience, a service that is both action and passivity, giving and receiving, responsibility and response; it is both patience and endeavor. As I stated and examined in *The Politics of Discipleship*, prayer is our most political act:[63] a participation in the mind of Christ written into all of creation—a mind that infuses all things with the task of communicating each to the other (even so-called "inanimate" things like Robinson Jeffers' "Mysticism of stone").[64]

---

63. See Ward, *Discipleship*, 280–83.
64. Jeffers, "The Rock and the Hawk," 502.

## Bibliography

Arnold, M. B. *Emotion and Personality*. New York: Columbia University Press, 1960.
Augustine. *Confessions*. Translated by William Watts. Cambridge: Harvard University Press, 1912.
Barr, James. *The Garden of Eden and the Hope of Immortality*. London: SCM, 1992.
Blackwell, Albert L. *Schleiermacher's Early Philosophy of Life: Determinism, Freedom, and Phantasy*. Chico, CA: Scholars, 1982.
de Gruyter, Walter. *On Freedom*. Translated by Albert L. Blackwell. Lewiston, NY: Mellen, 1992.
Durrell, Lawrence. *The Alexandria Quartet*. London: Faber and Faber, 1962.
Ekman, Paul. "Facial Expression and Emotion." *American Psychologist* 48 (1993) 348-92.
Gibson, J. J. *The Senses Considered as Perceptual System*. Boston: Houghton Mifflin and Co., 1966.
Goleman, Daniel. *Emotional Intelligence: Why It Can Matter More than IQ*. New York: Bantam, 1995.
Heidegger, Martin. *The Phenomenology of Religious Life*. Translated by Matthias Fritsch and Jennifer Anna Gosetti-Ferencei. Bloomingdale, IN: Indiana University Press, 2004.
Hegel, G. W. F. "Glauben und Wissen." In *Jenaer Schriften 1801–1807*, edited by Eva Moldenhauer and Karl Markus Michel, 287–433. Frankfurt: Suhrkamp, 1970. English translation by Walter Cerf and H. S. Harris, *Faith and Knowledge*. Albany, NY: SUNY, 1977.
———. *System of Ethical Life (1802/3)*. Edited and Translated by H. S. Harris and T. M. Knox. Albany, NY: SUNY, 1979.
Jeffers, Robinson. "The Rock and the Hawk." In *The Collected Poetry of Robinson Jeffers*, edited by Tim Hunt. Stanford: Stanford University Press, 2001.
Johnson, Aubrey R. *The One and the Many in the Israelist Conception of God*. Cardiff: University of Wales Press, 1961.
LeDoux, Joseph. *The Emotional Brain: The Mysterious Underpinnings of Emotional Life*. London: Weidenfeld & Nicolson, 1998.
Nathanson, Donald. *Shame and Pride: Affect, Sex, and the Birth of the Self*. New York: Norton, 1994.
Otto, Rudolph. *The Idea of the Holy*. Translated by John W. Harvey. Oxford: Oxford University Press, 1923.
Panskepp, Jaak. "Toward a General Psychobiological Theory of Emotions." *Behavioural and Brain Sciences* 5 (1982) 407–67.
Prinz, Jesse. "Which Emotions are Basic?" In *Emotion, Evolution and Rationality*, edited by Dylan Evans and Pierre Cruse, 69–88. Oxford: Oxford University Press, 2004.
Rosenkranz, Karl. *Georg Wilhelm Friedrich Hegels Leben*. Darmstadt: Wissenschaftlishe Buchgesellschaft, 1963.
Rothschild, Babette. *The Body Remembers: The Psychophysiology of Trauma and Trauma Treatment*. New York: Norton, 2000.
Schleiermacher, Friedrich. *The Christian Faith*. Translated by H. R. Mackintosh. Edinburgh: T. & T. Clarke, 1989.
———. *On Religion: Speeches to its Cultured Despisers*. Translated by Richard Crouter. Cambridge: Cambridge University Press, 1988.

———. "Über die Freiheit." In *Kritische Gesamtausgabe*, I/1, edited by Günter Meckenstock, 219–356. Berlin: de Gruyter, 1984.

Ward, Graham. *The Politics of Discipleship: Becoming Postmaterial Citizens*. Grand Rapids: Baker Academic, 2009.

Wright, Terence C. "Edith Stein: Prayer and Interiority." In *The Phenomenology of Prayer*, edited Bruce Ellis Benson and Norman Wirzba, 134–41. New York: Fordham University Press, 2005.

# 3

# On the Natural Desire of Seeing God

*Louis Dupré*

### The Loss of the Natural Desire of God

IN OUR SECULAR SOCIETY the idea of a natural desire of seeing God appears highly problematic. Yet until the fourteenth century most Christian, Jewish, and Muslim philosophers, as well as several ancient ones, accepted the existence of such a desire. Why has what once appeared so obvious, become so questionable?

#### *The Idea of God*

As long as philosophy formed an integral unity with theology, as it did during the early and the high Middle Ages, thinkers would have found it hard to conceive of nature without a transcendent orientation. Not before the rediscovery of the works of Aristotle in the twelfth and thirteenth centuries did philosophy begin to loosen its link with theology. In order to harmonize theology with Aristotle's newly accepted philosophy, Christian thinkers were forced to grant philosophy a formal independence. For that purpose they subordinated the finite end of Aristotle's *Ethics* to the Christian's ultimate end. The synthesis remained fragile, because a philosophical concept as basic as that of human nature remained also directly attached to the Christian's ultimate end. Which definition should prevail: the theological or the philosophical?

Modern philosophy rejected this *intrinsic* dependence of philosophy upon theology. How could philosophy remain subordinate to what, in its modern definition, falls outside its field of knowledge? Even the idea of God, the alleged source of a natural desire, originates *not* in philosophy, but in what believers refer to as a "revelation" of some sort, or at least in a mode of consciousness that is practical and worshipful rather than critical and rational. Philosophy encounters it as a *given*, not of its own making, which rightly or wrongly determines its own indeterminate notion of transcendence. A philosophy, then, that wants to be totally autonomous, that is, relying exclusively on the immediate intuitions and conclusions of reason, the moderns concluded, rules out any desire of seeing God as God is in himself, as falling entirely outside its field. Descartes considered such full autonomy a necessary principle if philosophy was to be reliable at all. Instead of accepting a theological idea of God, philosophy attempted to establish its own, by means of arguments attained by independent reason. At most, it might attempt to find some rational parallels with theological beliefs. Thus it grounded the idea of creation upon the ancient philosophical category of efficient causality, which had proven its effectiveness in the scientific interpretation of the world.

## A Different Causality

This notion of causality became the second cause of the idea of a natural desire of God losing much of its meaning. Problematic hereby was not the notion of causality as such. Ever since Plato, philosophers had interpreted the dependence of things on a transcendent first principle in causal terms. In Plato's thought, the phenomenal order rests on the foundation of ideal forms. This dependence of changing appearances on an unchangeable reality contains in essence what Aristotelians were later to call a *formal causality*. The cosmogonic myth of Plato's *Timaeus* misled many to regard the dependence of finite things on a transcendent foundation as having been *effectively caused* by that foundation. All too readily did they interpret the myth as if it referred to an instrumental *making* of the cosmos. In fact, Plato had used the myth of the Demiurge only to explain which metaphysical principles were needed for the constitution of a rational cosmos. Neither Plato nor Aristotle mentioned a "creation" of the world as Jews and Christians understood it: the ancient cosmos had no beginning, it was ever-lasting, even as the gods. In identifying the Hebrew idea of creation with instrumental action, Christian philosophers, following Philo, may have prepared a dangerous legacy.

They may have considered their interpretation confirmed by the fact that, for Aristotle, the causal relation between the First Mover and the lower spheres unquestionably implied an "efficient" causality. However, Aristotle did not restrict the relation with a supreme divine principle to be exclusively one of efficient causality. In *De anima* he describes the active principle of the human intellect as being itself divine. To become active, the intellect requires the impulse of a principle that is uninterruptedly cognizant and such a principle, he claims, must itself be divine. Indeed, once freed from the passivity of the body the soul itself will become divine. Moreover, in the *Nicomachean Ethics* Aristotle even claims that the highest mode of existence is the contemplative one—and that mode surpasses the merely human level. "Such a life would be too high for man; for it is not insofar as he is man that he will live so, but insofar as something divine is present in him; and by so much as this is superior to our composite nature is its activity superior to that which is for the theologian, no more than the exercise of a moral virtue. If reason is divine, then, in comparison with man, the life according to it is divine in comparison with human life."[1] Obviously, this surpasses the extrinsic relation of efficient causality typical of modern thought.

Neither for St. Thomas, inspired as he was by Aristotelian and Neo-Platonic thought, did the act of creation consist exclusively, or even primarily, in efficient causality, but rather in an internal, "quasi-formal" one. Repeatedly, Aquinas insists on the immanent presence of the creative cause, in the acting as well as in the every being of the creature. In the *Summa Theologiae* he writes: "God is the cause of action not only by giving the form which is the principle of action.... And since the form of a thing is within the thing, and all the more as it approaches nearer to the First and Universal Cause, and because in all things God himself is properly the cause of universal being which is inmost in all things, it follows that in all things God works inwardly," that is, not extrinsically as an efficient cause does.[2] And in his *Commentary on St. John's Gospel*: "God who operates by conveying being, operates in all things in the most intimate way."[3]

---

1. Aristotle, *Ethics*, 1177b.
2. Aquinas, *Summa Theologiae*, I, 105, 5c.
3. Ibid., *Commentary*, ch. 1; I, 5.

Createdness for Aquinas consists in the first place in God's immanent presence in the creature's *being* and acting

## A Different Concept of Nature

This immanent concept of divine causality, the only possible basis, I think, for a natural desire of God, became jeopardized when modern thought began to conceive the notion of nature independently of this transcendent presence. Earlier Christian thought knew only one *finis ultimus*, that was both natural *and* gratuitously given, namely the vision of God. It never conceived of nature as isolated from its more-than-natural foundation and orientation. A natural desire of God can exist only if the mind itself is in some respect connatural with the divine, since such a desire presupposes an intimate acquaintance with God. It assumes, as Augustine wrote, that the mind has already found God. Nature cannot desire that with which it is totally unacquainted.

For St. Thomas and other medieval thinkers, the term "supernatural" does not refer to a separate *reality*, but to a quality of strictly divine actions, forces, events, by means of which God allows humans to attain their end in nature as well as in grace.[4] His philosophy establishes the *possibility* of a natural desire of God. Does he also recognize its reality? In the *Summa contra Gentiles*, Aquinas treats the theme from two different, yet related points of view. One the one hand, he posits that each being seeks to realize the full potential of its nature.[5] But truth and goodness are perfections that a spiritual being naturally desires, even though its limited capacity prohibits either from ever fully attaining them. The desire (*appetitus*), then, is natural, even though its complete realization lies beyond the potential of human nature. In the same article, St. Thomas claims that all creatures seek the kind of similitude with the Creator that corresponds to their nature. For intellectual creatures, their natural ideal consists in acquiring the highest knowledge. That, according to Aquinas, means knowing things in their ultimate principle, that is, in God's own being. The same applies for the ideal of moral goodness.

An intellectual dynamism, then, moves human knowledge toward a knowledge of God. "*Intelligere deum est finis omnis intellectualis substantiae.*"[6] In his excellent analysis of this question in St. Thomas,

---

4. See Dupré, *Passage*, 167–89.
5. Aquinas, *Summa contra Gentiles*, III, 25.
6. Ibid., II, 25; cf. also III, 52.

Georges Cottier, O.P., writes, "[t]he natural desire has its source in the metaphysical nature of the intellect: its object is *being* in its full extent. However much a knowledge that attains the first being only through inferior analogates may fall short of this idea; by nature it spontaneously moves toward the perfect knowledge of the cause of being."[7] It is this very desire that propels the dynamism of thinking and knowing. Beyond each limited good or object of knowledge the mind implicitly pursues an unlimited one. St. Thomas assumes that a natural desire cannot remain unfulfilled, even though the human mind is incapable of satisfying it by its own force. Still, the mind cannot *demand* the satisfaction of a desire the fulfillment of which lies entirely beyond its capacity. The desire for seeing God, then, may be called "natural" only to the extent that it seeks its fulfillment in general, not in a theologically specific way.

If all human spiritual activity already implies a transcendent goal, it establishes some initial, natural union with this goal, even though its full attainment exceeds the capacities of human nature. Desire in some way anticipates an attainment even of a goal that never ceases to surpass human powers. To the extent that the person remains conscious of the dynamism that drives this desire, he or she already in some measure partakes in its fulfillment. If I understand this correctly, for Bonaventure, Aquinas, and Scotus, philosophy and theology become reunited in a mystical bond. They interpreted the natural desire for an ever-greater cognition and an ever-greater goodness as being driven by a more-than-natural dynamism. The natural desire for God thus became intrinsically transformed into a "supernatural one" of divine origin. Perhaps the same holds for artists pursuing the perfect formal expression of an idea, although they know it to lie beyond their reach. Yet while striving for its realization, they may become conscious of the supernatural impulse of their desire.

The nominalist theology of the later Middle Ages rejected the paradoxical idea of a natural desire of a supernatural gift. If, as Occam claimed, God can save the unrepentant sinner and reject the saint, God's decisions are unrelated to our expectations and the desire for God disappears altogether or must have grown in an already divinely sanctified nature. Indeed, nominalist theology split nature from the supernatural, as if it was a separate realm of reality. The empirical methods of the new science of nature grew out of the need to find another source of knowledge than the previous, now rejected arguments about how things *ought to be*

---

7. Cottier, "Désir naturel," 695–96.

in a divinely created nature. Those arguments had ceased to be persuasive because of the unpredictability of the nominalist God. Henceforth scientists had to rely on empirical observation and on the support of their mathematical skills.

There were exceptions. Nicholas of Cusa, whose life spans the entire fifteenth century, reunited what nominalist thinkers had divided, yet did so on the basis of an entirely new synthesis of philosophy and theology. He attempted to show how the human self, as *imago Dei*, naturally participates in the divine qualities of being both infinitely great and infinitely small. As such it feels naturally attracted by the divine prototype, which it mirrors. Indeed, all intellectual and all moral acts are driven by the mind's natural desire of its origin. The desire to know is a desire to know oneself and to know oneself requires to know one's divine prototype. If I am not mistaken, here even the distinction between the natural and the supernatural begins to lose all meaning. In *De filiatione Dei* Nicholas describes the road of knowledge as headed toward a mystical union with God.

Indeed, all search for understanding, according to Cusanus, is motivated by an implicit desire to comprehend God, and particular objects are no more than "symbolic signs of the true."[8] No knowledge is ever intrinsically secular. Human nature can be fully understood only as a dynamic tendency toward *theiosis*. "God, who is in all things, shines forth in mind when mind, as a living image of God, turns to its own Exemplar and assimilates itself thereto with all its effort..."[9] In *De sapientia* he argues that God's eternal wisdom attracts us by granting the mind a foretaste (*praegustatio*) of what she can achieve and thereby arouses a marvelous desire for her. Since this wisdom constitutes the very life of spiritual understanding, she incites us to seek the source of this life. Without that foretaste the mind would not seek its source. It might not even know that it had received it, if indeed it had done so. The mind is moved to it as to its own life.[10] While seeking its own unity (the norm by which it measures all things) the mind finds it in that principle in which all things are one.[11] In its search for unity and self-identity the mind expresses a fundamental desire for *unification with God*, in whom it knows *itself*. Only in the mystery of God's being does the mind grasp its unity and its distinctness. In the mirror of God does the

---

8. Nicholas of Cusa, "On Being a Son of God," II, 61.
9. Ibid., "Idiotae de mente," VII, 106.
10. Ibid., I, 10.
11. Ibid., IX, 123.

mind recognize itself.¹² The drive toward unification in God propels the entire progress of thought. The intellect reaches its destination only when it becomes divinized.

Later thinkers in the Platonic tradition, including Ficino, Malebranche, Berkeley, Rosmini, and, to some extent, such non-Platonists as Newman and Maine de Biran, continued to conceive of the intellect as moved by an implicit desire of God, while modern Scholastics continued to separated nature from the supernatural as if it were a wholly distinct domain of being. This led to the controversies about the existence of a *desiderium naturale*. A summary and defense of their efforts appears in Lawrence Feingold's massive study.[13] According to Feingold, the recent attempts by Henri de Lubac and his followers to restore Aquinas's alleged position, while ignoring the work of the commentators during half a millennium, rest on a mistaken principle. Feingold's study starts with a careful analysis of Aquinas's texts, followed by a lengthy analysis of the commentaries written by Scotus, Dennis the Carthusian, Caietanus, and Suarez.

Most of the commentators posit that a natural desire may be aroused (*elicited*) by some *knowledge* of God's existence. Others call the desire an innate, unconditional *appetite*. A great deal of disagreement divides the commentators concerning the nature of the vision of God, which is the object of the "natural desire." Some advocate that an innate natural desire is formally directed at a *vision* of God as God is in himself. This rules out the existence of a state of "pure nature" detached from man's supernatural destiny in grace. Such has been the position of de Lubac, von Balthasar, and John Milbank. Others, of whom Sylvester of Ferrara comes perhaps closest to Aquinas, argue that even an innate desire can be no more than a desire to know the ultimate causes and essences of reality. Such a desire stems from an appetite for extending knowledge beyond its natural limits. The position assumes a state of pure nature at the root of man's (purely) natural desire of God.[14] The alleged foundational desire of *seeing* God consists in the desire of an intellect that cannot be satisfied before resting in the infinite, but in a manner totally proportionate to its nature.

Most of the Scholastic commentaries, whatever their internal differences, end up with a duality of two states and two natures. This duality is

12. Dupré, "Mystical Theology," 105–17.
13. Feingold, *The Natural Desire of God*
14. I have profited greatly from Aaron Riches' intelligent analysis of Feingold's work. I have to take sole responsibility for the simplifications of this report.

less obvious in the position of Dennis the Carthusian, a follower of Ruusbroec's mystical theology, who may also have been influenced by Nicholas of Cusa, whom he accompanied during Cusa's inspection travel through the Netherlands. Aquinas's position remains ambiguous however we attempt to interpret it.

## Signs of the Restoration of the Idea of a Natural Desire

*The Readmission of Transcendence as a Legitimate Philosophical Category*

The main reason why the idea of a natural desire has disappeared from modern philosophy is the narrowing of the field. Philosophy has come to define itself as reflection on reality as it presents itself to our immediate observation or calculation. The idea of transcendence has thereby been withdrawn to a dark territory to which philosophy claims to have no access. Recently, however, it appears that it may be regaining its former place in modern thought and with it, the legitimacy of the idea of a natural desire. Several philosophers have accepted that no philosophical discourse about reality can succeed without a discussion of what defines its limits and hence what surpasses them. Heidegger strongly asserted that philosophy's main task consists in exploring the transcendent horizon of the known. He even compared the philosophical attitude with the mystical one, articulated by Eckhart.[15] In Jaspers' philosophy also, the notion of *Transzendenz* occupies a central position. Existence, for him, must be defined through the relation to what transcends it. From a very different, cosmological position, Bergson argued that the evolutionary process of the real requires a *divine* impulse. Contrary to Heidegger and Jaspers, he conveys to this transcendence a traditionally religious sense.

Christian thinkers, such as Blondel, Maréchal, and Rahner, have equated this transcendent horizon with God. Still, they hesitate to embrace the traditional idea of a philosophical *desire for seeing God*. They were all aware of the fact that transcendence allows other than religious interpretations. Is an equation of transcendence with God still philosophically justified? If philosophy must a priori be detached from any link with the religious experience, the answer is obviously negative. Philosophy, however, ought to reflect on the entire range of experience, not merely on the processes of reason, but also on the experience of faith, of which a desire for God is constitutive. Once the idea of transcendence has been

---

15. See Heidegger, *Gelassenheit*.

restored as a legitimate, indeed, essential part of philosophy, the question of a natural desire of an infinite ideal, constantly pursued yet never attained, in all spiritual activity re-emerges.

### The Natural Desire Revived

Indeed, Max Scheler argued that such a desire lies at the ground of the very affirmation of God's existence. "Only a real being with the essential character of divinity can be the cause of man's religious propensity that is the propensity to execute in a real sense acts of that class whose acts, though finite experiences cannot fulfill them, nevertheless demand fulfillment."[16] Note, Scheler does not pretend that God exists because the desire for God has to be *satisfied*, but the very *existence* of the desire presupposes a transcendent reality. Without God's existence, the religious aspirations of humankind would be self-contradictory. Even this modified form of Scheler's argument, in my opinion, goes too far. The fact that the mind's intellectual dynamism surpasses the immediate object of knowledge and desire, does not necessarily lead to any conclusion about the *nature* of this transcendence. The equation of the transcendent with a monotheist idea of God does not follow from an argument, but takes place *within* the act of faith. Karl Rahner is more cautious in establishing the religious nature of the idea of transcendence. For him, all knowledge presupposes a "pre-apprehension" (*Vorgriff*) of *absolute being*. "The pre-apprehension of this *being* is not an a priori knowledge of an object, but the a priori horizon against which the perception of a sensuous [or any other] object ex-posteriori appears. It constitutes the very condition for an a posteriori appearance."[17] The idea of infinite *being* that functions as the horizon against which we know all beings, cannot but be transcendent. To the objection that a purely negative concept of the infinite would suffice for that function, Rahner responds that the *priority* of the infinite horizon with respect to the cognition of the finite requires that the horizon *actually* exists. Already Descartes had responded in a similar way to the objections leveled against the thesis of the primacy of the infinite with respect to the finite he had advanced in his Third Meditation. The background of an *existing* infinity is a necessary condition for the mind to recognize the finite as finite.

The question remains whether the necessity of an infinite horizon requires the infinite being to exist *independently* of finite beings, as the

16. Scheler, *On the Eternal in Man*, 261.
17. Rahner, *Hörer des Wortes*, 176.

traditional idea of God implies. In itself the idea of *being* is neither finite nor infinite: it is indefinite. To posit that an infinite reality can exist independently of the finite is a religious *assumption*, not a philosophical conclusion. Logically, a pantheistic or a panentheistic answer would be equally possible. Yet, the metaphor of a transcendent horizon appropriately introduces the metaphysical question: What conditions the finite? The monotheistic answer that identifies the unconditioned conditioner with God, though not the only possible one, imposes itself to the philosopher's attention by having long been accepted in the West as well as in all monotheist cultures. Maurice Blondel therefore called it "a necessary hypothesis"; that is, a religious interpretation of transcendence, which the philosopher is not allowed to ignore and whose consistency he is bound to investigate, even if it does not, a priori, exclude other alternatives. To one who insists on a religiously *neutral* proof, that is, a purely logical argument that neglects the *given* nature of the religious experience, the monotheist answer is not likely to find acceptance as the only, or even the most satisfactory one. However, to one who is *personally* acquainted with the religious experience, the religious interpretation will be compelling.

## *Explicit and Implicit Natural Desire of God*

What does the preceding imply concerning the justification of the natural desire of God as God is in himself? If one maintains a strict separation between a supernatural sphere and a pure nature, such a desire seems hard to justify, even for a believer living in a thoroughly secular environment. However, that separation itself rests on the false presumption that the notion of nature can be conceived independently of any intrinsic relation to a transcendent horizon, or of any information attained within the experienced relation to that horizon. To be sure, the philosopher may make a formal and always provisional abstraction from the *nature* of that horizon, as Aquinas did when he accepted most of Aristotle's ethics and metaphysics without even raising the question whether his idea of God agreed with, or differed from, Aristotle's. When in later centuries, however, this merely *formal* abstraction developed into a *real* separation between two domains, it led to a closed concept of nature in which the question of a desire for God could not even arise. With few exceptions, modern thought has drawn the conclusions from this separation. For the secular philosopher the term *supernatural* lost its meaning because of the unproven character of the claims attached to it. Theology, on its side, has of late given up the strict separation of nature and grace as if they were two distinct realms of being, of which each one pursues a different end.

The situation, then, has drastically changed in the last decades. Metaphysics is once again actively engaged in an analysis of the *transcendent horizon* of being. If philosophy allows itself to be enlightened by a reflection upon the religious experience (as it did before it severed its ties with theology) and thereby admits the possibility of giving a positive, religious content to its own idea of transcendence, then, in my judgment, it reinstates the philosophical legitimacy of the mind's natural orientation (both in being and in acting) toward a transcendent terminus. Nor is the interest of investigating this horizon limited to believers: the question of God is, as the secular thinker Edmund Husserl affirmed, the most significant one in philosophy.

Two positions, however, do not seem to follow from the restoration by Henri de Lubac and his followers of this new formulation of the *desiderium naturale visionis Dei*. First, that all humans experience an *explicit* desire for God, such as some medieval philosophers appear to have implied. Many of our contemporaries would not know what to make of a desire for what remains totally alien to them. Even religious men and women living in non-monotheist cultures might find the idea of a single or a personal God genuinely puzzling. At the time when the concept of a natural desire of God was formulated, the West recognized monotheism as the only philosophically legitimate form of transcendence. These conditions have ceased to exist. Equally vanished, however, is the modern rationalist obstacle against the idea of the desire of God, implied by the philosophical dogma that what cannot be strictly proven by reason or experience deserves no place in philosophy. Nothing entitles philosophy to restrict its investigation to what can be established by scientific truth or logical argument. Philosophy had ceased to be the science of "reason alone," as understood in the various forms of rationalism of the last three centuries (the most recent of which was positivism). It now consists primarily in a rational *reflection upon experience*—from whatever sources the experience may draw its content. Phenomenological and linguistic analysis, as well as the radical empiricism of American philosophy, resist, at least in principle, any dogmatic, a priori, about the content of experience: they analyze it as it actually occurs, and in so doing prepare the way for a more comprehensive metaphysical reflection. In the new philosophical constellation, the mind's religious desire finds its place in the intellect's natural search for the nature of transcendence, and so would be implicit in human activity toward the *true* and *good as such*. No rational *a priori* prevents this search and this impulse to be specified by the idea of God, as presented in monotheist religion. Yet already St. Thomas cautioned that the object of the desire was much less defined than later Scholastics formulated it. It was, he claimed, a desire for a *beatitudo in communi*—a general idea of beatitude.

## Bibliography

Aristotle. *Nicomachean Ethics*. Translated by Robert C. Bartlett. Chicago: University of Chicago Press, 2011.
Aquinas, Thomas. *Commentary on St. John's Gospel*. Still River, MA: St Bede's, 1999.
———. *Summa contra Gentiles*. Notre Dame: University of Notre Dame Press, 1991.
———. *Summa Theologiae*. London: Eyre and Spottiswoode, 1963.
Cusa, Nicholas. "Idiotae de mente." In *On Wisdom and Knowledge* VII, translated by Jasper Hopkins, 51–601. Minneapolis: Banning, 1996.
———. "Idiotae de sapientia." In *Nikolaus von Kues, Werke, Vol. 1*, edited by Paul Wilpert. Berlin: De Gruyter, 1967.
———. "On Being a Son of God." In *Miscellania of Nicholas of Cusa*, III, translated by Jasper Hopkins, 51–369. Minneapolis: Banning, 1994.
Dupré, Louis. "The Mystical Theology of Cusanus' De visione Dei." In *Eros and Eris: Liber Amicorum for Adriaan Peperzak*, edited by Paul van Tongeren, 105–17. Dordrecht: Kluwer, 1992.
———. *Passage to Modernity*. New Haven: Yale University Press, 1993.
Feingold, Lawrence. *The Natural Desire of God according to St Thomas Aquinas and His Interpreters*. Rome: Appolinaire Studies, 2001.
Heidegger, Martin. *Gelassenheit*. Pfullingen: Neske, 1959.
Rahner, Karl. *Hörer des Wortes*. Munich: Kösel, 1963.
Scheler, Max. *On the Eternal in Man*. Translated by Bernard Noble. New York: Harper, 1960.

# 4

# Life, or Gift and Glissando

## Evolution, Vitalism, and Transcendence

*John Milbank*

~

### Evolution and Design

EVER SINCE DARWIN, AT a popular level the terms "creation" and "evolution" have been set against each other. In this lies little rationale, but we must ask for the rationale behind the constantly re-staged debate. It is indeed as if one has a kind of lobster-like double articulation, with superficial hostility between the two pincers, of a single episteme. On the one hand, there is the legacy of post-Newtonian Christian natural theology; on the other hand, there is the explanation of the phenomena of life in terms of the operation of the law of natural selection.[1]

In the first case one has to do with "creation" only in a bastardized sense. Newton no longer conceived of God as Being as such, and as the source of finite being produced from nothing, but sharing by various degrees in his infinite simple *esse*. His God was rather a supremely powerful

---

1. Even as sophisticated an academic as John Dupré gets this whole area hopelessly wrong, simply because he has no knowledge of the history of theology and the real nature of its interaction with science. Hence, he assumes that "the argument from design" is the strongest traditional argument for the existence of God, whereas in the most authentic Christian theological tradition (Augustine, Maximus, Aquinas, Cusanus, Pascal, etc.) it simply did not figure at all. See John Dupré, "Human Origins."

entity who had shaped alongside himself other entities with whom he communicated through a shared dimension dubbed his "sensorium," manifest to us as an inferred absolute space and absolute time. According to the, as it were, "old covenant" of the laws of motion, celestial as well as terrestrial bodies traveled in infinite straight lines unless otherwise interrupted, a movement that is perfectly reversible. But according to the, as it were, "new covenant" of gravity, celestial bodies were regularly bent back from this course to move cyclically in relation to each other. In the case of both "covenants" one has, on the one hand, an absolutely regularly operating and universal law. On the other hand, one has also the direct presence of God, however precisely conceived, whether in the one case as the absoluteness of space and time, or in the other case as the attractive and repelling force of gravitation. In the latter case, Newton the hermeticist was always in self-conflict with Newton the voluntarist theologian: the latter would have liked to reduce gravitation to mechanism; the former toyed with the notion that God had introduced into reality certain inscrutable and quasi-vital "active principles."[2]

This "designing" God is not the God of classical Catholic theology because his causality operates on the same plane as finite causes even though it is all powerful. One can trace the beginnings of such a way of conceiving of divine causality as far back as Bonaventure and Duns Scotus, but it displaced an older and essentially Neoplatonic way of looking at things, still holding good for Aquinas, in which the divine cause was a higher "influence" which "flowed into" finite levels of causation, entirely shaping them from within, but not "influencing" them or conditioning them on the same plane of univocal being, as a less metaphorically-rooted meaning of "influence" tends to imply. Put briefly, the ontological versus ontic difference between primary and secondary causality was lost sight of.[3]

It is still this post-Scotist and Newtonian God who is invoked by advocates of "creative design" all the way from Paley through to some recent evangelical and other Christian biologists. Just as motion and the planetary system appeared to be organized like clockwork in the Newtonian universe, so likewise Paley saw in organisms far more complex mechanisms whose instance could only be explained by the notion of direct and continuous divine causal influence. Similarly today, biologists like Michael

---

2. See Oliver, "Motion," 163–99.

3. See Funkenstein, *Scientific Imagination*, 23–117; and Jacob Schmutz, "La doctrine medieval," 217–64.

Behe argue that even the most primitive component of a light-sensitive nerve that permits "seeing" to arise is already so complex that only an extrinsic divine designer will explain its existence.[4] The scandal of "creationist science" is indeed the idea that God could become an empirical hypothesis, experimentally verifiable, but the scandal is still more theological than it is scientific and in fact, all the way at least from Newton to Faraday, the main current of natural science was centrally shaped by such scandalous confusion.

In the second case, one has the Darwinian tradition itself. It is, of course, not at all the case that Darwin displaced the ancient monotheistic doctrine of creation with the thesis of evolution by natural selection. To suppose that it is, would be to remain within the terms of the bastardized theological assumptions of Paley and the divine design tradition. Yet within the terms of this tradition, it is possible also to argue that Darwin was in one respect modifying received theology rather than simply standing it on its head. His project shares an important feature in common with the Christian apologetic *Bridgewater Treatises* (particularly the section by William Whewell), which he indeed cites positively at the outset of *The Origin of Species*. For both works, the Paleyite perspective on life is insufficient in terms of its Newtonian analogue. For in the latter case, while absolute space and time and the force of gravity represent the direct divine presence, this is still manifest in a totally regular fashion expressible by comprehensible laws. There appeared to be no biological equivalent to this regular divine governance. So both treatises are interested in compensating for this lack in terms of discovering more regular immanent processes at work in features exhibiting apparent organic design. This included processes leading to the constant creation of new species, such that *both* treatises exhibit a break with the Aristotelian focus upon fixity of species and the search for explanation of variation within species only, in favor of the attempt to account genetically for the variation of species itself. The difference is that in the case of *The Bridgewater Treatises* divine design ultimately explains the mutual adaptation of species and environment, while in the case of *The Origin of Species* the immanent law of one-way selective adaptation of species to environment becomes a sufficient *explanans* unto itself.[5]

---

4. Behe, *Darwin's Black Box*.

5. See Brooke, *Science and Religion*, 192–226; and Anthony Baker, "Theology and the Crisis," 183–215.

Nevertheless Darwin, if no doubt for largely expedient reasons, still left open the possibility that he had discovered a "law of creation." More decisively, the phrases in which he does so at the end of the *Origin* manifestly echo the design tradition in terms of its conviction that the pain and struggle of natural selection is justified by the beneficial "good" of later outcomes.[6] For a crucial aspect of the design tradition was theodicist: local and temporary ills were explained as necessary for the emergence of long-term or higher goods—indeed in Paley's case the divine ethics are wholly utilitarian. And for Paley already, long-term or higher goods are conceived in highly ascetic and stoic terms: "a family containing a dying child is the best school of filial piety" as he joyfully informs us.[7] This same emphasis is consummated by the work of Malthus: the latter is quite misread if we suppose that he thought his gloomy demographic conclusion posed a problem for theology, which he then had to solve. To the contrary, it is more as if the dire conclusion is uncritically embraced by a natural theology that thinks of virtue as emerging from a cosmic training in hardship.[8]

Darwin's central move was to extend Malthusian political economy to the economy of life as such. In doing so, he at last completed the Newtonian ambitions of the English design tradition—which one might describe as a bizarre fusion of a rather tame picture of nature, on the one hand, with the idea of a nature as a "hard school" of training in order and excellence, on the other. On the one hand, watercolors; on the other hand, cross-country runs. For now one had the equivalent of Newtonian motion in a straight line in the form of the *glissando* of constant variation of species. And one also had the equivalent of Newton's law of gravity in terms of the law of the survival of the fittest, as Darwin expressed it after Spencer.

This is certainly, nevertheless, an oversimplification: for Darwin variation is still by and large a physically imposed alteration of a lingering (Aristotelian) biological and sexual selection, while inheritance of acquired characteristics play some minor role in mutation. Nevertheless, the twin general model is overwhelmingly the norm: the ceaseless *glissando* along an absolute vital continuum; the emergence of relatively stable biological types interrupting this continuum by virtue of the law of struggle.

---

6. Darwin, *The Origin of Species*, 458–60.
7. Cited by Baker, "Theology and the Crisis."
8. See Milbank, *Theology and Social Theory*, 42–45; Baker, "Theology and the Crisis"; and Hanby, "Creation without Creationism," 654–94.

To what extent can one say that not just Darwin, but the entire Darwinian tradition remains informed by this Newtonian-Malthusian amalgam? In the case of the latter component, the law of struggle in the face of scarcity, it is not difficult to produce quotations from Richard Dawkins that show he is essentially a Malthusian: every genetic or phenotypic success will eventually engender a further increased general scarcity to ensure the continuity of refinement produced through competition. Without some continuous dimension of radical shortage rendering terrestrial reality less than infinitely shareable, natural selection could not be the basic process at work.[9]

In the case of the former component, ceaseless chance variation of species, the situation is more complex. Quickly after Darwin came the thermodynamic and probabilistic revolutions in nineteenth-century physics. This could be seen as problematic for Darwinism insofar as it began to move away from the dominant Newtonian paradigm of clearly defined mechanical causation exhibiting a perfectly regular function, towards a looser sense of statistically verified constant conjuncture that might indicate an entire gamut of co-conspiring causal forces at work.[10] On the other hand, critics like Darwin's friend William Herschel had already pointed out that Darwin's selective mechanism could not, like Newtonian law, be deployed to make clear advance predictions, nor be experimentally manipulated—for this reason he described the Darwinian natural norm as "the law of higgledy-piggledy."[11] Thus it appeared to many that Darwinianism could be more naturally correlated with the new probabilistic scientific paradigm. However, this immediately suggested that "natural selection" was something more diverse than originally intended and perhaps not exclusively focused upon the law of struggle. This has then bequeathed a huge and often suppressed ambiguity to modern biology: in so far as Darwinism remains pure, it belongs to old-fashioned, possibly outmoded Newtonian science; insofar as it can be correlated with modern physics, it ceases to remain, exactly, Darwinism. (And arguably, the further physics later drifted away from the Newtonian model, the worse this ambiguity has become.)

The new physics in its aspect as thermodynamic also encouraged the idea in biology that the *glissando* of organic variation is not Newtonian

---

9. See Baker "Theology and the Crisis"; Hanby, "Creation without Creationism."

10. For all the following discussion on the probabilistic/thermodynamic revolution and its impact upon biology, see Depew and Weber, *Darwinism Evolving*, 167–329.

11. See Hanby, "Creation without Creationism."

mechanical inertia plus Newtonian mechanical rupture, but rather a series tending to *crescendo* or *diminuendo*, to concentration or dispersal. Indeed, the new perspectives in physics offered a greater chance of integration with biology: organisms could be seen as instances of declining energy seeking a temporary refuge in relative equilibrium on the way to final entropy. And when these new perspectives were combined with the newly discovered science of genetics, then Darwin's organic variation could be understood in terms of genetic drift, as random bundles of genes exhibiting collectively certain tendencies measured in terms of statistical probability.

Lack of any understanding of heredity had clearly been a weakness in Darwin's theory. The hypothesis of genes can be seen as shoring it up by providing a precise physical location for organic variation. However, this only helps to confirm the first "Newtonian" element of *glissando*; it does not necessarily confirm the second "Newtonian" element, which is the law of survival.

It only unambiguously does so if, as with Richard Dawkins, one seeks to show natural selection at work fundamentally on the genetic level. Yet in fact, it is far more likely that natural selection works at *every* level—genotypic, phenotypic, species-wide—and indeed, contrary to what Dawkins would have the British population believe, the general tendency of genetic theory from its origins until now has actually been to modify orthodox Darwinism.[12] And it is for just this reason that one *can*, I think, claim that mainline Darwinism is Newtonian-Malthusian and therefore is in a strange collusion with its Christian fundamentalist enemies. For genetic theory suggests, first of all, that the *glissando* of continuous variation is essentially vital rather than mechanically physical; secondly, it suggests that this can result in genetic mutations that are not expressed at the phenotypic level and therefore never subject to the tests of natural selection, while further on down the generational line they will of themselves issue in phenotypic alterations. At the macro level of the scale, attention to the properties inherent only in populations, as with the great inter-war Russian-American biologist Theodosius Dobzhansky (incidentally—or not—a devout Russian Orthodox), has long encouraged attention to auto-poetic and internal shifts in animal constitution that are more to do with adaptation to an environment than with struggle for scarce terrain. Indeed, such a perspective has brought to the fore how species actively modify their own environment and can sometimes modify it in harmony with other species with whom they form a yet larger quasi-grouping. Perception of

---

12. See Cunningham, *Darwin's Pious Idea*.

natural agonism is not, of course, wrong, but it can be overstressed by too exclusive a preoccupation with the biological individual, rather than the smaller and the greater drifts within which it is swept up.[13]

What is more, one can go beyond Dobzhansky's nominalism, which defined a species in terms of a local inter-breeding population. For after all, do we not first of all only *recognize* such a self-generating group because of an inescapable shared likeness?[14] Yet perhaps such recognition only records an "accidental" not essential resemblance between members of a single biological lineage. This would suggest that the basic unit of the processes of evolution and natural selection is the individual. But then the question arises: what makes this individual *biological* in nature? The answer must have to do both with the inner inertial drive to organic self-development, and the drive to reproduce within certain regular parameters. Yet in that case, if one is to evade the most nakedly teleological construal of the biological individual (granting it a kind of "quasi-intention"), then an entire gene population and sequence, or else an entire population group or sequence, becomes the more likely subject of the evolutionary plot. But if the group assumes priority in this way, then resemblance between individuals reverts from accident to essence, and biological existence must still be construed in metaphysically realist terms.

Accordingly, one must still think of the living individual as in some sense instantiating a formal essence. But this is further to imply that, as for Aristotle, specific form itself (however mysteriously) "explains" in an ultimate and unsurpassable fashion. Moreover, since the nature of living form is to grow and to reproduce within certain regular and yet not entirely theoretically delimitable parameters (as gardeners and parents know) then this form is inherently "teleological" in the sense that its collective nature as internally moving and self-replicating across time (which is "its own point"—a goal beyond goal) is participated in by individual living organisms, who in this non-intentional sense "aim towards" their pre-defined fulfillment and flourishing.

For this sort of reason, Etienne Gilson argued that Darwin himself had not really escaped the teleological perspective that defines biology as such.[15] Even Darwinism cannot escape the question of why there is a "drive to survival"—which sounds just as anthropomorphic as the drive to appear or to appear as beautiful—and so forth. One might say that, of

13. Depew and Weber, *Darwinism Evolving*, 161–497.
14. See Hanby, "Creation without Creationism"; Grene, "Introduction," 1–15.
15. Gilson, *From Darwin to Aristotle*.

course, nothing is seeking to survive; it is just that certain random mutations turn out, within given equally accidental conditions, to be able to persist. But this still begs the question of the ontological character of the living unit. Why does a "single" gene or pool of genes remain single such as to "underlie" ("substantively") a process of mutation? Still more, why do genes and animals self-replicate over time in an organic way that produces constantly new individual instances of a recognizably "same" species? These questions mean that one cannot really stop asking exactly what is it that in some sense seeks to survive and to increase, or simply to sustain an inertia beneath variety? Why should there be any tendency in nature consistently to remain rather than endlessly to disintegrate, disseminate and re-form only momentarily? In other words, why is not the *glissando* of continuous variation *far more* absolute than it appears to be? Why are there any consistent living things at all? For if variation were more absolute, if no continuities in growth and reproduction were readily discernible, then there would be no reason whatsoever to speak of "life" in any sense whatsoever.

But once one has admitted that the drive to survive is teleological, then there is no reason not to suggest that there is equally a biological drive to expand self-manifestation in terms of growth and engendering—an extension of a drive to manifestation that may indeed characterize the individuation of all of physical reality as such.[16]

If, to the contrary, one really seeks to rid biology of all teleology, then, as with Dawkins, one must imply that all of life is epiphenomenal, a mere apparent cover for fully determined chemical and physical processes. Yet no-one has discovered exactly what these processes are that issue in such an upshot, still less exactly how such processes throw up this sort of an illusion. And arguably, it is transcendentally impossible for the latter discovery ever to be made, since the phenomenological experience of a supposed illusion—like that of color in Locke's philosophy—always occurs in a "language" that is incommensurable with the language of explanation of what is "really" going on: nothing within mere mechanical interactions in any way anticipates or could give rise to the appearance of a tree anticipating Spring, despite the fact that, at least to begin with, one cannot perceive a tree in any other way. Moreover, physics itself has abandoned the notion of all-pervading mechanism and all-pervasive efficient causality by recognizing, at the most fundamental of all levels, spontaneities, elective affinities, and obscure tendencies of matter to persist in certain

---

16. See von Uexküll, *Theoretical Biology*.

regular patterns. It becomes more plausible to read biological life in terms of an intense manifestation on the surface of a transcendental "life" that undergirds all of finite reality and is even coterminous with being as such.

Strict Darwinism therefore remains a dubious, unphilosophical, and unscientific ideology. It is still ultimately undergirded by exploded Newtonian physics and questionably pessimistic Malthusian demographics and political economy. In both respects it is secretly a first cousin of its necessary enemy, the divine design hypothesis.

But what does this mean in practice? In either case one has a biological underwriting of the capitalist market system. In the Darwinian case it is true, certainly, that the refusal or minimalization of the inheritance of acquired characteristics does not lend itself as easily to "social Darwinism" as do vitalist Lamarckian principles.[17] Nor does the inhumanly long timescale in which variation can issue in mutation. Nevertheless, Darwinism underwrites the picture of the struggling individual as the main social unit; of human groups struggling against each other; of eugenic manipulation as improving along a measurable scale of value (namely survivability), something (namely humanity) that is but an accidental upshot of accidental processes. Left-Darwinians like Dawkins seem to have to project a possible human self-invention without any ontological basis in their scientific conclusions: quite coherently then, everyone knows about Dawkins' selfish gene, but few about his recommended socially-altruistic human being.[18]

It is striking that most, though by no means all, contemporary Christian evangelical opponents of evolution (perhaps by contrast to the past) are enthusiastic supporters of the capitalist market. One can suggest that one latent reason for their horror at Darwin is that, in perhaps a very Anglo-Saxon way, it encourages tragic resignation in the face of market competition and not an unambiguous celebration of it as a glorious providential instrument for the training of freedom and independence.[19]

And both Darwinism and divine design envisage a political economy of nature and for this reason further share in common a reduction of the vital to the mechanical: Dawkins still has a watchmaker; it is just that he is now blind, like the secularized hidden hand of the marketplace.[20] In

17. See Depew and Weber, *Darwinism Evolving*, 193–217; and Bowler, *Darwinism*.

18. Dawkins, *The Blind Watchmaker*. For important critiques of Dawkins and Darwinism see Berlinsky, "The Deniable Darwin," 27–28, and McGrath, *Dawkins' God*.

19. See Jim Wallis, *God's Politics*, for a discussion of the Christian new right by a left-wing evangelical.

20. Dawkins, *The Blind Watchmaker*.

essence they view animals as complex mechanisms and organic struggles as processes of mechanical action and reaction. Beneath even genetic appearances for Dawkins, as I have already suggested, there presumably lurks chemical and then atomic and sub-atomic processes. Life itself then must be an epiphenomenon: we are all always already dead, along with our cats, dogs, and geraniums.

But does not the spectacle of the fight between the two fundamentalisms, biological and religious—a fight between first cousins—occlude from view an alternative vitalist way of understanding evolution? Darwin's mechanical reductionism was actually quite politically respectable and, as we have seen, it could readily be given back a theological gloss. In the seventeenth century it is often observable that a vitalist or "hylozoist" atheism was seen as yet more threatening than the mechanical variety. A machine is implausibly self-constructed and self-operating, unless it is a vitally inspired automaton: but an underlying vital force truly can displace God or at least immanentize him. And this story was repeated in the nineteenth century. Many have argued that Darwin's bias towards design and mechanism was, in fact, a mode of distancing himself from the evolutionism of political radicals in France like Geoffroi St-Hilaire, for whom there was a kind of forceful (but not strictly "teleological" he supposed) bias in matter itself towards greater and greater organization and self-awareness favorable to collective organization.

## Vitalism and Immanence

One can then suggest that the modern story of evolution concerns not just the fate of a Newtonian God and the meaning of a biosphere without God, but also a vitalist and sometimes even semi-mystical conception of the biosphere, which has taken many forms. The question of what happens now to a more traditional Catholic notion of God I shall advert to at the end of this chapter.

Quite simply and briefly, the vitalist view makes more sense than the Darwinian one. To reduce consciousness and life to epiphenomena is not science, but mystification. An adequate ontology has to be able to accommodate the arrival of these emerging realities. A living thing, as Leibniz realized, has parts that, in so far as they are living, reflect to infinity the organization of the whole organism and its infinite relations to all the rest of physical reality—this precisely distinguishes nature (the divine art) from human art, for which the parts of a machine are not in themselves machines as reflecting the organization of the whole. (He also argued that every physical substance, or "monad," is organic and so infinitely organized.) This infinite referral is the result of a self-sustaining action, an auto-poesis. Life endlessly engenders life and does not *as* life die—for if death cannot generate life, then the priority of life over death renders it immortal; there is no life without resurrection, as Russian philosophy has often argued.[21] Nor is it born, since it is not caused. More and more, most significant biologists recognize that a vital genetic drift and even the feedback of random phenotypic alteration are the major factors in the evolutionary process, with natural selection confined to an ever more minor role.[22]

Nor does current biology any longer need to choose between pure chance, on the one hand, or divine intervention, on the other, in order to explain microcosmically complex phenomena like the eye. Instead, it can appeal to mathematics and to musical theory for the insight that chaos is a phantom mirage: processes can only exist as organized series and patterns, since every "random" instance already contains patterns discernible for a selective gaze or a repeatable action—and these are the only possible modes of response, even if they are impersonal. What is it that causes selection and why are certain patterns favored—not just at the organic level but at the sub-organic also? It is very hard to know, but it is at least impossible now not to conceive of ceaseless organic variation as truly a *glissando* and moreover as one constantly interrupted by mysterious preferential selections that seem to have the force of "revelations"—as they do for the human composer of music when he selects from an infinite myriad of possible combinations.

These sorts of considerations have rightly tended to give a new currency to the thought of Henri Bergson.[23] One could read him as offering a double criticism both of orthodox scientism and of orthodox theology (or rather as he supposed it to be), which pinpoints their hidden collusion. For Bergson, to suppose that reality is measurable and predictable like Cartesian space is to deny to it any auto-originative dimension and to encourage the deistic hypothesis of an ultimate originator and sustainer. (One can add here that if capitalism is the mechanization and spatialization of social reality—its reduction to statistical outcomes and maximum possible

---

21. See Leibniz, *Monadology*, 64; Leibniz, *Principles of Nature and Grace, Founded on Reason*. For the Russian perspective, see Bulgakov, *Philosophy of Economy*.

22. See Depew and Weber, *Darwinism Evolving*, 479–97.

23. See especially Bergson, *Creative Evolution*.

abstract repeatability—then we should not be surprised if a certain sort of deistic or voluntaristic God will always be re-invoked in every neo-liberal historical moment.)

As against this, Bergson reasonably suggested that life and consciousness, since they are upshots in excess of the merely physical, themselves offer a re-manifestation on the surface of the world of processes at work in its deepest depths. When we gather up our forces to will and to create, we obscurely fuse past, present, and future and directly intuit something that, in striving to bring about, we already see. In this fashion we directly experience in temporal *durée* the fundamental work of the *élan vitale*. Human art and action is not then an epiphenomenal illusion, but neither is it a sudden alien intrusion upon reality. The consequence of this view—drawn by many of the greatest modernist artists, and perhaps supremely by the Catholic composer Olivier Messiaen and his pupils Iannis Xenakis and Pierre Boulez—is that the artist realizes in the free creation also the most revealing experimental work of science.[24]

The priority of the vital over the physical can then be seen as essential to the securing of immanentism—even if this will tend to mean that the *élan vitale*, however named, becomes an immanent deity, or even a quasi-transcendent one.

Peter Hallward, in a penetrating summary, has shown how most modern French philosophers are in this respect the heirs of Bergson.[25] They tend to identify the absolute as a creative force that consists in a *glissando* of constant variation (or absolute heterogeneity or internal self-differentiation) that is a perpetually non-identical repetition. While, in the case of Gilles Deleuze, this is an immanent absolute named variously "a life" or "pure composition" or "the plane of immanence" or "the abstract machine," the virtuality rather than actuality of this absolute is paralleled in philosophers like Michel Henry or Christian Jambet by the henological or "beyond being" character of their notion of transcendence. But in either case, one has a resulting dualism in terms of the contrast between a "good" transcendental creative factor, on the one hand, and a "bad" static and representable created element, on the other. This dualism is virulent precisely because the virtual creative factor is only actualized or self-realized in terms of the static element that inevitably obfuscates (both

---

24. For ideas on Messiaen and the entire question of musical ontology on which the current article is substantively drawing throughout, see Pickstock, "Quasi una Sonata." See also Darbyshire, "Messiaen," 33–55, and Fabbi, "Theological Implications," 55–84.

25. Hallward, "The One or the Other," 1–33.

in terms of being and of knowing awareness) the very forces that sustain it and always exceed it.[26]

And already, in Bergson himself, the vital impulse does not truly exist apart from its tendency to constantly run into reverse, to look backwards, laying out time as memory and thereby engendering the spatial field that is studied in physics.[27] Picking up on post-thermodynamic notions of evolution, Bergson saw organic life as reverse entropy, temporarily recuperating its diminishing series, although also as that which constantly recuperated the self-renewing ultimate source of being (transcendental "life") beyond the grasp of physical science as such.

In a similar fashion, Deleuze and Guattari see life as decoding the formally organized circular flows of physical *milieux* and thereby as establishing "territories." In their reading of the latter process in the case of animals, they are radically non-Darwinian and learn from both Bergson and the composer Messiaen. A bird singing his song is not primarily defending a territory, according to the chapter "On the Refrain" in *A Thousand Plateaus*, but is rather continuously establishing it, for territorial animals make more explicit a decoding that removes a haeccity from the organized flux in order to restore and release energy that is endemic to life as such. A territory is, for Deleuze and Guattari, literally a sacred space established by animal art before it is an assurance of sufficient food and security, since animality *need not* seek these things through a process of individuation—it simply happens to do so, or even in some fashion *chooses* to do so.

Again, in keeping with Bergson, the territory is for Deleuze and Guattari already a reaching beyond itself, a deterritorialization precisely because its drawing of a circle in order to contain energy has conjured the power of absolute heterogeneity whose virtual capacity exceeds the circle that it draws on in the very process of drawing it. The refrain that the bird sings is equivalently a folding back upon itself of the uninterrupted *glissando* of life in order to establish a theme, a cry that represents animal identity and wards off the threat of destruction. Yet the territorial refrain can already be expanded into a song of courtship and even into pure variations that have lost sight of all function, as Olivier Messiaen had already concluded.

26. Deleuze, *Pure Immanence*, 25–35. See especially, 31: "Events or singularities give to the plane all their virtuality, just as the plane of immanence gives virtual events their full reality. . . . A wound [an instance of the Stoic 'incorporeal'] is incarnated or actualized in a state of things or of life; but it is itself a pure virtuality on the plane of immanence that leads us into a life."

27. Bergson, *Creative Evolution*, chapter 3, 186–272.

For Deleuze and Guattari, this same process is simply taken further in human beings: our highest effort is to conjugate forces which send milieus and territories spinning into free-play but without disappearing altogether into chaos or invoking the heterogeneous as a new sort of closure. One could say that, for them, this is a new sort of post-human and ecological sociality. It is intended to resist both narrowly defended terrains, on the one hand, and entirely abstract universal modes of capture like that of capitalism, on the other. It concerns the "betweens" of reality and the "diagonals" that exit from the vertical spatial and horizontal temporal coordinates within which they are inscribed. This is their "path of flight"—not really one of straightforward escape, but rather of escape both from stifling enclosure and the vacuous loneliness of mere escapism—escape for the sake of escape. In so far as it aims somehow magically to capture the forces of the cosmos itself, it is apparently unlike Derrida's appeal to an "impossible" donative *différance* that is merely regulative and cannot be in any sense realized. It is also somewhat unlike the usual Marxist injunctions merely to negate the given or await its immanent collapse. It is rather a Spinozistic injunction to individuals already and always to create a positive joyful conjugation of forces.

In this manner (Bergsonian or Deleuzian) vitalism seems to combine a sophisticated reading of modern science with a continuing role for metaphysics and an ontological ground for the human pursuit of hopeful social projects.

## For a Transcendent Vitalism[28]

But is this entirely the case? We saw that the eighteenth- and nineteenth-century Anglo-Saxon God of intelligent design is a half-immanent God interacting on the same plane with what he influences. From this there results a fundamental dualism of the creative and designing, on the one hand, and the inert and the designed, on the other. This dualism is *not* the result of having a transcendent principle, a transcendent *esse-intellegere-volere* from which finite being is entirely derived in all degrees of its existence, including secondary causality and creaturely freedom. It is rather the result of dividing up the finite world into spheres of influence between a quasi-transcendent principle, on the one hand, and sheerly finite causal process, on the other.

---

28. I have borrowed this term from my colleague at Nottingham, Agata Bielik-Robson.

But this means that vitalism, by switching to the apparent monism of pure vitalist immanentism, does not get rid of this dualism, but rather augments it by rendering it aporetically virulent. In a hypostasized double negation the fixed and apparent is merely the phenomenal guise for the virtual and dynamic, which nevertheless only exists at all through its phenomenal self-occlusion. It is all rather like Thomas Carlyle's deconstructed account of German idealism and romanticism: the phenomenal world is the "clothing" of the real ideal world; and yet the examination of human culture reveals that the entire realm of thought is itself a matter of "fashionable clothing" or temporarily preferred image and metaphor. Hence, by implied analogy the cosmic clothing conceals a null energy that is merely the power to clothe and so to disguise itself.[29]

Any immanentism whatsoever tends to succumb to this model of double disguise—of the real by appearance, but more fundamentally of appearance by the supposed real. In constantly "uncovering" the illusion of uncovering itself, postmodernism does little more than expound the grammar of such immanentism, which it never calls into question. For, to repeat, in any immanentism there is the whole or the director of the whole, which is the truly real—for Bergson it is the *élan vitale* that is absolutely self-differentiating—with an absoluteness not without *some* kinship with the absolute time of Isaac Newton. But this "absolute"—as with Spinoza's substance, Heidegger's Being, Deleuze's "a life," Derrida's *différance*, etc.—is only "actual" in another subordinate realm that it ceaselessly erects and dismantles.[30] In Bergson's case this is the realm of space, which is all that ordinary cognition ever represents.

Since subordination is involved here, even if the subordinating requires the subordinate in order to be at all, then this *schema* involves always not only dualism, but also hierarchy between a higher conditioning power and a lower conditioned reality. One can try, like Francois Laruelle, to be more avant-garde than all the avant-garde in thinking a purer immanence by constructing and invoking an absolute that exists purely as self-presupposition that is immediately a self-positing without any conditioning of an "outside."[31] Yet Laruelle is still led to say that this process itself, in order to attain a thinkable actuality, throws up the spheres of conditioning/conditioned that are conventionally constructed and theorized by both practical life and philosophy, even if these are not supposed

29. Thomas Carlyle, *Sartor Resartus*.
30. See Cunningham, *Genealogy*.
31. Laruelle, "What Can Non-Philosophy Do?" 169–91.

to feed back into the ultimate unthinkable nullity that is also everything. Dualism and hierarchy are therefore the secret heart of all immanentisms.

Why should this matter, politically? It matters because immanentist vitalism cannot really think an advance to a better world. Deleuze's intentions were in many ways admirable, but his notion of composition is inherently unstable and contradictory—pulled in two opposite directions at once. To the degree that the path of flight deterritorializes, it also tends to a void, nullity, or chaos that will either swallow it up or be recruited as an abstract basis for totalizing rule. Inversely, to the degree that, to use the musical example deployed by Deleuze and Guattari, atonality remains rooted in the tonality of territory, it will still affirm local prejudices. That there *needs* to be, ethically and politically, a mean between the concretely local and the merely void and abstract universal is correct, as Deleuze to his credit recognizes. And yet his Bergsonian outlook cannot really think in this medium.

Why? Because a univocal process of pure self-differentiation is only realized through the very realities that it must also constantly negate: milieus, aggregates, and territories. The "mechanosphere" includes both these things, and to pursue a line of flight is in the end to be resigned to evil as well as good, enclosure as well as freedom—so this it is only personal and stoic liberation after all.[32]

Crucial here is a point made by Peter Hallward that supplies a second reason for concern. Absolute heterogeneity is self-generating difference and therefore it is the many in so far as it one, and the one in so far as it is many, but not in any sense a mediation between the two. It contains no *relation*—and this is not a plea for Hegelianism. Rather, it is a demonstration that even Deleuze's differential metaphysics reduces to an oscillation that is also a coincidence between the one and the many (or the subject and the other). This is actually still the dialectical *failure* to think mediation or "the between"—as William Desmond has argued with respect to Hegel.[33] By contrast, in the spatialized or territorialized level of Deleuze's "chaosmos" there are apparent relations and representations, but these relations are not originally constitutive since each spatial reality is ultimately directly engendered by absolute heterogeneity—the acausal deterritorializing force that establishes the real primarily as difference in excess of any preceding continuities of essence. Their harmony is not, indeed, exactly pre-established, but it is constantly re-established by continuous

32. Deleuze and Guattari, *A Thousand Plateaus*, 501–17.
33. Desmond, *Hegel's God*.

occasional intervention, even if the spatial things do not really occupy any ground independent of such intervention, and even if the intervention is only "there" in the intervening. Hence Deleuze declares that, while his differential monads are no longer discrete, they remain, in their (Whiteheadian) "prehending" of each other (non-relationally) "windowless."[34]

But without real relations, human beings and all other organisms are reduced to the subservience of a vital flow: their only possibility of salvific self-escape must consist in self-abolition through identification with this vital flux. And if relations themselves cannot mutually constitute something that discloses ultimate reality, then there is no real hope for a social and ecological transformation that acknowledges both individuals and their vital bonds to others without which they could not live nor express any values.

The question here is, if the *glissando* of the vital process is actualized only through "notes," "scales," and "metres," then do we necessarily need to see the latter as *in any sense at all* interrupting or completing the *glissando* rather than as serially constituting it? This is the same as to ask, *does* the vital process exist in a pure heterogeneity that always expresses the same univocal One, or does it rather consist, as William Desmond has suggested (in a bold attempt to "dynamize" and temporalize Thomistic analogy), in endless analogical relations that express simultaneously identity and difference? In the first case, as with Hegel, one has only an apparent coincidence of opposites whose constantly renewed *aporia* in point of fact still respects formal logic. In the second case, one has a more radical and irreducible coincidence of opposites precisely because there is as much persisting pleasurable tension as there is reconciliation—a tension that sustains, as Desmond puts it, the agapeic distance of the other (in its relatively "univocal" singularity) within and yet beyond the erotic moment of fusion (which, unlike the philosophers of difference, he does not moralistically deny). This coincidence of the genuine *metaxu* can truly be "heard" rather than thought, as Desmond suggests, in poetry or music.[35] And perhaps it can be heard in the most maximally strained and so verifying degree in the most extreme of modern or post-modern musics, where "harmony" remains in some extended sense despite all the disharmony and complexity. Certainly in Messiaen, if not in Xenakis, the continuous perpetual variation of unpredictable rhythm is not superior to, but

---

34. Deleuze, *The Fold*, 81: "Prehension is naturally open, open onto the world, without having to pass through a window." See also 121–37.

35. Desmond, *Being and the Between*, 177–225.

is rather something constantly arriving with, the invocation of a spatial coloration invoked through sound. This "synaesthesia" renders his always programmatic music "poetic," if one takes poetry to be the instance of blending the various sensory mediums—a blending which, as "common sense," one can see as giving rise to language as such and so thought as such. (Here also one has an ineffable "between," without which, nonetheless, thought would not really operate.)

By contrast with this synaesthetic and metaxological blending of "organizing" time and organized space, it is arguable that the continuing downgrading of space and visibility in modern French thought is still basically Cartesian in character. Bergson had not really felt the force of the new physics—which, in effect, from the mid-nineteenth century onwards, precisely restored the hermeticism and Neoplatonism that Newton (who was precisely *not* the last of the magicians) had tried to keep at bay: the primacy of light; the role of descending series; action at a distance; apparently unmediated harmonization; the coincidence of opposites; the irreversibility of a time that is not absolute; the multiplicity of finite infinites. (There are anticipations of most of these things in Robert Grosseteste, Giordano Bruno, etc., as recent research shows, and it is also the case that early twentieth-century physics was imbued with the spirit of the second wave of romanticism that mutated into modernism.)[36] By contrast, Bergson still saw physics as concerned with the precisely measurable and did not explore the *aporias*, given ecstasies, and mysterious relationality of space in the same way that he explored the paradoxes of time. (Perhaps for this reason he not only read, perhaps validly, Einstein's space-relative time as only spatialized time and not true *durée*, but he also failed to read *durée* as itself relative to eminent extension.)[37]

This meant that he did not consider the possibility that the irreducibly relational interfolding of past, present, and future is not simply the work of a temporal self-differentiation, but might equally be the work of a spatial "laying out" of such moments in a display, such that "relation" lies not simply "inside" a thing (G. E. Moore's "internal relation")—else it would be that thing, or the totality of all things, negating event and contingency—nor simply "outside" that thing (Moore's "external relation"), in which case it would merely belong to another thing or again to all things

---

36. See Mackenzie, "*The 'Obscurism'*"; Gatti, *Giordano Bruno*; Cushing, *Philosophical Concepts in Physics*; and Penrose, *The Road to Reality*.

37. See Bergson, *Duration and Simultaneity*.

with the same upshot.[38] For there to be events in time, there must be a spatial "laying out" of temporal moments, but their mutual ecstasy is not thereby simply abolished, but instead is expressed in a different way in the mystery of the "between" that is real relationality—neither internal nor external. Temporal ecstasy is the "erotic" inwardness and savor of mutuality; but spatial mutuality is the "agapeic" externality and reaching endlessly out towards the ecstatic goal. And each is relative to the other.

The third criticism concerns the question of series and gift—two names for the same thing in the writings of the pagan Neoplatonist Proclus.[39] If complexity always falls out as an ordered series, then it is a rising or a falling, has inevitably a greater or lesser focus or foci. For this reason the usual "radical" objection to hierarchy as such is the worst naivety—for phenomenologically and ontologically speaking there is always hierarchy, and equality can only be achieved by the subtle blending of asymmetrical ascendencies. (Most of our current political thought fails to see precisely this.) It is notable that "hierarchy" was only the name given by Dionysius the Areopagite to the "series" of the pagan Neoplatonists, which always had a mathematical dimension.[40] So I do not altogether complain of Deleuze's immanentist hierarchy—only of its stasis and absolute non-reversibility. Whereas the Neoplatonic series was always psychically ascendable, one must climb Deleuze's stoic staircase to the sole end of subjective annihilation. This means, in consequence, that if Deleuze's vital series "gives," like Plotinus's One, what it does not have (since it is beyond being, which is nonetheless derived from it), namely all the various ontological actualities which he isolates (milieus, territories, and so forth), it also takes away what it gives, does not allow any return gift of gratitude to the absolute, and finally calls one beyond any generous reciprocity.[41] In this way the human creative act might, as with Bergson, invoke the absolute, but it cannot as gift invoke an absolute giving and sharing. Yet art is perhaps distinguished from science as gift; as Iannis Xenakis declared in his thesis defense, *Arts/Sciences: Alloys*, to select is to receive a revelation as if "by grace." And to offer a work of art is to offer delight and so a gift "meritoriously," not just the usefulness of instruction.[42]

38. See Deleuze, *Pure Immanence*, 35–53.

39. See, for example, Proclus, *Elements of Theology*, propositions 18, 20, 42.

40. Dionysius the Areopagite, *The Complete Works*.

41. For a critique of Plotinus in relation to the gift, see Bruaire, *L'être et l'esprit*, 95–107.

42. Xenakis, *Arts/Sciences Alloys*, 27–47, 61–79 (dialogues with Olivier Messiaen and Michel Serres, respectively).

The political advantage of vitalism is that the creative human effort is here in tune with, even disclosive of, the ultimate. But the hope for positive social construction demands more than this heroic individualism—it demands that our mutual love, relating and surprising in order to forge new bonds, be also in tune with the ultimate.

But supposing that we were to hear the music of Messiaen, whose thoughts about territory and the refrain are invoked at the most pivotal point of *A Thousand Plateaus*, otherwise than he was heard by Deleuze? In his own voluminous but fragmentary writings, the composer constantly tries to fuse the thought of Bergson on time with the thoughts of Aquinas on the relation of time and the cosmos to eternity.[43] He certainly embraces the notion that music is primarily non-identical repetition, continuous variation and so manifests *durée*, yet he denies that the latter is "immediately given" to consciousness—instead it is only experienced through all our corporeal and spatial interactions that alone produce continuous rhythm. And even though the latter is the temporal essence of music, sound has a synaesthesic aspect that conjures up for us colors, specific spatial sites, and objects of visual contemplation. Hence for all the abstractness of Messiaen's rhythmic lines and for all his invoking of the non-narrative dimensions of intensity, timbre, polyrhythm, polydynamics, polyharmony, heteroharmony, and so forth (and arguably he neglects too much the narrative dimension, writing *no* liturgical music!) his music remains situated and representational. In keeping with this, the step-ways forward movements always simultaneously spread out into a vast and varied simultaneous sonority. As his pupil Pierre Boulez put it, what one should hear through all this is the strange "diagonal" where harmony and color blend with rhythm and melody.[44]

But in that case the diagonal is the mediation of the seemingly heterogeneous. It is, in fact, another name for the *metaxu*. And for Deleuze it is this diagonal that is the line of flight. But can this be the true diagonal, the true between, if it veers hopelessly between vertical arboreality and a never fully attained quality of the sheerly rhizomatic? This Deleuzian diagonal is not, indeed, a relation, since it seeks to escape from both traps—but really it can never escape from either and is stuck in a shuttle. Just because, in order to be a free, pure relationality without relation between points it must escape the vertical and the horizontal; its relationality is fully captured all the time by either pole. Moreover, its diagonality does

---

43. Messiaen, *Traité de Rythme*, especially 7–52.
44. Boulez, *Notes*, 231–32, 295–301, 382–83.

not *express*, participate in the absolute, since this is the sheer horizontality of the purely virtual.

In this way immanentism, in refusing a transcendent God, always winds up deifying an impersonal process and ontologically subordinating those concrete situations within which alone human beings can truly dwell as human.

So Deleuze finally failed to hear Messiaen's diagonal as ultimate—or as on the way to an infinite diagonal. Messiaen's diagonal remains truly a pure relation just because it does not seek to escape its two co-ordinates and yet is still the "surplus" to them, which alone links them in order to render them elements of a complex, perhaps cosmic music.

Hence Deleuze mis-reads the line of flight. It goes just as much upwards with the trees as it burrows along with the roots of the prairie. If it is to escape and yet remain, it must continue to relate and never abandon one pole of this relating for the other. This means that its flight *denies* the ultimacy of any immanent process or any partially immanent Godhead, because this will always consecrate a duality that renders relationality subordinate. To say the givenness of spatial laws traps us in impersonal fixity and cold terroristic rule is true, but the idea of a one-way impersonal temporal gift that gives only itself to itself traps us just as surely.

Instead, we need to think of the vital as relational or metaxological. But in that case there is no controlling power within the finite world and there is nothing that inscribes a boundary round this world. There is only the sequence and pattern of inter-tangling diagonals in interaction with pattern-forming processes (horizontally) and open-ended, always-developing essences (vertically). To properly re-constitute this world diagonally is indeed to move along a horizontal path, as when one is ascending an inclined staircase, but it is also to climb upwards, to reach beyond this world altogether. Progress forward through time is possible because it is simultaneously a reaching to transcendence, not a re-invocation of a primordial impersonal process. We can therefore only reach towards better social relations insofar as we come to understand ourselves as participating in a higher source of relationality that constantly gives itself.

For if relations are to be ultimate within this world, they can only be grounded in relationality. But if this is something finite, then *either* it is a given set of spatial relations, which reduces to a totality and is not relation, *or* it is a giving temporal relationality, which reduces to the monism of time and again and is not a relation.

No, if relationality or "the between" is to be ultimate within the world, then the world itself must be purely relation, purely a medium—down to its ground something received, such that it is at bottom a relation to itself as other, a reception of itself as gift, which it must then give to itself—this allows that the inner reality of the cosmos is vital, even psychic in Bergson's sense.[45] But it additionally ensures that the autopoetic is from the outset also relational, also social, also a response, also involved in giving and receiving. This alone ensures that hierarchic series are gifts and reversible—even the hierarchy of Creator and creation, since by perfect reception and response the human creature and the cosmos through her can be deified.

Within this conception, it does, indeed, remain true as for Carlyle and as recognized by Shakespeare in *The Tempest*, that finite reality itself is a flimsy garment, a theatre, a dream. But it also ceases to be the case that this dream apparently conceals a "real" spiritual dreamer, whose supposition in turn conceals the reality *only* of "concealment," of dreaming. This "postmodern" scenario was already mooted by the greatest Baroque dramatists, namely Shakespeare and Calderon, but they both also envisaged how it is outplayed within a Catholic dramaturgy.

For what matters in *The Tempest* within the magical artifice of Prospero's disclosure through fiction (allegorical masques) of the historical truth, and his conjuration of justice, is that both truth and justice must in the end subserve the higher and more voluntary magic of mercy and reconciliation. In this way, even though the cosmos remains a theatrical dream, Prospero can, in the end, abandon his "rough magic" because he now sees this dream as upheld by divine mercy and grace. In other words, the "dream" is real to a finite degree just because it allows some exercise of a non-compromising goodness that seeks a true "between," or analogical co-dwelling of creatures, human and bestial. So whereas the "dream" of appearance within immanence is constantly cancelled only to constantly reappear in a shuttle without meaning, the dream that creatively emanates from a transcendent source is granted a certain reality of its own, just to the measure that it is given, and gratefully returns, a certain share of the good. Here then, a being without the good is "mere dream" or illusion, but a being with the good is also a good that is (somewhat) actual (rather than merely being merely intended, or primarily an imperative, as for Kant, or a pre-ontological subjectively constitutive imperative, as for Levinas).[46]

---

45. This is argued by Bruaire, *L'être et l'esprit*, 51–87, and *passim*.
46. Nevertheless, a Levinasian thesis of the priority of good over being could be

It is the same dramatic argument in Calderón's *La Vida es Sueno*.[47] Here the protagonist Segismund, Prince of Poland, has been imprisoned without any human contact in order to forestall a prophecy that he will rule as a tyrant. His father Basil feels that, in justice, this prophecy should be tested and has Segismund released, but on the merciful condition that if he should indeed prove tyrannous he will later be told that he has only dreamt that he was for a day a ruler. The prophecy is indeed fulfilled, and Segismund proves in one horrendous day of misgovernment to be both unruly and violent. However, he then himself concludes that whether or not he was dreaming during this interlude is irrelevant: for each of us only dreams what happens to us or what we are, insofar as we are always performing a role (as for Carlyle) and the entire creation is itself a divine artifice in which we play our allotted parts. This means that, for Calderón, beneath the idea of disguise lies the reality that if there is *only* disguise then whatever role we are performing we are, after all, only performing ourselves as some mask or another. Thus in this instance Segismund only dreams that he is a ruler, but ironically he truly is, by destiny, just this ruler (so that he is, in fact, dreaming who he really is), but then again such a role is purely an artifice, a seeming.

However, Segismund finally repents and is released to become a worthy ruler. It is realized that human beings are not bound to tragic fate and that the attempt to evade the prophecy itself ensured that Segismund became the inhuman monster that the prophecy foretold. Segismund declares that all that matters, awake or dreaming, is the doing of justice and the granting of mercy, for in this way finitude is granted its true measure of significance, and so of reality, in accordance with the divine intention: "To act with virtue / Is what matters, since if this proves true, / That truth's sufficient reason in itself; / If not, we win us friends against the time / When we at last awake."[48] This is expressed in terms of absence of any true human life, if it is "without honor," and honor in turn is seen as a preparedness to receive gifts and, still more, liberally to grant them. Thus within the perspective of transcendence, appearances and temporary states are "saved"

---

seen as partially confirmed here. See, Shakespeare, *The Tempest*, Act IV Scene I, 148–56: "These our actors / as I foretold you, were all spirits, and [note] / are melted into air, into thin air; / And, like the baseless fabric of this vision, / The cloud-capped towers, the gorgeous palaces, / The solemn temples, the great globe itself, / Yea, all which it inherit, shall all dissolve, / And, like this insubstantial pageant faded, / Leave not a wrack behind." See also, Act V Scene I, 40–57.

47. Calderón, "Life is a Dream," 407–40, esp. 456, 466, 477.

48. Ibid., Act III, 462.

because they are seen as instances of gift that can be recognized if this founding generosity is taken up and perpetuated.

It follows that, if one allows the seemingly greater dualism of Creator and created, there ensues, paradoxically, no unbridgeable dualism, and no psychically unclimbable stairway. Within immanence one has to choose between the less real appearance of the vertical on the one hand and the less actual but more finally real truth of the horizontal on the other. But if the *metaxu* of diagonal relation is truly ultimate, then there is no duality in this world between appearance and reality or actuality and virtuality, for *all* is now, *more radically than for postmodernism*, ephemeral shadowy image; and yet the shadow can still in itself bear the trace of goodness, and therefore can fully participate in and not occlude the real, just in so far as the theatre of shadows becomes also the scene of an enactment of cosmic justice and mercy (towards all creatures, not just human ones).

As for the duality between God and the world ... it does not exist in any simple fashion. For in leaving this world for God along the diagonal of Jacob's ladder one receives back this world with more intensity and more advance towards its eschaton. As Maximus the Confessor put it: if the visible things refer always to the invisible, the invisible things refer always back to the visible.[49]

But is not relation abolished in God as the ultimate source? Not according to Catholic understanding. To the contrary, it argues—and I am thinking especially of John Scotus Eriugena here—that if God is the one who creates and receives back from the creation its tribute of praise, then he *is* this, as himself outside himself, but also he *is* this, as not merely himself within himself. We are given to ourselves vertically always in the mode of a simultaneous cosmic and social ecstasy towards finite others, because God is in himself both vertical interchange of gift and horizontal absolute continuity. God is at last *entirely* the diagonal medium because the Father is only "above" the Son in generating the Son, and the process of engenderment is nothing but the Son in his vertical iconicity. (For this reason an "entire" diagonal medium is, in an extraordinary sense, "univocally analogical," because the Son is a "perfect" likeness to the Father and univocally at one with him in infinite being, as Eckhart taught.)[50] This diagonal line is infinitely and entirely expressed in the Father-Son absolute substantive relation, but as infinite expression it is also infinitely unexhausted and like a fractal line winds on, as it were, from two to three and

---

49. Maximus the Confessor, "Mystagogy," chapter 2, 189.
50. See Mojsisch, *Meister Eckhart*.

then presumably infinite dimensions in the Holy Spirit, whose substantive relation to Father and Son forms a "square" on the base of their mutual love.

In the New Testament, the name of the receptive and exchanging Holy Spirit as the ultimate transcendental "between" is therefore "gift," but it is also therefore "life." For if God is the infinitely sustained exchange of gift, then he is also supremely life, as that which is self-sustaining, self-increasing, and self-engendering. And if God supremely gives to the creation the gift of being, then he must also give to it life since, also in finitude, to be without remainder gift is to be likewise without remainder, yet here by the grace of another, perpetually self-renewing.[51]

Therefore, the only perfected metaphysics of vitalism must be a Catholic one, a philosophy that is equally a true exegesis of the gospel.

## Bibliography

Baker, Anthony. "Theology and the Crisis in Darwinism." *Modern Theology* 18 (2002) 183–215.
Behe, Michael, J. *Darwin's Black Box*. New York: Simon and Schuster, 1996.
Bergson, Henri. *Creative Evolution*. Translated by Arthur Mitchell. New York: Dover, 1998.
———. *Duration and Simultaneity: Bergson and the Einsteinian Universe*. Translated by Robin Durie. Manchester, UK: Clinamen, 1999.
Berlinsky, David "The Deniable Darwin." *Commentary* 101.6 (1996) 27–28.
Boulez, Pierre. *Notes of an Apprenticeship*. Translated by R. Weinstock. New York: Knopf, 1968.
Bowler, Peter J. *Darwinism*. New York: Twayne, 1993.
Brooke, John Hedley. *Science and Religion: Some Historical Perspectives*. Cambridge: Cambridge University Press 1991.
Bruaire, Claude. *L'être et l'esprit*. Paris: PUF, 1983.
Bulgakov, Sergius. *Philosophy of Economy: The World as Household*. Translated by Catherine Evtuhov. New Haven: Yale University Press, 2000.
Calderón, de la Barca. "Life is a Dream." Translated by Roy Campbell. In *The Classic Theatre, Vol. III: Six Spanish Plays*. Edited by Eric Bentley, 409–80. New York: Doubleday, 1959.
Carlyle, Thomas. *Sartor Resartus: The Life and Times of Herr Teufelsdröckh*. Introduced by Alasdair Gray. Illustrated by Edmund J. Sullivan. Edinburgh: Canongate, 1987.
Cunningham, Conor. *Darwin's Pious Idea*. Grand Rapids: Eerdmans, 2010.

---

51. Michel Henry has explored this in an indispensable way, despite the fact that his dualism of "inner" life versus external embodiment (alluded to earlier in this article) and his concomitant claim that "auto-affection is transcendentally prior to mediation by external sensation" (a conclusion that is importantly disputed by Chrétien) gives a certain quasi-Manichean cast to his exegesis and theological reflections. See Michel Henry, *I Am the Truth* and "Phenomenology of Life."

———. *Genealogy of Nihilism: Philosophies of Nothing and the Difference of Theology.* London: Routledge, 2002.
Cushing, James T. *Philosophical Concepts in Physics the Historical Relation between Philosophy and Scientific Theories.* Cambridge: Cambridge University Press, 1998.
Darwin, Charles. *The Origin of Species.* Edited by J. W. Burrow. Harmondsworth, UK: Penguin, 1979.
Dawkins, Richard. *The Blind Watchmaker: Why the Evidence of Evolution Reveals a Universe without Design.* New York: Norton, 1996.
Deleuze, Gilles. *The Fold: Leibniz and the Baroque.* Translated by Tom Conley. London: Athlone, 1993.
———. *Pure Immanence: Essays on a Life.* Translated by Anne Boyman. New York: Zone, 2001.
Deleuze, Gilles, and Felix Guattari. *A Thousand Plateaus.* Translated by Brian Massumi. London: Athlone, 1987.
Desmond, William. *Being and the Between.* New York: SUNY, 1995.
———. *Hegel's God: A Counterfeit Double?* London: Ashgate, 2003.
Depew, David J., and Bruce H. Weber. *Darwinism Evolving: Systems Dynamics and the Genealogy of Natural Selection.* Cambridge: MIT, 1997.
Darbyshire, Ian. "Messiaen and the Representation of the Theological Illusion of Time." In *Messiaen's Language of Mystical Love*, edited by Siglind Bruhn, 33–55. New York: Garland, 1998.
Dionysius the Areopagite. *The Complete Works.* Translated by Colm Luibheid. London: SPCK, 1987.
Dupré, John. "Human Origins and the Decline of Theism." In *Darwin's Legacy: What Evolution Means Today*, 41–62. Oxford: Oxford University Press 2003.
Fabbi, Roberto. "Theological Implications of Restrictions in Messiaen's Compositional Processes." In *Messiaen's Language of Mystical Love*, edited by Siglind Bruhn, 55–84. New York: Garland, 1998.
Funkenstein, Amos. *Theology and the Scientific Imagination: From the Middle Ages to the Seventeenth Century.* Princeton: Princeton University Press, 1986.
Gatti, Hilary. *Giordano Bruno and Renaissance Science.* Ithaca, NY: Cornell University Press, 1999.
Gilson, Etienne. *From Darwin to Aristotle and Back Again: A Journey in Final Causality, Species and Evolution.* Notre Dame IN: Notre Dame University Press, 1982.
Grene, Marjorie. "Introduction." In *Dimensions of Darwinism: Themes and Counter-Themes in Twentieth-Century Evolutionary Theory*, edited by Marjorie Grene, 1–15. Cambridge: Cambridge University Press, 1983.
Hanby, Michael. "Creation without Creationism: Toward a Theological Critique of Darwinism." *Communio* 30 (2003) 654–94.
Hallward, Peter. "The One or the Other: French Philosophy Today." *Angelaki* 8.2 (2003) 1–33.
Henry, Michel. *I Am the Truth: Toward a Philosophy of Christianity.* Stanford: Stanford University Press, 2003.
———. "Phenomenology of Life." *Angelaki* 8.2 (2003) 97–111.
Laruelle, Francois. "What Can Non-Philosophy Do?" *Angelaki* 8.2 (August 2003) 169–91.
McGrath, Alister. *Dawkins' God: Genes, Memes and the Meaning of Life.* Oxford: Blackwell, 2005.

Mackenzie, Iain M. *The "Obscurism" of Light*. Norwich, UK: Canterbury, 1996.
Maximus the Confessor. "The Church's Mystagogy." In *Selected Writings*, translated by George C. Berthold, 183–225. New York: Paulist, 1985.
Messiaen, Olivier *Traité de Rythme, de Couleur et d'Ornithologie*, Tome I. Paris: Leduc, 1994.
Milbank, John. *Theology and Social Theory: Beyond Secular Reason*. Oxford: Blackwell, 1990.
Mojsisch, Burkhard. *Meister Eckhart: Analogy, Univocity and Unity*. Translated by Orrin F. Summerell. Amsterdam: Grüner, 2001.
Oliver, Simon. "Motion according to Aquinas and Newton." *Modern Theology* 17.2 (2001) 163–99.
Penrose, Roger. *The Road to Reality: A Complete Guide to the Laws of the Universe*. London: Cape, 2004.
Pickstock, Catherine. "Quasi una Sonata: Postmodernism, Religion and Music." In *Theology and Music*, edited by Jeremy Begbie, 190–211. Cambridge: Cambridge University Press, 2006.
Proclus. *Elements of Theology*. Translated by E. R. Dodds. Oxford: Oxford University Press, 1963.
Schmutz, Jacob. "La doctrine médiévale des causes et la théologie de la nature pure" (XIIIe—XVIIe siècles). *Revue Thomiste* I–II (Jan–June 2001) 217–64.
Shakespeare, William. *The Tempest*. Edited by Anne Barton. Harmondsworth, UK: Penguin, 19
von Uexküll, Jacob. *Theoretical Biology*. Translated by D. L. Mackinnon. London: Kegan Paul, 1926.
Wallis, Jim. *God's Politics*. San Francisco: Harper, 2005.
Xenakis, Iannis. *Arts/Sciences Alloys: The Thesis Defence of Iannis Xenakis before Olivier Messiaen et. al*. Translated by Sharon Kanach. New York: Pendragon, 1985.

# 5

## *Analogia Naturae*
### What Does Inanimate Matter Contribute to the Meaning of Life?

D. C. Schindler

~

### Schelling and the Challenge of Mechanism

THE DEVELOPMENTS IN THE science of nature that crested in the seventeenth century are commonly referred to as a "revolution" because they involved not just a set of discoveries or a new theory, but a fundamental change in the conception of nature simply, even if the implications of the change have taken centuries fully to unfold.[1] One aspect of this transformation is what has been called the "democratization" of the natural world,[2] wherein the classical hierarchy of being was flattened out so that all things in the cosmos, no matter how base or how celestial, were seen to be composed of essentially the same "stuff" and were all equal under the law of nature, eventually codified in Newton's mechanics. The revolution occurred in waves, each laying low in succession one level of the classical

---

1. And, to be sure, the "revolution" began several centuries before Galileo. As Analiese Maier has shown, the emergence of "physicalist thinking" that separated physics, not only from Aristotle, but from philosophy and theology more generally, reached a first crescendo among the Parisian nominalists in the fourteenth century: *Die Vorlaüfer Galileis*, 1–2.

2. Mutschler, *Spekulative Physik*, 22–23.

triad of being-life-intellect, which Plato introduced in the *Sophist*. Initially, while Galileo sought to provide a better account of projectile motion, he established principles that presumed to describe the behavior of all being precisely insofar as it partook of motion—that is, insofar as it is physical at all.³ Darwin's theory was a revolution arguably not because of the claim that the forms of natural things change over time but more fundamentally because his explanation of the manner of the change extended mechanism into biology.⁴ It thus recast the very meaning of life, suggesting that life does not have a reality in itself but is rather an epiphenomenon of the mechanistic interaction of material parts. If Darwin did not draw out all the implications of his ideas, it did not take long for others to do so. The third wave that has been occurring in our age, namely, the extension of mechanism into the specifically human spheres of existence—for example in "sociobiology" and evolutionary psychology—is rarely called a revolution, perhaps because the first two waves have left so little to overturn. Ultimately, mechanistic interpretations of love, faith, reason, and so forth, have become almost a matter of course.

The fact that this represents a crisis need not be belabored here; the existence of this conference, and the interest it has generated, already bears witness to the urgency of the challenge mechanism poses to life, and what is at stake in it. But we are not the first to reflect on this challenge, and our own reflections can be aided by a consideration of the fate of other attempts. Especially instructive in this regard, I would suggest, is the philosophy of nature developed by F. W. J. von Schelling in the early nineteenth century, initially through some collaboration with his friend Hegel.⁵ Schelling anticipated in some ways the ramifications of the scientific revolution we just indicated. He believed that if a connection to life were removed altogether from matter even at its most rudimentary

---

3. Henri Bortoft explains that Galileo's theory of motion entailed a radically new way of seeing nature more generally: *The Wholeness of Nature*, 160. See the general presentation of Galileo's concept of nature in Burtt, *Metaphysical Foundations*, 72–104.

4. Christoph Cardinal Schönborn set off a maelstrom of controversy for having pointed out the distinction between the fact of evolution and the theory concerning its causal mechanism, saying that, while the church has accepted evolution, she has never endorsed a blind mechanistic explanation for it. The ferociousness of the controversy suggests that the essence of the matter is indeed the mechanism, and thus the concept of nature (and the concept of being more generally), that lies behind it. See Schönborn's original *New York Times* editorial published July 7, 2005.

5. Though it lasted only a year, Hegel and Schelling founded the *Critical Journal of Philosophy* in Jena in 1802, in which they published mostly their own pieces on the philosophy of nature.

level, it would never be able to be reintroduced later, and that the loss of life in nature would in turn evacuate the meaning of human existence. For him, the problem is not materialism *per se*, but the supplanting of the ancient materialism that recognized vital properties in matter by the lifeless materialism of modern mechanism. Schelling describes the gradual encroachment of mechanism and its culmination in a kind of technological reconstruction of nature from top to bottom in his dialogue *Bruno* in the following way:

> Since men agreed that, in the beginning, matter was dead, it was decided that death was the principle governing all things, and that life was just a derivative phenomenon. And after matter had succumbed to death, nothing remained but to banish the last witness to its vitality, that is, to transform light, the universal spirit of nature, the form of forms, into an equally corporeal entity, to divide it up mechanistically just like everything else. Now since life was extinguished in all the members and organs of the universe, since even the living manifestations that connect bodies to one another were reduced to lifeless motions, there now remained only the final and grandest task, namely, to bring nature, already dead in its innermost parts, back to life again, mechanistically.[6]

This was written in 1802. Rather presciently, Schelling thought that the reinterpretation of light that we have, for example, in Newton's optics would eventually entail a revolution in man's own self-understanding.[7] To drive life out of matter, and so out of nature simply, is to render nature the fundamental opposite of freedom. In other words, in a mechanistic world freedom becomes wholly unnatural, an empty, arbitrary spontaneity without substance, and so its products are nothing more than "superficial facts," not expressions of a deeper meaning but events that have only external intelligibility. The implication is a dissolution of the universe, which has its symbolic expression in the fragmentation of the university:

---

6. Schelling, *Bruno*, 209–10. His argument in the *Bruno* is that, strictly speaking, materialism, intellectualism, realism, and idealism, are not four different philosophies, but, properly understood, one absolute philosophy interpreted from four different angles. In this case, true materialism is not a study of the body as opposed to the soul, but includes within itself both body and soul, understood from the perspective of matter, which means that matter is essentially living.

7. Schelling presented Newton's optics in his *Lectures on the Method of Academic Study* as the greatest proof of the possibility of a complete and internally consistent construction of false inferences that is grounded from top to bottom on experience and experiment: see ibid., 564.

the "hard" sciences collapse into mechanistic materialism and the "soft" sciences collapse into historical positivism. Schelling described this two-fold collapse with great pathos in the *Lectures on the Method of Academic Study* he delivered likewise in 1802.[8]

It seems to me that the gist of Schelling's judgments resonate rather broadly with our experience of the contemporary world. To respond to the conception of nature that is presented by the leveling of being in mechanistic materialism requires a renewed reflection on the relation between inorganic and organic matter, and indeed on the relation between life and human being.[9] Schelling's response to the scientific revolution was to retrieve the ancient notion of the World Soul in a way that made sense of modern discoveries in the study of nature.[10] He placed life at the center of his conception of the cosmos, and attempted to think through the structure and behavior of matter in relation to this center. Ultimately, he was led to reinterpret matter, not as inert stuff opposed to life, but rather as a lower degree of the living, a kind of ossification of vital activity.[11] As such, it possesses an inherent drive toward the dynamic complexity of life and ultimately of spirit. Schelling thus sought to reinstate a hierarchy of being that took full consideration of the developments in modern science, but reinterpreted them according to a view of the whole. This is what he and Hegel together in their early collaboration called "speculative physics." But whatever scientific value Schelling's ideas may still have—this is a matter of continuing controversy[12]—and however attractive his reversal of the revolution may seem, it is difficult to deny a basic criticism that has been

---

8. Schelling, *Method of Academic Study*. Schelling's aim in these lectures was to recover the central role of philosophy, defined as the science of the absolute, as a precondition for the integration of the disciplines. Each discipline can have life in itself only to the extent that it understands itself as a particular reflection of the whole.

9. Iain Hamilton Grant helpfully observes that, if we have a dualism at the level of physics (between inorganic and organic matter), we will necessarily also have a dualism between nature and spirit. As he puts it, a "two-worlds" physics entails a "two-worlds" metaphysics. See his *Philosophies of Nature*, 15. The key is to overcome the dualism without collapsing in turn into a monism.

10. Schelling, *Weltseele*.

11. In the *Weltseele*, he claims that life is what is *essential* in things, and that "dead" matter is not dead in itself but merely "extinguished life," ibid., 190. In his *First Sketch* (*Erster Entwurf*, vol. 7, 87), Schelling explains that matter is a particular degree of action. In his 1801 *Darstellung meines Systems*, he says that "dead matter" does not exist as such; it is simply matter insofar as it is not raised to the form of the existence of absolute identity (101–2).

12. The main debate on this has occurred between Bernd-Olaf Küppers, *Natur als Organismus*, and Marie Heuser-Kessler, *Die Produktivität der Natur*.

made of his *Naturphilosophie*: Schelling overcomes modern mechanism's tendency to reduce biology to physics only by reducing physics to biology.[13] Even his supporters admit that the sea of life in his dynamic view of nature exposes no dry land for the "thingness" of things that it does not then flood again in the very next moment.[14] The value Schelling gives to life he precisely takes away from material being as such. What seems to be lacking in this rare attempt in modern philosophy to reflect on the meaning of life in the face of mechanistic science[15] is a way to overcome separation without losing genuine, irreducible difference. In other words, Schelling's great—we might say "tragic"—experiment in the philosophy of nature reveals the need for a truly analogical conception of nature. This is what we will attempt to sketch out in a very rudimentary way in the following pages.

## Nature Conceived Analogically

According to Aristotle, nature is an internal principle of motion and rest (*ta men gar onta panta phainetai echonta en heautois archēn kinēseōs kai staseōs*).[16] He derives this definition from a consideration of what appears to be common to the various things that are generally affirmed as existing "by nature," namely, animals (and their parts), plants, and "the simple bodies [*ta hapla tōn somatōn*], such as earth, fire, air and water." Now, it is clear in what sense animals and plants betray an internal principle of motion, and so qualify as natural. But there are a couple of peculiarities about

---

13. See Küppers, *Natur als Organismus*, 88. Certainly, this is a problem that Schelling sought vehemently to avoid, but arguably his general strategy to resist the higher reduction of nature to spirit, and so the real to the ideal, not by affirming the goodness of matter per se, but by absolutizing the *living* character of nature, continued to undercut his intention. It seems that the "positive philosophy" that Schelling developed toward the end of his life had some potential for recovering the specifically *material* dimension of the physical world as philosophically significant, but this philosophy occupied itself with religion and mythology rather than with natural science. His later discussions always included the philosophy of nature within the negative moment of reflection. I. H. Grant has argued that Schelling does not reduce the inorganic to the organic, but rather all of the beings in the world are "regional expressions" of a fundamental opposition of immanent forces: Grant, "Introduction," 62. But even this qualification does not suffice for the analogy of nature we will be proposing here.

14. See Heuser-Kessler, *Die Produktivität der Natur*, 101–4.

15. Hans Jonas observes that modern philosophy lacks altogether a genuine philosophy of nature; he appears to overlook Schelling's contribution, but the observation remains a striking one: see his *Philosophical Essays*, xii–xiii.

16. Aristotle, *Physics*, II.1.192b13–15.

this list with respect to the definition Aristotle offers of nature that call our reflection back to reconsider the meaning of that definition. On the one hand, while Aristotle very clearly includes human beings among the things of nature as a species of animal, that which is highest in man and unique to him in the natural world, namely, intellect (specifically as *nous*, and ultimately as *nous poiētikos*) is not exactly a principle of motion and rest.[17] Indeed, as is well known there have been centuries of controversy over the question of the extent to which the intellect is "in" the natural world at all. On the other hand, although Aristotle insists that the elements are natural and so distinct from the artifacts that they can be arranged to constitute, it is not clear in what sense these things may be said to have a specifically *internal* principle of motion and rest insofar as they in fact do *not* move themselves in an active sense. As Aristotle himself says later in the *Physics*, they have a principle, not of moving or producing, but of *suffering* movement (*ou tou kinein oude tou poiein, alla tou paschein*).[18] We might say that the definition Aristotle offers of nature finds itself stretched at the two extremities in a non-trivial way; or perhaps in more technical language, Aristotle does not posit a single, univocal concept of nature that he then applies mechanically to the members of the class of natural beings. Instead, the differences among the beings called natural are such that they prompt us to reinterpret at each level the meaning of the unity of nature, sometimes in a quite basic way, but nevertheless without simply doing violence to that meaning and so to the unity.

## Simple Bodies

Let us reflect, then, on nature's manifest difference in unity as it comes to expression in the ontological constitution of things—specifically, in terms of the relation they present between form/matter, unity/difference, interiority/exteriority, and particularity/universality—and in how this constitution bears on their characteristic activity, i.e., their particular expression of motion and rest. We may begin by comparing the beings on Aristotle's

---

17. Ibid., *De anima*, I.3.407a30–35; I.4.408b15–20.

18. Ibid., *Physics*, VIII.4.255b30–31. Aristotle here is trying to explain how the motion of the elements can be essentially externally caused, and yet still remain distinguishable from violent motion—which requires him to qualify the distinction normally made between natural and violent as that between the internally generated and the externally imposed. On the meaning of motion in Aristotle in relation to his general metaphysics, see Oliver, *God and Motion*, 29–50.

list of natural things, and delve more deeply into human being, following some observations from Hegel.

There are, first of all, evidently different degrees of ontological complexity among these types of beings: simple beings, the natural elements, are of course homogenous by definition, which means that what they are as a "whole" is indistinguishable from the parts of the thing: every part of water is water.[19] If the form represents the quality of a thing and the matter that out of which a thing is, or comes to be what it is, simple bodies seem to lack a significant distinction between form and matter. Their form is essentially their matter and their matter is their form. In this case, as the form does not significantly transcend the matter, the unity of a simple body does not significantly transcend the difference of its parts: every part of it is essentially the same. This is why it does not affect the being of water to be divided; no damage is done to water that is poured out into a number of cups. Hegel defined matter (i.e., the natural elements) as "externality," though he said that one could just as well think of matter as exhibiting a pure immanence.[20] In another text,[21] he characterized matter as possessing its center outside of itself, a characterization that echoes the scholastic description of material being as *"partes extra partes."* There is no center to

---

19. It may be objected that this observation has been rendered altogether obsolete by the discovery of the molecular structure of matter (and in turn the further "analyzability" of molecules, and so forth); in this case, water is evidently *not* homogenous, but can be broken down into the component parts of hydrogen and oxygen. There are two responses to be given here. First of all, the point being made above is that there is a relative indistinction between form and matter in the "simple bodies," not that there is an absolute identity between the two. The point allows room for further differentiation and qualification among the different classes of elements and compounds, homogeneous and heterogeneous matter. At the end of the essay, we will make a further comment about the sorts of material beings that are sufficiently complex that they immediately bear a certain analogy to organisms. Second, it is important to keep in mind that the atoms that constitute the elements do not *exist* except in a qualified sense: in fact, we can isolate them only in abstraction, and indeed in a certain respect only by doing a certain violence to matter. Atoms have their real being in the specific matter that they constitute. In other words, we have to avoid ascribing a univocal concept of being to both atoms and the natural elements that make up the world of experience. In this respect, Wolfgang Smith's distinction between the physical (subatomic particles and the like, which Smith associates with the metaphysical principle of potency) and the corporeal (the bodies that represent objects of sense experience) is helpful: see chapters 2 and 3 of his *The Wisdom of Ancient Cosmology*, 37–70. Smith's observations echo, in contemporary language and concepts, a view championed by Goethe.

20. Hegel says that nature, at the level of the elements, "is precisely the merely internal, and for that reason also the merely external, connection of mutually independent existences": *Philosophy of Mind*, 381; *Zusatz*, 9.

21. Hegel, *Philosophy of History*, 17.

the "being" of elements, because each part is equally center; we thus have a complete immanence of form. At the same time, this means that the "being" of matter is "ex-centric," that the form is in a sense externally divided from itself horizontally. This is why matter can qualify as a substance (*ousia*) only in an analogous sense,[22] since unity and the capacity to exist self-sufficiently, according to itself, is what defines Aristotelian being.[23]

One of the implications of this relative indistinction between form and matter in the "simple bodies" is a curious dialectic between the particular and the universal. On the one hand, they collapse into each other since there is no real difference (beyond mere spatial and temporal location) between water here and water itself—water is water—and, on the other hand, there is an extrinsicism in this relation: because there is no intrinsic unity, a unity that would transcend and so gather the parts up into an integrated whole, we cannot speak of an "individual water" that possesses the nature of water; possession requires an interiority, a definite being (a "substance," i.e., "*ousia*"), to which the nature would belong. It is just as true to think of water as being possessed *by* its nature. This "dialectic" between the material particularity of water and its formal universality casts an important light on the essential movement or behavior that characterizes simple bodies. It is often asked whether the simple bodies are "self-moving," and there is quite a bit at stake in this question:[24] if we say that they do move themselves, we seem to blur the distinction between inanimate and animate matter, and so fall into a universal vitalism. But to the extent that we lack this distinction we will be unable to avoid interpreting the evidence of mechanistic behavior in material being as a threat to the teleology that belongs to life simply, and so we will find it necessary to deny Newton's first law of motion (the so-called "law of inertia") in

---

22. This is the fundamental misunderstanding in Helen Lang's otherwise excellent discussion of Aristotle's natural philosophy: Lang, *The Order of Nature*. Though her text claims to be a treatment of Aristotle's physics, and though she presents her approach precisely as a reaction to the tendency to interpret Aristotle anachronistically, through the lens of classical physics, Lang separates Aristotle's discussions of the elements from his discussions of plants and animals, which she refers to as his "biology"—as opposed to his physics proper. She thus takes the elements to be the paradigm of substance, and then explains that all other things are substances to the extent that they are made up of the elements. What is lacking here is a properly analogical concept of substance. This is what leads Lang to give what may be described as an aggressively materialistic interpretation of Aristotle.

23. Aristotle, *Metaphysics*, IV.2; VII.1–3; *Categories*, 5.

24. See the classic text by Furley, "Self-Movers," 3–14. See also Lang *Order of Nature*, 40–50, and Oliver, *God and Motion*, 35–41.

order to protect the integrity of the organism. On the other hand, if we say that the simple bodies are *not* "self-moving," we would seem to take them out of the realm of nature altogether, since nature is defined as an "internal principle of motion and rest."[25] In this case, we gain a distinction between life and inanimate matter only by forfeiting an essential distinction between nature and artifice. We end up conceding, in other words, the mechanism of the scientific revolution we mentioned at the outset, and all of its implications. If matter does not have an internal principle of motion, how are we to understand the relationship between living things and their material parts? Life in this case would have to be a kind of "energy" that lies outside of matter, but this means it would be able to interact with matter only in the form of an extrinsic force. To separate life from matter is paradoxically to reduce it to a material force.

So what, then, is the answer to the question, Are simple bodies self-moving? It seems to me that the answer is to point out that the question is improperly put: it implies that simple bodies have a "self" to which motion can be either ascribed or denied. The question, in other words, presupposes a univocal notion of being (and nature) that requires equal application indifferently to all the "beings" of nature: animals, plants, and elements. But our reflection on the relative indistinction of form and matter in the elements suggests, by contrast, that they have a relatively "abstract" kind of being, and this abstraction has implications for the nature of the order displayed in its characteristic behavior. It is sometimes said that modern thought is distinguished from ancient thought in that it conceives of physics as the conformity of "stuff" to mathematically formalizable laws rather than as the variegated and qualitative activity that springs from the hierarchy of different natures—i.e., extrinsic order imposed from above vs. order that arises from the interplay of spontaneous, internal principles.

---

25. An alternative way of responding to the dilemma we are describing here is to insist that, while the verb that Aristotle uses to describe nature, "*kineisthai*" (see Aristotle, *Physics*, 192b22), can be read either as a middle voice (nature is an internal principle of *moving itself*) or as a passive voice (nature is an internal principle of *being moved*), the passive reading is more comprehensive, since it includes the elements, which Aristotle, as we saw above, explicitly says do *not* move themselves, but instead suffer movement—see Lang, *Order of Nature*, 41. While this way of reading Aristotle is certainly not false, it threatens to dissolve the analogy: we would be led to think of the self-motion of animals as something *external* to their nature, the whole of which would be expressed in their *being moved*—in this case, by themselves. In other words, their active generation of movement would be accidental to their nature. The broader implication is that life would be removed from the center of nature, and replaced by the elements. The response we are proposing would resolve the dilemma without this consequence.

But our analysis suggests that these two perspectives converge in an essential way, not for all physical being, but *solely at the level of the elements qua homogenous matter*. The behavior of earth or water, for example, can be conceived as conformity to a law, not because it is inert "stuff" being acted on wholly from without by external forces, but because the order of its nature lies (relatively) "outside" of it. In other words, water is natural because it has an "internal principle of motion and rest," but it is not living because, while the principle is internal to the nature of water, that nature is (relatively) external to any particular instance of water. This is why elements can be said to *suffer* movement rather than *produce* it. This interpretation opens up room, it seems to me, for all of the external relations that characterize "mechanics," but without breaking the analogy of nature and the centrality of life. A recognition of the specificity of elemental "being" allows us to distinguish it both from life and from artifice. How precisely the difference of inorganic matter is *good* is a question we will return to at the end.

## Plants

A plant reveals greater complexity than the natural elements insofar as it has a certain differentiation of parts and therefore a unity that transcends them sufficiently as to be able to gather them up into an intelligible whole, a real being or substance. The parts, however, are not radically different from the plant itself—as Goethe observed in his morphological studies, the parts of a plant are a certain repetition of the whole.[26] This is why, on the one hand, a plant can lose many of its parts without fatal injury to its being (one can tear off a leaf), and also why in some cases with certain types of plant it is possible to break off a part and replant it. The part then generates an entirely new and independent whole, which reveals a certain "diffuse" existence of vegetable unity.

There is, here, an "internal" being, so that we can speak of an individual plant, and this interiority implies, of course, an exteriority that is different. While in the elements the center is identical to the parts, in plants the center is *not* in fact the same as the parts, but the difference

26. "Researchers have been generally aware for some time that there is a hidden relationship among various external parts of the plant that develop one after the other and, as it were, one out of the other (e.g., leaves, calyx, corolla, and stamens); they have even investigated the details. The process by which one and the same organ appears in a variety of forms has been called *the metamorphosis of plants*," Goethe, *Scientific Studies*, 76.

does not have significant content beyond that fact. Plants are not mere externality, but their being is rather constituted by the simple difference between internal center and external parts. The essential movement of a plant, then, is, as it were, the spanning of this difference, the unfolding or manifestation of its being: it is proper for a plant to *grow*. But because the unity is only relatively different from its parts, the plant does not have a drive to move beyond the unfolding of its parts, and indeed it cannot reverse this movement (while a plant can die, it cannot "ungrow").[27] The relationship between the center and the parts is, thus, unilateral, the form moves outward to the extremities. Nature, which is expressed at the level of the elements as (relatively extrinsic) form, begins to acquire the character of efficient causality to the extent that the defining form is internalized (though of course one could describe the same reality as the change from a purely immanent form to one that transcends the matter). The now "internal" possession of its (universal) nature by the (individual) natural being comes to expression in the phenomenon of reproduction. The individual plant exhibits "self-motion" in its growth; the species exhibits "self-motion" in the generation of new individuals. The self-motion in both cases belongs to the form, but the difference between these two is due to the fact that the form is not yet self-possessed. The relationship between the universal and the particular therefore remains extrinsic, which is evident in the fact that vegetable reproduction occurs outside of the plant and does not require the active involvement of the individual plant in the process. The acorn simply *falls* from the tree, even if it does not fall far.

### Animals

With animals, we have a leap in both unity and difference. The parts of an animal are significantly different from one another; there is no mere repetition of the same. Indeed, we make a vital distinction between internal parts (the organs) and external parts. At the same time, however, the parts of an animal are more profoundly interdependent, so that the loss of any one can be quite damaging and even fatal. One can graft a plant part onto a plant, but one cannot do the same with animals. As a rule, animal parts do not grow back once lost, and they cannot be turned themselves

---

27. This is not to deny that certain plant parts can "re-form" themselves under particular circumstances, and thus exhibit what Goethe calls "a backward step, reversing the order of growth," ibid.

into new organisms.²⁸ The unity of an animal, its "center," is thus more radically interior to the organism than in the plant, which means that it transcends all of the parts in a more complete way than in a plant. Indeed, the unity of an animal transcends its different parts to such an extent that it not only, so to speak, pours itself out into the parts (growth), but at the same time relates the parts back to itself: this is sentient consciousness, the rudiments of a self. The form of the animal, its center, is thus extended into its outward parts, not simply in the unilateral movement of growth, but also without, so to speak, abandoning its interiority, and this is what transforms its external parts into organs of perception. The transcendence of the animal form, in short, is the cause both of its conscious self-hood and its capacity to feel.

But this "vertical" transcendence entails a horizontal transcendence. The unity of an animal spills out, as it were, beyond even its physical boundaries. Above we saw that the internalizing, the gradual self-appropriation, of form turns what is at the lowest level the imposition of order in the manner of formal necessity (what comes to be called the laws of nature) by degrees into the efficient causality of motion. In a plant, the movement arises from the center; now, at the level of the animal, the individual being moves itself according to its center, it actively generates its acts from itself. The transcendence of the animal's unity thus accounts for its locomotion. It can move to a new place beyond the place it stands at present because its reality exceeds its physical being and therefore its location in space. According to Hegel, the excess of an animal's unity beyond its physical boundaries entails a contradiction, insofar as the animal becomes thereby *more* than what it is: it both *is* and *is not* the world beyond itself at the same time. We will consider an alternative interpretation of the ecstatic character of animal being in a moment, but Hegel's account of this state of affairs is illuminating. The need to resolve the contradiction that constitutes the being of the animal entails the two activities that Aristotle says make up the life of the animal: feeding and procreation.²⁹ On the one hand, the animal attempts to overcome the externality of matter that confronts it as both itself and not itself in a particular way: by consuming it. Here we have a philosophical explanation of the essential connection between locomotion and appetite, for which Aristotle offers a more practical explanation. Indeed, Hegel expands this point to account

---

28. Cloning is only apparently an objection to this claim; whatever else cloning is, one thing it is *not* is the generation of a new whole out of a simple part.

29. Aristotle, *History of animals*, VIII.1.

also for the phenomenon of sexuality. Consumption does not resolve the contradiction of the animal because the elimination of the otherness of the matter *qua* food reinforces the self of the animal, and so simply posits the contradiction anew and indeed more forcefully. Here, then, arises the second way the transcendence of the animal's unity gets manifest: in the sexual relation, the animal resolves its ontological contradiction by means of a unity with an externally other that is nevertheless the *same*. This union, however, is essentially a *physical* one, a matter of sensible appetite, which finds its terminus, as Aristotle says, outside of the soul.[30] The animal has a sensible awareness of the union, but cannot be said to "know" it, which means the union is achieved only outside the animal's soul and not also properly inside it. The relation between the universal (the species), to which this union therefore belongs, and the individual animals that unite in this case remains extrinsic. There is a true sense in which we could say that the species makes use of the individuals to propagate itself.

### Humans

When we move to the human being, we enter into a radically different order in this regard. There is a sense in which life, presented in the difference between animals and plants, represents the paradigm of nature, i.e., the internal principle of motion and rest; it establishes the "base-line" meaning of the notion (though, of course, not in a univocal way). But if vegetable and animal beings represent the essence of nature, the spiritual life of man *exceeds* that, and yet it does so in a manner that turns out to bring life to a higher and perhaps unexpected fulfillment. (The Neoplatonic triad distinguishes intellect from life, but then again Aristotle identifies thought as a kind of living,[31] and indeed self-thinking thought as perfect life.[32]) How does this work? The unity of human being betrays first of all a transcendence of a qualitatively different sort. The form of man is so transcendent, we could say, that it not only lies beyond the organic parts of his being so as to be able to gather them up into a conscious self, like an animal, but it lies beyond even *itself* so as to be able to grasp even its own grasping: the human being is not merely conscious, but is *self*-conscious; the human being can meaningfully say "I."[33] The radical kind of interiority

30. Aristotle, *De anima*, II.5.417b20ff.
31. Ibid., II.2.
32. Ibid., *Metaphysics*, XII.7.
33. It may be said that the dialectic that grew from Kant's notion of the

that self-consciousness implies is required for a being to possess its nature rather than simply being possessed by it. Nature, we recall, is an internal principle of motion and rest; but nature remains extrinsic to itself at the level of the natural elements and is only gradually internalized up the chain of being. It is only at the level of man that the internal principle truly becomes internal *to itself*. This is a basic reason why human beings have a special dignity; every "I" is not only an individual, but at the very same time is universal.[34] We talk of a person's *humanity*, and we do so as if it were a characteristic he possessed, something that belongs to him. But we don't talk about a cat's "felinity" except when we're trying to lighten the mood in a philosophy class.

The scholastics understood the intellect that represents the specificity of the human soul as a *reditio completa*, a movement that returns perfectly back to itself.[35] (And therefore is necessarily *not* a motion, which Aristotle defines as the actuality of potency *as* potency and so as essentially "incomplete."[36] This is why materialistic cognitional theory will always and inevitably be a chasing after wild geese.) Interpreted according to an analogical concept of nature, the *reditio completa* shows itself to be the

---

transcendental unity of apperception to form the heart of German Idealism, namely, the objectification of subjectivity that occurs in reflective self-consciousness and must be overcome, fails to see the radical nature of the transcendence at issue here. It is of an altogether different order than the "speculative" (from *speculare, speculum*) split into subject and object. At the same time, because of the transcendence, the self-consciousness of the "I" does not have to be *opposed* to all reflexivity and relation and the otherness this implies, such as seems to be the case in the pure immediacy of radical immanence in Michel Henry's notion of self-affection. On this, see Zahavi, "Subjectivity and Immanence in Michel Henry," in *Subjectivity and Transcendence*, 133–48.

34. Hegel seems to ascribe universality to the "I" in a merely extensive sense: "When we say 'I,' we mean, to be sure, an individual; but since everyone is 'I,' when we say 'I,' we only say something quite universal," *Philosophy of Mind*, 11. But we mean the coincidence of individuality and universality in a more directly ontological sense: the "I" *is* the perfection of the natural form's self-possession, and so a complete coincidence of individual being and universal nature. This does not mean that each human being is its own species, as Aquinas says of the angels, who lack matter altogether, but only that, in the human being, the species grasps itself as universal.

35. To say that the human spirit is constituted by a perfection "redition" is an ontological claim, and does not imply that every human being is perfectly transparent to himself, or in possession of perfect self-knowledge. The failure to make this distinction accounts for much of the confusion in postmodern thought that takes classical philosophy to be founded on self-presence. The ontological structure of spirit as a *reditio completa* is in fact necessarily implied even in the claim that human beings always *lack* self-knowledge. It is not meaningful, for example, to complain of the absence of self-knowledge in a table.

36. See Aristotle, *Physics*, VIII.5.257b5–10.

completion of the self-appropriation of form that *defines* nature simply. This is why man's understanding of himself brings insight into the nature of nature. Such an interpretation also allows us to see that the efficient causality that represents an essential aspect of human freedom is not arbitrary spontaneity but rather the perfection of formal causality. The human being can be an *author* of action precisely because the center from which his acts proceed is a self-possessed unity. In this case, freedom is not a "subjective" power that *acts on* the outside, "objective" world. Rather, it is a further extension of internal unity: while the unity of an animal is present, so to speak, as far as its skin (which is what makes it sentient), beyond its skin, as we saw above, the animal can only "feel" the other that therefore remains external to it. But the human being can be present as a unity even in his external acts, which is why this self-transcendence in action continues to "belong" to the person, and we can call what he does genuine acts of self-expression.

Because of this transcendent unity, a human being is capable both of growth and locomotion, but at the same time he has the capacity for a much more profound encounter with otherness. As Hegel observed, an animal's excessive unity causes a kind of restlessness that leads it to seek satisfaction in something outside of itself, first food and ultimately a mate. The restlessness is due to a unity that spans the difference between the individual and the species (this is the essence of the Aristotelian form).[37] With the human being, however, the individual self-consciously possesses human nature, the universal, and so is capable of a more contemplative relationship toward the otherness of the world. The form of man, the rational soul, is not just one form among many (like, for example, the other animal and plant souls) but is a form of forms: the soul is *panta pōs*, in a certain sense all things.[38] It can thus internalize the "other," the things in the world that are different from itself, both without destroying those things (i.e., consuming them and so reducing them to oneself), and also, so to speak, without leaving itself (i.e., in the self-transcending movement of sensible appetite). The human being can achieve an ontological intimacy with things without having physically to cross a distance to make contact with them. This represents a transformation of the meaning of nature, once again: it is an internal principle that is capable, because of its

---

37. The classic discussion of this paradoxical feature of Aristotelian form is Owens, *The Doctrine of Being*, 379–400.

38. Aristotle, *De anima*, III.8.

excessive interiority and so self-transcendence, of including motion so to speak within its encompassing rest.

It bears remarking, at the end of this brief sketch of the analogy of nature, that the differences between the various "levels of being" are not to be interpreted *nominalistically*, i.e., non-analogically. A nominalistic interpretation would see the differences as defining separate classes of things, and would thus be embarrassed whenever a defining trait appeared in some class other than the one it supposedly defines. For example, to the extent that one finds evidence of intelligence in the animal world one is unable to claim intelligence as a defining property of human being. But if we take the differences in a *non* nominalistic fashion, then we expect a certain "porosity"—to use William Desmond's fertile term—among the different classes. The differences that constitute the various levels of being we have been discussing are not separate properties, but different ways of possessing, participating in, one and the same nature. As such, the properties are not possessed exclusively by one class in opposition to the others, but—if we may put it thus—possessed by each on behalf of them all.[39] In this case, similarities abound throughout the spectrum, without this fact disturbing the distinctiveness of the levels of being: we have not only the recapitulation of the lower by the higher, but also a certain anticipatory participation in the higher by the lower. Animals display genuine traces of intelligence, for example, not because intelligence is not a trait that defines human being, but because, by virtue of the ontological unity of nature, animals are in some real way "like" man. Because of this non-reductive "porosity" of boundaries, due to the transcendence of the unity of "types" and the ontological oneness of the cosmos, there will always be an abundant variety of expressions at each level of nature, which underscores the unity of the whole. Nature is so thoroughly analogous that even the individual levels of nature show forth an analogical structure: some plants, for example, will behave like animals in a certain respect, others like the elements in a certain respect, all without surrendering their "plantness," and so forth. We will return to this important point at the end.

---

39. We might compare this "distribution" of qualities in nature to the "propriation" of properties in God: we attribute power most properly to the Father, and gift most properly to the Spirit, etc., even though in fact these properties are shared by all the divine persons by virtue of the absolute simplicity of God's nature. Each person possesses his properties *for* the others, as it were.

## The Goodness of Matter and the Natura Analogiae

At the "top" of the analogy of nature we described in the previous section lay the universality of the human spirit.[40] It is interesting that Hegel, after contrasting this comprehensive and so concrete aspect of spirit to the abstractness of matter,[41] passes directly from this contemplative union of the soul with all things in principle to man's coming to know God—a movement from finite to infinite spirit—and thus passes over the relation between the individual and the universal that comes to expression in human community.[42] While the relation between the individual and the species at the animal level finds its consummation quite literally in the union of the sexes, for Hegel one could say that every human being is already in himself the unity of the individual and the universal insofar as he is spirit. The dignity of spirit, for Hegel, lies in what he calls its "triumph over externality."[43] If matter has its center outside of itself, spirit finally has its center wholly *within*. Hegel's description of spirit as the culmination of the natural world, which passes beyond nature, reveals that he conceives of the analogy of nature in a strictly unilateral fashion, wherein the inorganic represents a lower level of the organic, and the organic, in turn, reveals itself to be a lower level of spirit. Progress thus occurs as an intensification of interiority, the gradual widening of the scope of unity. But as we suggested above, this conception misses an essential aspect of analogy, namely, the positivity of difference. What "positivity" means specifically here is that the lower level not only reflects the higher at a diminished grade, but that, at the same time, it *adds* something to the higher and so contributes something genuine to the meaning of nature. Thus, while it is clearly true that, in the hierarchy of being presented by analogy, the higher reveals the meaning of the lower, it is *also* true that the lower reveals something essential about the higher. There must be a reciprocity in addition to hierarchical asymmetry in genuine analogy.

So, what in the present case does the "lower" add? We come here to the question in the title of our essay. As we saw above, what characterizes

---

40. This sketch does not necessarily exclude the "separate intelligences," the angels, but as transcending the physical world altogether they belong in a much more distant way to nature.

41. Hegel, *Philosophy of Mind*, 11–12.

42. This leap in Hegel's description at this point is discussed at greater length, with an attempt to "fill it in" on the basis of Hegel's own principles, in a chapter from my new book, *The Perfection of Freedom*.

43. Hegel, *Philosophy of Mind*, 10.

the mechanical relations of simple bodies is externality, parts outside of parts. But to speak of externality in this context is to say that difference exceeds unity. Now, while there is clearly an imperfection in externality so expressed, which justifies our thinking of simple bodies as a base kind of being, if we were to include inorganic matter as at the same time an expression of nature precisely *in* its inorganicity and so precisely in its irreducible distinction from life—in contrast, we recall, to the tendency in Schelling to include matter in nature only to the extent that and the degree to which it bears some relationship to life—we affirm that what is unique about it is indispensable to our understanding of the whole. In this case, it is the relative subordination of unity to difference that specifies the inorganic, which we may perhaps describe as a kind of "heteronomy": the elements are wholly subject to their nature, which they do not possess in an internal way. Affirming the goodness of the mechanical qualities of the inorganic brings to light the fact that the integration of unity and difference at higher levels of being does not mean that the achievement consists *merely* in the unifying of greater and greater spheres of difference but at the very same time in the increasing differentiation of unity. Rather than describing the hierarchy of nature simply as a gradual "triumph over externality," a properly *analogical* concept of nature allows us to see the integration of unity and difference instead as a mutual submission of each to the other. More concretely, we might say that positing the lifeless elements as an indispensable expression of the meaning of nature reveals at least two things:[44] first, that having one's center outside of oneself—i.e., ecstatic being—is something positive; and second, that it is good not only to possess one's nature, but also to be *possessed* by one's nature. This twofold revelation allows us to offer a different interpretation, for example, of sexual union from that of Hegel. For Hegel, this union is the resolution of the contradiction of animal being: sex accomplishes what eating does not, because the other, which the animal internalizes, remains other even in its sameness. But this view threatens to make sex simply a higher form of consumption. And such a view shows why this union can simply be surpassed, for Hegel, by the *knowledge* relation that constitutes the highest life of spirit. By contrast, if we affirm externality as a positive expression of nature, then we see the goodness of sexual union not merely in the fact

44. These are, of course, not the only two. It would also be quite fruitful to reflect on the significance for the whole of the temporality and spatiality that characterizes matter: according to Aristotle, the defining quality of matter is belonging to a particular place (earth below, fire above, and so forth). One might think of the importance of place and history in human existence as due in a particular way to our material being.

that difference has been overcome by unity but at the same time in the fact that unity is thereby extended, brought beyond itself. In this case, what is good in sexual union is never simply surpassed in the transcendence toward spirit, just as the goodness of matter and its mechanistic properties is never simply surpassed in the transcendence toward life.

There are some immediate implications of this analogical concept of nature for our understanding of human existence, which we have space here only to list. Most obviously, we come to see that the unity of the universal and particular in the soul of man, the form of forms, which Hegel describes as the "triumph over externality," shows itself to be only half of the picture, so to speak.[45] Sexual union represents the converse reconciliation of the individual to the common. Indeed, at the human level, sexual union becomes *marriage* and *family*, which is not only a physical coming together (a union of necessity only temporary and periodic), but a spiritual/bodily union that involves—to invoke the language that John Paul II made famous—a "gift of self" through the permanent commitment of freedom. Such a view depends on the meaning of freedom we sketched above, but highlights not the fact that the outward act remains within the unity of the self, but that the unity comes to expression even here, outside the self. The truth of marriage is a dual unity: a person not only takes the other to himself, but he henceforward also *belongs to* the other, who remains a spirit forever irreducible to his own. Indeed, the union of persons in marriage, far from reducing difference, is fruitful of further persons. As a paradigm of love, this is a heteronomy without alienation. In love, as Ferdinand Ulrich once said, one has one's center outside of oneself, which is a recapitulation at a higher level of the distinctive being of matter.

Second, a unilateral interpretation of nature could lead one to understand the ascent of the hierarchy of being as a progressively complete possession of nature that reaches a perfection in man's self-consciousness. In this case, man would represent pure mastery over his own nature. What the externality of mechanism shows is that, as we saw above, it is good not only to possess one's nature but also *to be possessed by it*. We might suggest that the "allergy" (from *aliud*, other) to heteronomy that one finds in the Enlightenment (quite thematically in Rousseau and then in Kant) is the

---

45. And, of course, the half that it shows is also significantly altered: in light of the analogical conception of nature, we are led to interpret the unity of knowledge not simply as an appropriation of the truth of things into oneself but at the same time as a kind of ecstasis by which one joins oneself to the things known. For a sketch of what this sort of knowledge might look like, see my "Towards a Non-Possessive Concept of Knowledge," 577–607.

result of a loss of analogy. If human being represents the internalizing of nature, perhaps we ought to say that it is also by the very same token his internalizing *by* nature, which is to say that in the human being nature becomes internal to itself. Human being in this regard represents a kind of perfection of subjectivity *and* a perfection of objectivity; thus conceived, we have an ontological ground for the inviolability of human dignity, a fundamental respect for the very nature we possess in ourselves, that does not rely on a dualistic separation of man from nature (such as we find in many, if not most, personalistic philosophies). And we also have an ontological ground for the study of nature *in light of* human existence.[46]

Finally, insofar as it valorizes difference, and not simply as a function of unity, the analogy of nature provides a positive ground for limit, and so for the unsurpassable goodness of the finitude of human existence. It is revealing that Hegel has no place, ultimately, for non-infinite spirit; the very meaning of spirit is the infinite that reconciles finitude to itself. One of the most fruitful aspects of Hegel's thought is that he brings to light the necessity of the finite for the infinite. But it is precisely a necessity rather than a generously conceived *good*. The finite is necessary to the absolute, i.e., good *for* the infinite, in Hegel's understanding, rather than being good simply, in and for itself *qua* finite. Only an analogy of nature that has room for the inanimate character of matter will be able to accommodate the abiding finitude of the human being.

This last point brings us to our conclusion: though there is no space here to show how it is so exactly, our final reflections suggest that, in the end, there cannot be a "beyond" without at the same time an "outside." In the created world at the very least, transcendence and externality share a common fate. Both of these dimensions are necessary to a properly analogical concept of nature. It is not an accident that Schelling both conceives of the inorganic as a lower degree of life and that he comes to identify God (in his middle period) with nature,[47] while Hegel, unsatisfied with an organic dynamism, collapses nature into spirit and man into God.[48] The externality of matter is a resistance to such a collapse, it is the "physical presence" of discontinuity within the continuity of life, which

---

46. See, for example, Spaemann, "Wirklichkeit als Anthropomorphismus," 13–35.

47. In his 1804 work *On the System of Philosophy in General and the Philosophy of Nature in Particular*, Schelling describes the universe as God's self-affirmation, and denies that God is the *cause* of the universe, arguing instead that he *is* the universe, understood in a particular way.

48. See Desmond, *Hegel's God*.

then dramatically anticipates and prefigures the discontinuity of spirit's transcendence of life. But this reveals that the model for analogy is not a pyramid, a simple ascent toward the ever more perfect; instead, the model is a formal meaning that gets dramatically interrupted by a reality that both transforms and fulfills it. Analogy, so it seems, is essentially *cruciform*. Thus conceived, the analogy allows for the various reversals that receive such profound significance in the Christian tradition.

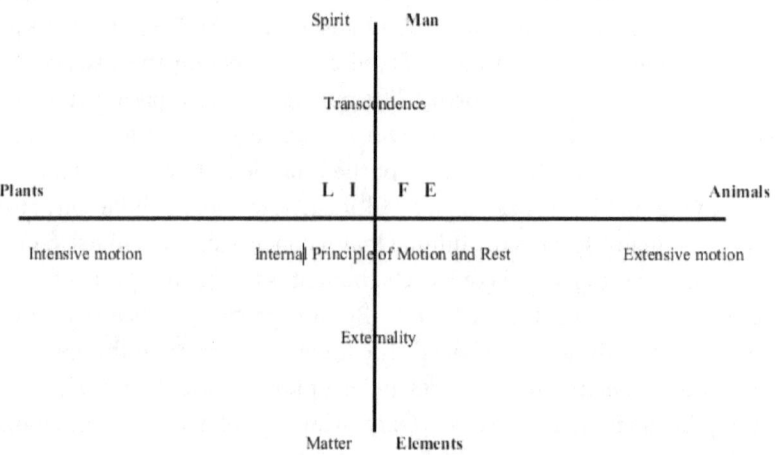

## THE ANALOGY OF NATURE

The dramatic nature of analogy that has emerged through our reflections allows us, at the end, to give a nuanced response to the question of the relationship of "external" matter to the inwardness of life. Is there no sense in which we might say that even inorganic matter shares in the properties of life? Is it simply "metaphor," in the conventional sense of *fiction*, of poetic imposition, to describe a stone statue as *living* or to perceive in a magnified droplet of water a perfection of shape, which, as it gathers up and reflects an infinity of light, evokes the internal unity of an organism? There are two responses to make here. In the first place, the "porosity" of real boundaries we spoke of above allows us to affirm a genuine sharing of properties, so that just as animals display in a true way characteristics that belong properly to human beings—for example, the capacity to play or to communicate their inward states[49]—so too may elements display in their own way what belongs properly to organisms. Indeed, as we suggested

49. See Portmann, *Animal Forms*, 196–201.

above, there is an analogy even within the various levels of being: if earth is matter in a paradigmatic sense, then we might say that fire represents matter in a more living form. The higher form, even here, brings out a dimension of the lower form without rendering the lower form superfluous. The important thing is to avoid claiming without due qualification that life is the *essence* of matter, in a manner that would deprive matter of its own essence, and so of the positivity of the difference that gives matter its proper place in the cosmos. And this leads to the second point: maintaining the proper essence of inorganic matter as distinct from the organic is what allows us to see the elevation of matter in art, or in the bodies of living beings, as a kind of *grace*. The organic unity and dynamic life of a beautifully constructed space, the transparency of matter to spirit in a joyful human face, is something of a miracle, in the sense that it has an "event"-like character, and it radiates a certain gratuity. This does not make the elevation an alienating imposition precisely because of the unity of nature expressed in analogy. In this we have a prefiguration of the transformation of nature by grace: grace, as the church affirms, is not the opposite of nature that threatens to eclipse or destroy it. Rather, grace both presupposes nature and brings it to a higher perfection, a more complete state of naturalness beyond what it could achieve by itself. In this respect, the very ecstatic quality that material being contributes to the meaning of life, it also receives back from life in a surprising, but fulfilling way. And all of this belongs to the profound exchange of being that constitutes the analogy of nature, which thus reveals the whole cosmos to be suffused with the meaning of gift, a creatively reverberating echo of the original gift at its source. It is this wondrous exchange that represents the adequate response to the challenge of the scientific revolution.[50]

## Bibliography

Aristotle. *Categories. On Interpretation. Prior Analytics.* Loeb Classical Library. Cambridge: Harvard University Press, 1938.

———. *History of Animals, Books VII–X.* Loeb Classical Library. Cambridge: Harvard University Press, 1991.

———. *Metaphysics, Books I–IX.* Loeb Classical Library. Cambridge: Harvard University Press, 1933.

———. *Metaphysics, Books X–XII. Oeconomica. Magna Moralia.* Loeb Classical Library. Cambridge: Harvard University Press, 1935.

---

50. I would like to thank the participants at the "What is Life?" conference, and especially John Milbank, Simon Oliver, and Chris Hackett, for their questions and comments on this paper, which helped me clarify some of the ideas presented here.

———. *On the Soul. Parva Naturalia. On Breath.* Loeb Classical Library. Cambridge: Harvard University Press, 1957.

———. *Physics, Books I–IV.* Loeb Classical Library. Cambridge: Harvard University Press, 1957.

Bortoff, Henri. *The Wholeness of Nature: Goethe's Way toward a Science of Conscious Participation in Nature.* New York: Lindisfarne, 1996.

Burtt, E. A. *The Metaphysical Foundations of Modern Science.* New York: Anchor, 1954.

Desmond, William. *Hegel's God: A Counterfeit Double.* Burlington, VT: Ashgate, 2003.

Furley, David. "Self-Movers." In *Self-Motion: From Aristotle to Newton,* edited by Mary Louise Gill and James G. Lennox, 3–14. Princeton: Princeton University Press, 1994.

Goethe, Johann Wolfgang von. *The Collected Works.* Volume 12, *Scientific Studies.* Translated by Douglas Miller. Princeton: Princeton University Press, 1988.

Grant, Iain Hamilton. "Introduction" to the translation of the preface to *On the World Soul. Collapse* 6 (2010) 59–65.

———. *Philosophies of Nature after Schelling.* New York: Continuum, 2006.

Hegel, G. W. F. *The Philosophy of History.* Translated by J. Sibree. New York: Dover, 1956.

———. *The Philosophy of Mind.* Translated by William Wallace. Oxford: Clarendon, 1971.

Heuser-Kessler, Marie. *Die Produktivität der Natur: Schellings Naturphilosophie und das neue Paradigma der Selbstorganisation in den Naturwissenschaften.* Berlin: Duncker und Humblot, 1986.

Jonas, Hans. *Philosophical Essays.* Englewood, NJ: Prentice Hall, 1974.

Küppers, Bernd-Olaf. *Natur als Organismus: Schellings frühe Naturphilosophie und ihre Bedeutung für die moderne Biologie.* Frankfurt: Klostermann, 1992.

Lang, Helen. *The Order of Nature in Aristotle's Physics: Place and the Elements.* Cambridge: Cambridge University Press, 1998.

Maier, Annaliese. *Die Vorläufer Galileis im 14. Jahrhundert.* Volume 1 of *Studen zur Naturphilosophie der Spätscholastik.* Rome: Editioni di Storia e Letteratura, 1949.

Mutschler, Hans-Dieter. *Spekulative und empirische Physik.* Stuttgart: Kohlhammer, 1990.

Oliver, Simon. *Philosophy, God, and Motion.* New York: Routledge, 2005.

Owens, Joseph. *The Doctrine of Being in the Aristotelian Metaphysics.* 3rd ed. Toronto: Pontifical Institute of Medieval Studies, 1978.

Portmann, Adolph. *Animal Forms and Patterns.* New York: Schocken, 1967.

Schelling, Friedrich Wilhelm Joseph von. *Bruno, or On the Natural and the Divine Principle of Things.* Translated by Michael Vater. Albany: SUNY, 1984.

———. *Historisch-Kritische Ausgabe.* Im Auftrag der Schelling-Kommission der Bayerischen Akademie der Wissenschaften begründet von Hans Michael Baumgartner†, Wilhelm G. Jacobs, Jörg Jantzen, Hermann Krings†, Francesco Moiso† und Hermann Zeltner†. Herausgegeben von Jörg Jantzen, Thomas Buchheim, Jochem Hennigfeld, Wilhelm G. Jacobs und Siegbert Peetz. 40 volumes (planned). Stuttgart: Frommann-Holzboog, 1976–.

———. *Sämmtliche Werke.* Nach der Original Ausgabe in neuer Anordnung [in a new arrangement]. 6 vols. and 6 supplementary vols. Edited by Manfred Schroter. Munich: Beck and Oldenbourg, 1927–59.

Schindler, D. C. *The Perfection of Freedom: Schiller, Schelling, and Hegel between the Ancients and the Moderns*. Veritas. Eugene, OR: Cascade, 2012.

———. "Towards a Non-Possessive Concept of Knowledge: On the Relation between Reason and Love in Aquinas and Balthasar." *Modern Theology* 22 (2006) 577–607.

Smith, Wolfgang. *The Wisdom of Ancient Cosmology: Contemporary Science in Light of Tradition*. Oakton, VA: Foundation for Traditional Studies, 2003.

Spaemann, Robert. "Wirklichkeit als Anthropomorphismus." In *Grundvollzüge der Person: Dimensionen des Menschseins bei Robert Spaemann*, edited by H. G. Nissing, 13–35. Munich: Institut zur Förderung der Glaubenslehre, 2008.

Zahavi, Dan. *Subjectivity and Transcendence*. Tübingen: Mohr Siebeck, 2007.

# 6

# A Short Meta-Critique of Quentin Meillassoux's Divine Nihilism

*Conor Cunningham*

~

Philosophy believes in God because God does not exist.[1]

QUENTIN MEILLASSOUX

IN MANY A TRENDY Parisian café, and in many an austere Anglo-Saxon philosophy lecture hall, there is a rumor afoot, uttered in conspiratorial tones: *there is nothing but matter*. Like some scary bedtime story (Brothers Grimm, no doubt), we are supposed to both enjoy this story and be fearful of it. Enjoy it, because it is supposed to be radical, emancipatory even, because such materialism is thought to topple every church, making a mockery of all religions, for how can you have religion in the face of materialism—where would you locate the soul, after all, not to mention the mind? All our culture skates on very thin ice: love, poetry, literature, intercourse, for they are but a façade, behind which lies the truth, the truth of us all, and of everything, the *réel* hiding behind every face, our closest yet most foreign neighbor. As Jacques Lacan says,

> What we see in there, these turbinate bones covered by a whitish membrane, is a horrendous sight; . . . there's a horrendous

1. Watkin, *Difficult Atheism*, 135.

discovery there, that of the flesh one never sees, the foundation of things, the other side of the head, of the face, . . . the flesh from which everything exudes, at the very heart of the mystery . . . formless . . . Spectre of anxiety . . . the final revelation, you're this—You are this, which is so far from you, this which is ultimate formlessness.[2]

Without any solid reference points (solid self, or definite soul) disorientated, material man, stumbles around the rooms of his own house—his own body, and life—as if it were someone else's home. What was once familiar seems strange, odd, threatening even. Sigmund Freud refers to this as the Uncanny, which contains two inferences: "*Heimlich*" (home-like, or familiar) and "*Unheimlich*" (eerie, or strange).

According, then, to those who peddle the rumor of materialism (and thus nihilism), the truth of our situation is like that of Rene Magritte's painting *La Reproduction Interdite* (1937) in which the man looking in the mirror sees only what appears to be the back of his head, because the truth is that the face is merely material; in other words, the face as some sort of special, iconic site is a fiction generated not by what is real, but only by the nominal play of language, for it is language which fools us into thinking we exist; its seduces us into being. But behind the grammar of such conjurations lies the *réel*, namely, matter. And matter is always threatening to reveal itself, doing so at times in the stain, the corpse, the disease, the smell, breaking out of all and any contrived vessels. This reveals an apparent nominalism in our pretence to order and classify, to parse the world, in real terms. As Kojève says, "the conceptual understanding of empirical reality is equivalent to murder."[3] He gives the example of the concept "dog." The point being that for such a concept to work it must, on the one hand, be something of a lie, insofar as the concept "dog" is not itself a dog, and in truth, any actual dog is not identical with that concept. In this way, every time we say "dog" we betray reality, we betray, and therefore violate the entity which we are forcing to fall under its explanatory powers; this what Lacan referred to as *manque-a-être*.[4] In addition, the concept "dog" just to work requires that all dogs must die, they must be mortal, otherwise we could not detach the concept and any particular dog—they would be eternally the same, and in so being would be unthinkable. Instead we require finitude, or mortality, just to be able to think at all: you are thinkable only

2. Lacan, *Seminar II*, 154–55.
3. Kojève, *Introduction to Hegel*, 323
4. Lacan, *Seminar II*, Book VII, 294.

because you will die (and, of course, for Hegel this seems to be true of God also: God must have the world so that God is thinkable, for if God were merely an empty infinite, without a finite that stands over and against it, it would be the equivalent of nothing, as there would simply be no traction, so to speak, for God to be intelligible). To some degree, this was partly what Hume (or at least Philo) was arguing in the *Dialogues concerning Natural Religion*, because there Hume makes the point that if God were unique, a singularity, so to speak, then God would be beyond all analogical thinking; that is, God would be unthinkable. This also stands for the "universe"—and here Hume anticipates Alain Badiou—for if the universe is everything, and is real, it is immune to thought; that is, it cannot be thought, for if it could, it would not be everything. Therefore "the universe" is not a legitimate concept (it is what Jean-Paul Sartre had already called a "detotalized totality." Lacan speaks of "*L'Une-en-moins*" and Badiou will say, the One is not; see below).[5] That being the case, just as for Hegel (or at least Kojève's Hegel), if God were real—that is, if God were truly infinite and eternal—then God would in effect be dead, as God would be unintelligible. Here then, atheism and theism (or theology and nihilism) begin to look very similar, even exchangeable (what Jean-Paul Sartre had already called a "missing God") and this crucial ambiguity is what those such as Gianni Vattimo, Giorgio Agamben, Jean-Luc Nancy, Alain Badiou, and Quentin Meillassoux will build on (see below).[6] Alas, forms, essences, and natural kinds all fade away. In their wake is the now ubiquitous threat of dust, pure matter, merely arranged, maybe *thus* rather than *so*, even if we colloquially and parochially call such arrangements "rape," "cancer," "life," "death," or indeed, "the Holocaust." As Badiou says, "The void proper to life, as death shows, is matter."[7] In other words, "everything that is bound testifies that it is unbound in its being."[8] This unboundedness is what Sartre called "the being of the slimy."[9]

In light of the above, we ought to heed the words of Robert Spaemann, who seeks to develop ways of thinking that offer "resistance against this oblivion."[10] But at the same time, does nihilism offer an opportunity for theology? For does it not free us from many idols, or indeed does it

5. Sartre, *Being and Nothingness*, 623; Lacan, *Seminar XX*, 129.
6. Sartre, *Being and Nothingness*, 623.
7. Badiou, "The Event as Trans-Being," 99.
8. Ibid., quoted in Brassier, "Nihil Unbound," 50.
9. Sartre, *Being and Nothingness*, 610.
10. Spaemann, quoted by Zaborowski, *Philosophy of the Human Person*, 118.

not once again help reveal the *ex nihilo* from whence all came? Maybe then, it is fair to say that the overcoming (*Überwindung*) of nihilism is its consummation (*Vollendung*): the "first step toward the true overcoming of nihilism . . . we need to go expressly up to the limit of nothing."[11] Yet this, no doubt, is the danger of dangers (*die Gefahr der Gefahr*), both for nihilism and for theology.[12] As Nietzsche said, "The supreme values in whose service man should live, especially when they were hard on him and exacted a high price. . . . Now that the shabby origin of these values is becoming clear, the universe seems to have lost value, seems meaningless—*that is only transitional.*"[13] Maybe this is why Maurice Blanchot reluctantly concludes that "Nihilism tells us its final and rather grim truth: it tells us of the impossibility of nihilism."[14] In rest of this short article we will examine the work of Quentin Meillassoux in a bid to demonstrate the lengths that atheism and nihilism must go to; but the need to go to such lengths indicates what Blanchot says, namely, that nihilism is impossible, likewise atheism.

## Meillassoux

Echoing many of his fellow continental philosophers, according to Meillassoux, only by believing in God can you achieve atheism, because then nothing is beyond atheism's reach; there is no lack, no mourning, no loss—this is the only atheism there could possibly be. After all, the devil believes in God, but surely, the devil is the ultimate atheist, or anti-theist—he believes but still rebels. As Watkin points out, Meillassoux comes "tantalizingly close to implying that the only way to be rid of God is rationally to prove him."[15] (Something advocates of Intelligent Design have failed to grasp.)[16] Meillassoux insists that we must retain "a little absolute" (*un peu d'absolu*).[17] This is the case for a number of reasons, the most important, I would argue, is that if there is nothing absolute left, and therefore discourse falls not only into banality, but gibberish, then there is an absence, and therefore a gap to be filled, whether it will be or not. But of course, to

11. Heidegger, *Metaphysics*, 217–18.
12. See Nietzsche, *Will to Power*, 44–45.
13. Ibid., 10.
14. Blanchot, *Infinite Conversation*, 149.
15. Watkin, *Difficult Atheism*, 137.
16. See Cunningham, *Darwin's Pious Idea*.
17. Meillassoux, *After Finitude*, 49.

infer meaning from such an absence, to see gibberish as a lack, is already not to gibber.

In a striking quote, Meillassoux tells us that "Our inability to understand an ultimate reason is not a subjective incapacity but a capacity to grasp the objective impossibility of such a reason. This is not an index of man's wretchedness, but of his grasping grandeur."[18] This is a radical move, at least at first blush, but I don't know how the inference follows or, rather, let me ask this question: the significance that accompanies the inference, from where does it come? The excitement of the radicalness, the fact that this revelation is different from its opposite, or from the statement, "there is a cow in that field," does not stem, or cannot stem, from the revelation itself. If that is true, then the revelation is not pure, and is contaminated by a discourse, a logic other than that of its own—again, atheism fails, for as said, the devil may be the ultimate atheist, but after all, the pride is parasitic, just as rebellion is. Meillassoux very deliberately insists that he, the nihilist, is a rationalist: "I'm a rationalist and reason clearly demonstrates that you can't demonstrate the necessity of laws: so we should just believe reason and accept this point: laws are not necessary—they are facts, and facts are contingent—they can change without reason."[19] Let us ask, first of all, what is change? and, second, what's the significance of change being imputed here? After all, reason must not change for us to notice what Meillassoux is talking about. Indeed, as Watkin makes clear, Meillassoux is still operating with faith: "his demonstration still stands or falls on an unacceptable act of faith, the faith inherent in the proclamation that 'I'm a rationalist'..."[20] Two major theoretical planks in Meillassoux's philosophy are that of ancestrality and the arche-fossil: "I will call 'ancestral' any reality anterior to the emergence of the human species—or even anterior to every recognized form of life on earth.... I will call 'arche-fossil'... materials indicating the existence of an ancestral reality or event; one that is anterior to terrestrial life."[21] The point of these two concepts is to help undermine what Meillassoux calls correlationism: "the central notion of philosophy since Kant seems to be that of correlation. By 'correlation' we mean the idea according to which we only ever have access to the correlation between thinking and being, and never to either term considered apart from

---

18. Watkin, *Difficult Atheism*, 147.
19. Meillassoux, quoted in Watkin, *Difficult Atheism*, 160.
20. Watkin, *Difficult Atheism*, 161.
21. Meillassoux, *After Finitude*, 10.

the other."[22] The problem here is that this seems to mean that thought is forever barred from the absolute; that is, all thoughts are limited, finite, and partial, which means reason is likewise limited, and in so being it remains beholden to an *other* (whether or not we know what or who that other is, is not the point). The real fear here is that if reason is limited, atheism remains impossible, just as immanence will remain in the shadow of a possible transcendence, for, once again, immanence, like reason, cannot attain everything. Against this, Meillassoux wants to empower reason, empower it beyond the limits of correlationism, and at the same time to refuse all this talk of the overcoming, or the end, of metaphysics, which atheist philosophy has appealed to as a method of attack against religion. The point here being that any such attack is simultaneously a weakening of reason, and therefore of atheism: as a result, "even atheism . . . is reduced to a mere belief, and hence to a religion, albeit of the nihilist kind."[23] To repeat, atheism says, God is dead, religion is wrong, and as a consequence, we must give up on our silly endeavors to build a metaphysics, we must give up on truth, as all is now only a matter of perspective, and so on. Meillassoux employs the ideas of ancestrality and the arche-fossil to help demonstrate that just because something is not thought by the human— that it is impossible for the human to think it (the human didn't exist then, of course)—does not mean the unthought is impossible, that it did not exist. Thus for Meillassoux, every "materialism that would be speculative, and hence for which absolute reality is an entity without thought, must assert both that thought is not necessary (something can be independent of thought) and that thought can think what there must be when there is no thought."[24] Or put differently, "we are going to put back into the thing itself what we mistakenly took to be an incapacity in thought." Meillassoux wants to do this so that he can have what he calls a "principle of un reason." In other words, everything in the world is without a reason; that being the case, they can be otherwise: all that we see can perish. But this is so not because there is a superior law driving us to destruction. No! All can disappear or perish because there is no such law of perishing; for if there were, the perishing would be something of a chimera, as *the law that made all perish would not itself perish*. In short, Meillassoux is arguing for radical contingency, one based on nothing.[25] It should, however, be noted that

22. Ibid., 5.
23. Ibid., 46.
24. Ibid., 36.
25. Ibid, 53.

his understanding of existence in terms of hyper-chaos, should not make us think that for him the world lacks laws—it does not. The chaos, so to speak, lies at the level of the laws themselves, crudely put, *there is no law for laws*, they can change at any time, it's just that they may not, and seem not to. Here, at this level, the principle of sufficient reason collapses.[26] Take gravity, the apple that falls from the tree will obey the law of gravity, but, quite simply, there is no reason that the law of gravity obtains.

Somewhat counter-intuitively is that this is what leads to true atheism, one that will lead to God, to miracles, to resurrection—this then is nihilism, a truly counterfeit theology; that is, a fully colonized theology. For example, according to Meillassoux, miracles are possible, and that would lead you to think that this is support for the religious case, but no. Miracles are possible precisely because there is no order in the world; in other words, you have no reason to say "no" to a miracle. That being the case, every miracle disproves the existence of God, as it reveals existence as underwritten by hyper-chaos, or contingency.[27] "Every miracle thus becomes the manifestation of the inexistence of God, insofar as every radical rupture of the present in relation to the past becomes manifestation of the absence of any order capable of overseeing the chaotic power of becoming."[28] Notice, Meillassoux does not write about the *non*existence of God, but rather the *in*existence—the former would impoverish atheism or nihilism, doing so by locking it into a reactive dualism (see below). What is crucial here is Meillassoux's privileging of time, and his particular understanding of it. According to him, time is not governed, or does not unfold under the watchful gaze of some non-temporal principle, because there isn't one, and this means that time is "delivered to the pure immanence of its chaos, its illegality."[29] This pure becoming, the pure immanence of time, accommodates a world of laws, order, and so on; yet, in so doing, there is no reason for such order, and no reason why it might simply not disappear, and if it did, in a sense, nothing would have happened—there is never a reason. Interestingly, Meillassoux argues that "the living is not primarily the emergence of a power of interested choice, but the emergence of a massive disinterest in the real."[30] By this he means that the living ignores the real, the chaos, and instead it closes itself off from

26. See Harman, *Quentin Meillassoux*, 63.
27. See Meillassoux, "Potentiality and Virtuality," 80.
28. Ibid., 74, note 7.
29. Ibid., 73.
30. Ibid., "Subtraction and Contraction," 74.

pure becoming. Yet if they become too closed off from Chaos they would, in a sense, mortify, and therefore die. Nietzsche said something similar: "The beings who did not see exactly had a head start over those who saw everything in flux."[31] Moreover, "a human being that did not possess the power of forgetting (or here, contraction) would no longer believe in its own being and lose himself in the stream of becoming."[32] Consequently, "forgetting is essential for all organic life."[33] The task for the philosopher, according to Meillassoux, is, then, to "maintain oneself in the Outside, but to hold oneself close, thus to some degree closed, and thus to discipline into writing a chaotic experience."[34] Maybe it is a little like filling a vessel with water, but doing it too fast, and as the water gushes in, the sheer amount forces it out; *too much too fast*—so one runs the risk of dying of thirst, yet on the other hand, if you refuse the flow of water completely, then once again death would occur.

Turning now to Meillassoux's rather eccentric yet interesting understanding of God, one that will to some degree fulfill atheism, or better, nihilism. First of all, Meillassoux, like any good nihilist, rejects the atheism/theism dualism, doing so for a number of reasons, some that have already been mentioned. One that has not is that of despair. In short, if God does not exist then there is no chance of justice for those who have died—indeed, for those have died as victims of horrible atrocities, therefore despair reigns. But if God does exist, then despair still reigns, for we then have to ask the question, why did God let all those atrocities happen?[35] This situation is what he terms a spectral dilemma, one that can only be solved by way of a highly paradoxical move: we must argue for the resurrection of the dead (here siding with religion), yet only doing so by arguing at the same time that God does not exist, or rather that God is *in*existent; in other words, God does not exist *yet*. There is a shift in modalities, as it is now about a future existence, as God is possible, or God is virtual. Similarly, "since everything that is logically possible really is possible, then since the rebirth of bodies is not illogical it must also be possible."[36]

He tells us that "Following the three Worlds of matter, Life, and thought, the rebirth of humans ought to be distinguished as a fourth world;

---

31. Nietzsche, *Gay Science*, 171.
32. Ibid., "History for Life," 62.
33. Ibid., 62.
34. Meillassoux, "Subtraction and Contraction," 107.
35. Ibid., "Spectral Dilemma," 265.
36. Ibid., "Divine Inexistence," 189.

... it exists already as an object of hope, of the desire of every human qua rational being."[37] This fourth world is, according to Meillassoux, the world of justice. It seems to me that Meillassoux is wrong to assume a universal desire for rebirth; indeed, would the real question not be, what kind of world would they be reborn into? Is it a world still full of those people who perpetrated the crimes? Moreover, if it is world of justice, is it also a world of forgiveness? And lastly, is not Meillassoux not simply (culturally, and not philosophically) assuming a collection of goods or virtues—a sort of naïve presumption of the existence of the good—insofar as he thinks some things are good and some are evil? Indeed, he is presuming the existence of ethics, but how can he do this and be consistent with his own philosophy? After all, those who perpetrated the crimes would surely beg to differ with him. Meillassoux then goes on to argue that what is important is that more comes from less; for example, the living from the non-living, and so on. Then he infers from this that if God existed this would not be the case, as less would come from more, and in a sense, all events would be prohibited because they are absorbed by the preceding more of God—they cannot escape God's presence. Consequently, Meillassoux tells us, "the hope of rebirth is bound to the astonishing awareness of the inexistence of God."[38] True creation *ex nihilo* requires the absence of God, so there is actual freedom, actual novelty, or newness. There are so many things wrong with this that it is hard to know where to begin. First of all, let us just mention that this is a complete misunderstanding of what creation *ex nihilo* means—I shall return to that in moment. A second glaring problem is that Meillassoux's own position ends up being guilty of the very same crime, except in reverse; for every new birth, like this season's fashion or this year's model of some car or other, would, we all know, be overshadowed by that which will come after it. As Meillassoux tells us, *more follows less* and this axiom, if ontologized would mean that whatever is can never really be astonishing, because what's coming is superseding it. This way, freedom would require a form of *perpetual abortion* as we endeavored to prevent that which is *coming after us* from actually arriving, and that is meant in two ways: temporally and violently. Indeed, this is the logic of Capitalism writ large. Meillassoux can, of course, as we would expect him to, tell us that there is no necessity in the world, but then that applies to the *more follows less* mantra too, and that means that his whole argument about God having to be inexistent is wrong.

37. Ibid.
38. Ibid., 192.

Meillassoux further demonstrates his economy of abortion (or, more accurately, murder) when speaking of giving birth to God: "We bear God in our wombs, and our essential disquietude is nothing other than the convulsions of a child yet to come."[39] Once again, from the perspective of theology, what he is saying is interesting, but at the same time wrongheaded. The problem being that if such a child were to arrive, we would immediately have to crucify it and start waiting for the next Messiah, who would, of course, be more. From theology's perspective, the logic is different. First, this child to come is always already, for he is the eternal Son, the lamb slain before the foundation of the world, which signals to us that any metaphysics that would try to understand creation must employ *nonidentical repetition, recapitulation*, and lastly, *anamnesis* (see below). Also, this Son "is already" in a second sense; this child became incarnate two thousand years ago and we humans did bear this child in our womb—namely, Mary as *theotokos*. And lastly, the Son is to come again. To repeat, the Son is eternal, the Son became flesh, we killed him (probably because we employed an economy similar to that of Meillassoux, were more always follows less; therefore, we had, like some latter-day Herod, to slaughter the holy innocents, as they were an obstacle). Lastly, the murdered child of God rose from the dead still bearing the scars of their human life, thus validating history; and lastly, we are eschatologically directed to his return, one that will indeed usher in justice, judgment, and forgiveness. Maybe Franz Kafka is correct: "We are nihilistic thoughts, suicidal thoughts, which come into God's head." Suicidal because God ends up dying under our hands, either by the way Nietzsche understands it, or Christian orthodoxy.[40] The whole shape of such a metaphysics and its implications protect us from all reductive economies or logics, and any sense of Whiggish consumption and destructive accumulation.

Two lessons from Charles Péguy are telling. The first is that according to Péguy, and contra Meillassoux, *more does not follow less*. Péguy argued that we tended to misunderstand events, because we read them in too linear a manner. For example, it would be supposed that the fall of the Bastille is commemorated by Federation Day in France, which could be said to repeat that fall. Instead, Péguy suggests that the fall of the Bastille repeats and celebrates all subsequent instances of Federation Day. Another example would be a water lily painted by Claude Monet. For Péguy, the first painting executed by Monet of his famous water lilies repeats all

---

39. Ibid., 231.
40. Kafka, quoted in Benjamin, *Selected Writings*, 798.

subsequent paintings. These later paintings in some sense intensify the originary repetition of the first: "Everything which is beginning has a virtue which can never be rediscovered, a strength, a novelty, freshness like dawn. . . . [T]he first day is the most beautiful. Perhaps the first day is the only beautiful day."[41] This is Clio's law of *vieillissement,* in that things get older and decay. What Péguy wishes to oppose with this understanding is the logic of the hoarder—that is to say, accumulation—but this does not mean that a second painting is simply not as good as the first. For even Péguy's own work contradicts this notion, in that his second work on Joan of Arc is better than the first. The point to be made is that the second is better *because of* the first, so in this sense is less. The intensification is not a cumulative hoarding; instead, it is a lived realization of the beginning, just as Picasso realizes the potency of Cézanne, and so on. All artists do, then, in a sense realize the first artist (nature), which is itself the realization of God's artistic intention: the Word. At a mundane level, with regard to the fall of the Bastille, unless there was a certain potency in that event there would be no Federation Day. The event would not be commemorated if the fall had been followed by a reversal of royal fortune. It is the *poesis,* the potency, in the first Monet that gives rise to the non-identical repetition of all those that follow. All subsequent paintings are the event of the first, in so far as the first creates the place for these others through its own being. Therefore, there is, on the one hand, a non-identical repetition and, on the other hand, there is recapitulation, and this, rather than imprisoning, emancipates: "An eternal foundation does not exclude the need to begin anew. No degree of eternal foundation alters the fact that the foundation is, in some sense, in the world and eternity."[42] And this brings us to Péguy's second point. In one of his most beautiful works, he has God say, a number of times: "Even I, God, am surprised by hope." So Meillassoux is correct to speak of hope, a hope for justice, for rebirth; it is just that his metaphysics are, it seems to me, all wrong. By returning to his understanding of creation, his errors can be highlighted—at least, errors in his understanding of the Christian doctrine of creation. In fact, correct understanding of the doctrine of creation turns out to be crucial for assessing all the nihilist attempts to colonize theism. Let us conclude, then, with some final reflections about nihilism and creation *ex nihilo.*

There is, according to Augustine, no before or after to creation, for all temporal terms are a fruit of creation, an effect of creation, and not

---

41. Charles Péguy, quoted in Servais, *Charles Péguy,* 336.
42. Péguy, "Notre Jeunesse," 96.

a framework within which creation is to be understood. In other words, for Augustine *time itself was created*, and thus we creatures see things in temporal terms but these are inappropriate to God. If they were, in fact, appropriate then creation would not be *ex nihilo*, but would arise once again from the structuring of pre-existent material. Thus as Augustine tells us, "When a builder puts up a house and departs, his work remains in spite of the fact he is no longer there. But the universe will pass away in the twinkling of an eye if God withdraws his ruling hand."[43] In other words, just as creation does not have a beginning, it is, in a sense, never over (ontologically speaking). Aquinas, picking up on Augustine's thinking nearly a thousand years later, makes clear "God's relation to the creation is understood as a purely conceptual relation, while the creature's relation to God is real";[44] or again, "Every relation which we consider between God and the creature is really in the creature, by whose change the relation is brought into being; whereas it is not really in God, but only in our way of thinking, since it does not arise from any change in God."[45] With regard to the question of change, Aquinas expands on this elsewhere, saying, "Creation is not a true change, but is rather a certain relation of the created thing, as a being that is dependent on the Creator for its existence and that connotes succession to previous non-existence. In every change there must be something that remains the same although it undergoes alteration in its manner of being.... In creation this does not take place in objective reality, but only in our imagination."[46] This means that for us creatures, for all that is created, the temporal is a result of our createdness.

For Augustine, and even more so for Aquinas, our existence is not essential to us (what Aquinas calls the real distinction between our essence and our existence). Because we are created, because all we have is received, it is perpetually the case that in a sense our being is always naked. As Anselm says to God "You are in no way less, even if they should return to nothing."[47] Eckhart echoes this: "He could add the entire world to God and would have nothing more than if he had God alone."[48] This means that creatures are in a sense nothing, and both Eckhart and Aquinas concur: "All creatures are one pure nothing. I do not say that they are a little something

---

43. Augustine, *The Literal Meaning*, IV, 12, 117.
44. Aquinas, *Summa Theologiae*, I, q.45. a.3. ad.1
45. Ibid., III, q.2. a.7; see also, ibid., I q.28. a.1. ad.3; I q.6. a.2. ad.1.
46. Ibid., *Compendium*, 99; also see *Summa Gentiles*, II, c.18, n. 952.
47. Anselm, *Proslogion*, chapter 20.
48. Eckhart, *Omne datum optimum*, 65; my translation.

or anything, but that they are pure nothing";[49] "each created thing, in that it does not have existence save from another, taken in itself, is nothing."[50] As St. Augustine said of God; "But you are deeper than my inmost being and higher than my own height."[51] This intimacy, this non-invasive, divine concurrence, informs the world. Here we see in the starkest possible terms the non-dualism of Christian theology: God cannot be something alien to immanence, something simply different. Maybe then, it is better to conclude that we would rather answer the door to Christ, who is, in the end, a more "uncanny" guest than nihilism, with all its needs, and its diabolic destruction of the world. In this way, we must understand that nihilism is not the truth of Christianity, but, if anything, Christianity is the truth of nihilism, if, that is, there is any truth to nihilism. That possibility makes me pause to think that maybe Fyodor Dostoevsky is correct, "Nihilism isn't even worth talking about."[52] Nor maybe is Meillassoux's work, though no doubt in the industrial, bourgeois market for endless novelty—in terms of philosophy and its hubris, all of which pass into the mists of being old fashioned—his will last for a time.

## Bibliography

Anselm, St. *Proslogion*. Translated by M. J. Charlesworth. Oxford: Clarendon, 1965.
Aquinas, Thomas. *Compendium of Theology*. Translated by Richard Regan. New York: Oxford University Press, 2009.
———. *Summa contra Gentiles*. Translated by Anton Charles Pegis. Notre Dame: Notre Dame University Press, 1991.
———. *Summa Theologiae*. Translated by Anton Charles Pegis. London: Eyre and Spottiswoode, 1963.
Augustine. *Confessions*. Translated by R. Coffin. London: Penguin, 1961.
———. *The Literal Meaning of Genesis*. Translated by John Hammond Taylor. Mahwah NJ: Paulist, 1982.
Badiou, Alain. "The Event as Trans-Being." In *Theoretical Writings*, translated by Ray Brassier and Alberto Toscano, 97–102. London: Continuum, 2004.
Benjamin, Walter. *Selected Writings, Vol. 2*. Translated by R. Livingstone. Cambridge, MA: Belknap, 1999.
Blanchot, Maurice. *The Infinite Conversation*. Translated by S. Hanson. Minneapolis: University of Minnesota Press, 1993.
———. "Literature and the Right to Death." In *The Work of Fire*, 300–344. Stanford: Stanford University Press, 1995.

49. Quoted in Bernard McGinn, *Mystical Union*, 66.
50. Aquinas, *Summa Theologiae*, 1a, 2ae, q.109, a2.
51. Augustine, *Confessions*, III, 6, 11.
52. Fyodor Dostoyevsky, *Selected Letters*, 333.

Brassier, Ray. "Nihil Unbound: Remarks on Subtractive Ontology and Thinking Capitalism." In *Thinking Again: Alain Badiou and the Future of Philosophy*, edited by Peter Hallward, 50–58. London: Continuum, 2004.
Cunningham, Conor. *Darwin's Pious Idea: Why Ultra-Darwinists and Creationists Both get it Wrong.* Grand Rapids: Eerdmans, 2010.
Dostoyevsky, Fyodor. *Selected Letters.* Translated by A. MacAndrew. New Brunswick, NJ: Rutgers University Press, 1987.
Eckhart, Mesiter. "Omne datum optimum." In *Sermons, Vol. 1*, translated by Jeanne Ancelet-Hustache, 65–66. Paris: Éditions du Seuil, 1974.
Harman, Graham. *Quentin Meillassoux.* Edinburgh: Edinburgh University Press, 2011.
Heidegger, Martin. *Introduction to Metaphysics.* Translated by G. Fried and R. Polt. New Haven: Yale University Press, 2000.
Kojève, Alexandre. *Introduction to the Reading of Hegel.* Translated by James Nichols. New York: Cornell University Press, 1963.
Lacan, Jacques. *The Seminar of Jacques Lacan, II: The Ego in Freud's Theory and in the Technique of Psychoanalysis, 1954–1955.* Edited by Jacques Alain-Miller. Translated by Sylvana Tomaselli. New York: Norton, 1991.
———. *Seminar XX: On Feminine Sexuality. The Limits of Love and Knowledge.* Translated by B. Fink. New York: Norton, 1998.
McGinn, Bernard. *The Mystical Union of Meister Eckhart.* New York: Crossroad, 2001.
Meillassoux, Quentin. *After Finitude.* Translated by R. Brassier. London: Continuum, 2008.
———. "Divine Inexistence." In *Quentin Meillassoux: Philosophy in the Making*, by Graham Harman, 90–122. Edinburgh: Edinburgh University Press, 2011.
———. "Potentiality and Virtuality." *Collapse* II (March 2007) 55–81.
———. "Spectral Dilemma." *Collapse IV: Concept Horror* (May 2008) 261–75.
———. "Subtraction and Contraction: Deleuze's Remarks on Matter and Memory." *Collapse* III (November 2007) 63–107.
Nietzsche, Friedrich. *The Gay Science: With a Prelude in Rhymes and an Appendix of Songs.* Translated by Walter Kaufmann. New York: Vintage, 1972.
———. "On the Use and Abuse of History for Life." In *Untimely Meditations*, translated by R. J. Hollingdale, 51–124. Cambridge: Cambridge University Press, 1997.
———. *The Will to Power.* Translated by Walter Kauffmann. New York: Vintage, 1968.
Péguy, Charles. *Clio.* 1909–12. Reprint. Paris: Gallimard, 1931.
Sartre, Jean-Paul. *Being and Nothingness.* Translated by H. Barnes. Routledge: London, 2000.
Servais, Y. *Charles Péguy: The Pursuit of Salvation.* Cork, Ireland: Cork University Press, 1953.
Watkin, Alan. *Difficult Atheism: Post-Theological Thinking in Alain Badiou, Jean-Luc Nancy, and Quentin Meillassoux.* Edinburgh: Edinburgh University Press, 2011.
Zaborowski, Holger. *Robert Spaemann's Philosophy of the Human Person.* Oxford: Oxford University Press, 2010.

# 7

## Persons or Creatures?
### Sellars, Whitehead, and the Metaphysical Problem of Late Modernity

*Neil Turnbull*

~

As is well known, metaphysics has made a very significant comeback of late; an intellectual event that is likely to prove to be of real historical significance—especially given that its return has come as something of a disorienting shock to philosophers working within the often conceptually arid, "post-metaphysical" confines of academic philosophy, where the metaphysical has been largely disavowed only to have reappeared as morbid intellectual symptoms of various kinds (relativism, nihilism, the fetish of "analysis" for its own sake, the celebration of the post-human, and so forth). However, in this regard at least, change is now very much in the air. With the rapid emergence of the explicitly metaphysical philosophies of Sellars, Whitehead, and Deleuze, alongside the appearance of the quasi-theologies of the so-called contemporary "speculative materialists," to a new prominence in the contemporary philosophical field, metaphysical controversies are now re-emerging to proclaim a new autonomy of philosophical reason in relation to its self-imposed post-Kantian "critical" exile.[1] More specifically, after almost a century of intense criticism by

---

1. The recent French Bergson-inspired revival in metaphysics will not be discussed here. As we will see, this is largely because, with his preoccupation with the

positivist philosophical parvenus—alongside numerous, often seemingly redoubtable, dismissals of metaphysics as at worst a "linguistic anathema," at best little more than an "historic illusion" residing somewhere between "the implausible" and "the nonsensical"—metaphysics is once again being recognized as precisely what "good old fashioned metaphysicians" always thought that it was: an inevitable complement and presupposition to all authentic modes of thought, as well as a practical intellectual necessity required for resolving the many and various "conceptual agonistics" that have become the *sine qua non* of modern forms of historical existence. Thus, it is very important to point out right from the start that the contemporary turn to metaphysics is *not* philosophy *faut de mieux*, but rather a significant metastasis in the philosophical discourse of late modernity itself; one that may, as I show below, suggest an epochal return of an engagement between philosophy and theology.

## The Metaphysical Problem of Late Modernity

It is becoming very clear that our culturally particular (and ontologically highly peculiar) form of historical existence, "late modernity," is in fact a receptacle for a number of pressing metaphysical issues that cannot be "dissolved" into post-metaphysical discourses. More specifically our core contemporary intellectual problematics are now of such depth and intensity that they clearly require the *ultima ratio* of the global forms of philosophical reflection associated with work of the classical metaphysician.[2]

---

metaphysics of *temporality*, Bergson's work is very much determined by a key philosophical problematic of an earlier modernity; the "forwards-driven" modernity of the nineteenth century. Thus his philosophy, I suggest, no longer "resonates sufficiently" in late-modern cultural contexts where the metaphysics of space has regained paradigmatic priority over and above the earlier modern metaphysics of time. More specifically, although important, his work does not speak to the increasingly object-oriented ontological condition of those living in worlds determined by the spatializing logic of the techno-sciences. Neither will I discuss the recent "speculative materialist moment"—one that proposes a new modernist metaphysics in a combination of the Cartesian thesis that "thought thinks reality" (the basic metaphysical assumption of modern science) and the Leibnizian claim it is mathematics that allows us to "think the infinite." For these philosophers, we might say that science and mathematics undo the conditions of possibility of philosophy as it has been traditionally conceived (and in so doing, they allow for a new conditioning of the conditions that allow philosophy to emerge). My view is that speculative materialism does not take us beyond the ideas Sellars and Whitehead in any significant way (and in some ways, it is simply an antitheist misreading of the ideas of the former).

2. Although difficult to periodize precisely, "late-modernity," as it is defined here,

Whereas the old critique of metaphysics viewed itself as essentially an exercise in the attainment of "mental hygiene" (defined, in the end, as "conceptual conventionalism"), attempts to bleach the discourses of modern philosophy into a post-metaphysical poetics, mathematics, or therapeutics only made philosophical thought—and in the end historical life itself—sterile. Or as Whitehead put it, "if men cannot live on bread alone, still less can they do so on disinfectants"—to the extent that all those who desire to understand the philosophical truth of our particular form of historical existence, a desire that directs the philosophical impulse into the nature of science and its relationship to thought, need to "[e]ndeavour to frame a coherent, logical, necessary system of ideas in terms of which every element of our experience can be interpreted."[3]

Whitehead makes a telling point. The Kantian attempt to cleanse the modern conceptual terrain of its "residual" ancient metaphysics now seems like yet another modern epigone of the grandeur of older forms of philosophical insight. Moreover, demands for an empirically founded conceptual clarity and transparency (without recourse to wider metaphysical concerns) can only amount to an intellectual toxin within the tangled webs of today's contested conceptualities. It seems as though in our (later) modernity—one of heightened ontological complexity and radical epistemological under-determination and undecidability—the Kantian critical project fails; in the end collapsing into the same forms of Humean skepticism that it tried so valiantly to escape from. As such, in opposition to the Hume/Kant skeptical dyad, contemporary philosophy must begin from an appreciation of the tensions within late-modernity's most fundamental assumptions and seek out some kind of unitary, global, resolution to these in a new overarching metaphysics. More specifically, our particular intellectual situation—one that cannot, we now see, be reconciled via a liberal relativism that views all metaphysical orientations as essentially a "lifestyle choice"—can only be adequately resolved if it is understood in terms of a general philosophical scheme that informs us as to *what our*

---

is associated with the emergence of the mass-production/mass-consumption societies that emerged after the First World War—when science, culture, and the economy became integrated on the basis of a new modernist cultural-metaphysics. This is essentially a "conservative modernity" that strives to regulate modernity's disruptive temporalities by means of the scientific management of social life (it is, we might say, the era when an essentially authoritarian political arrangement ideologizes itself as the continuation of classical liberalism). This is a mode of modernity where the promise of emancipation is widely conceived in terms of techno-scientific forms of progress, and one where science itself has become "metaphysics."

3. Whitehead, *Modern World*, 74.

*epoch is* in an account of what it conceives as "ultimately real."[4] This is not to advocate a return to a new form of philosophical dogmatism, but rather, only, to recommend a new, concerted effort to go beyond the limits set by "autonomous reason" in a way that begins to remedy the chronic "dissociation of thought from the real" that was symptomatic of twentieth-century existence. As Whitehead put it:

> Philosophy will not regain its proper status until the gradual elaboration of categoreal schemes, definitively stated at each stage of progress, is recognised as its proper objective. There may be rival schemes, inconsistent among themselves; each with its own merits and its own failures. It will then be the purpose to conciliate the differences. Metaphysical categories are not dogmatic statements of the obvious; they are tentative formulations of the ultimate generalities.[5]

Following on from this important insight, in this chapter I want to suggest that the main "schematic rivalry" of today—one that demands a metaphysical resolution that "conciliates its essential differences"—is, by and large, that between the categorical framework that supports the theoretical endeavors of contemporary scientists and the one that sustains the more familiar hermeneutics of our late-modern modes of ordinary cultural life. More specifically, I want to suggest that the most significant metaphysical problem of late-modernity, and the issue that is emerging to threaten neat institutional divides within philosophy and between philosophy and "other disciplines," is the issue of how to generalize and resolve the antagonistic relationship between the naturalistic particulate metaphysics of the contemporary physical sciences and the experiential, personalist, and communitarian metaphysics that continues to sustain "mundane" thought and practice.[6]

---

4. The relationship between the "historical real" and "the absolute" is, of course, one of the key metaphysical problems of modernity, as Hegel recognized. In this context, I will suggest that the question can be elided because metaphysics' return suggests the "return of the real in both senses" (for an understanding of the absolute presupposes that the real, in some sense, exists). Thus the return of metaphysics amounts to a first moment in what will no doubt amount to a wider return of a historical forms of life as "seekers the absolute."

5. Whitehead, *Process*, 12.

6. It is important to mention here the recent attempt by those working within the tradition of science studies to collapse the distinction between the ordinary objects of everyday life and the esoteric objects of the theoretical sciences. The problem with such attempts is that they only succeed in relativizing this issue and ultimately undermining the very idea of the object itself.

Interestingly, in this context, a cursory examination of the contemporary philosophical scene seems to suggest that at present there are *two* metaphysical resolutions to this cultural-metaphysical situation being offered: one that attempts to resolve it by means of a "Kantian" preservation of the philosophy of culture via a new metaphysics of persons (and communities), conceived as prior and as somehow more fundamental vis-à-vis the spheres of the scientific; and another, "Neoplatonic," approach that takes a position that is more naturalistic, in a revised "cosmological" sense, in giving a certain priority to the "ontologically creative" functions of "the organismic"—especially to the forms of affective creativity that are seen as the essential characteristic of an essentially cosmic and cosmological reality.[7] The first option, associated with the metaphysical reflections of Wilfred Sellars—but not, strangely, those of his contemporary followers—looks towards what might be termed a revisionary metaphysics of personhood and community life that allows the theoretical claims of the theoretical sciences to be reconceived in ways that are "relevant" to both scientists and non-scientists alike. This way looks for a new language of science where science's theoretical concepts "appear" in a different, more "personalized" way, that is, in a way that does not deny the reality of the personal in the manner of contemporary forms of scientific conceptuality. The second, associated with the philosophical ideas of A. N. Whitehead, builds on the metaphysical potentials contained within contemporary theoretical science—especially biology, both evolutionary and cellular—in a way that aims to transform the metaphysical presumptions of everyday life in terms of a Platonized vitalism. The former, we might say, is a project to "humanize science," the second a project to redefine a traditional conception of the human in terms of a new biological ontology.[8] In what follows, I will outline these two metaphysical positions in more detail and examine

---

7. Here, of course, we need to make clear the nature of the relationship between naturalism and vitalism. In one sense, vitalism *is* a form of naturalism, but one that does not distinguish between human and non-human nature. We might then usefully view vitalism as a form of "ultra naturalism" that may in the end fail to preserve the dignity and integrity of the human. In its pure form, vitalism can give rise to highly dubious ethical and political visions—and this is one reason why another (alternative) metaphysics may be needed if we are to move beyond the current intellectual impasse.

8. An immediate reaction here is that these two positions amount to the same thing—arriving at the same place from different directions as it were. However, the wider cultural and historical implications of these two metaphysical schemes are quite different, as I hope to show. We might say that Sellars offers us a conservative resolution to this metaphysical problem in his desire to retain traditional conceptions of persons and communities; Whitehead's being a more radical proposal in this respect.

which of them seems the "more appropriate" with regard to the contemporary intellectual milieu outlined above.[9] In overall terms, I will suggest that when their philosophies are placed in conjunction, the question that is fundamental to the work of both these philosophers (and is now emerging as a metaphysical question, after the manifest failure of psychological naturalism in the twentieth century) is this: what is the human subject? Is it essentially *creaturely* (that is an "affective product" of a deeper creative process, and thus only a individual in abstraction) or is it essentially an *autonomous agent* (the product of a historical *telos* where we must conceive of any individual entity, in its "highest forms," as a unified center of rationality, autonomy and responsibility)?[10] In short, when placed together these philosophers allow us to discern that the basic metaphysical question of our times is essentially metaphysical and accidentally theological: what are we today when presented with the ontological commitments of the theoretical sciences—persons or creatures?

## First Resolution: Wilfred Sellars' Scientific Personalism

We can now begin to address a philosophical response to the metaphysical problem of late-modernity that provides us with perhaps the clearest statement of what is essentially at stake with respect to it (and here we can see the philosophical imagination at work in a powerful way).[11] This is the

---

9. Both, in the end, I want to say, amount to two distinct versions of what can be usefully termed *romantic positivism*: that is, an attempt to find a way of making the particulate and hitherto mechanistic metaphysics of modern science "resonate" with the interests, concerns, and intuitions of everyday lived experience. They are not scientistic philosophers in the strict sense, and it is important to separate positivism and scientism in this context. See Olafson, *Naturalism*, 24–45. The former being essentially a Hegelian dream of a unified and completed science, the latter a metaphysical thesis that scientific theories give us the "best steer" as to the true nature of the real. Romantic positivism offers us a dream of a unified and completed science, but without claiming that science, at least as we currently conceive of it, can inform us about the true nature of things. Romantic positivism is thus a version of positivism where science collapses back into a metaphysics that goes far beyond scientific naturalism as it is currently conceived.

10. Or: when it comes to contemporary metaphysical problematics, my question is this—who should we follow, Sellars or Whitehead?

11. There is a real need to habilitate Sellarsian philosophy of science today within a philosophical context where the dominant philosophical conception of science is one that has been shaped through a radical and uncritical (sociological) reading of Kuhn. Kuhn, informed by the notorious instrumentalist "under-determination" thesis, viewed scientific knowledge claims as "merely paradigmatic" and thus undermined by

response of the American "renegade Kantian" philosopher Wilfred Sellars. It has been long recognized that Sellars' seminal paper, *Philosophy and the Scientific Image of Man*, was an oasis of metaphysical insight in what was at the time a murky swamp of mid-century positivist banalities.[12] It was in this paper that Sellars attempted to provide a new, "synoptic," late-modern, metaphysical vision that encompassed the totality of late-modern worldhood within a single and unifying metaphysical scheme; an account of how, as he put it, "cabbages and kings ... numbers and duties, possibilities and finger snaps, aesthetic experience and death"—"things in the broadest sense of the term"—currently "hang together in the broadest sense of the term."[13] However, for Sellars, any such attempt at keeping a metaphysical "eye on the metaphysical whole" is rendered radically aporetic because of the emergence of new conceptualities and ontological commitments associated with theoretical physics.[14] More specifically, for Sellars, as late moderns we enter into conceptuality (and thus thought, reason, and so

---

a thoroughgoing "interpretative flexibility." Sellars' metaphysical account of science is the antidote to the "spurious professionalization" of the philosophical conception of science that this implies.

12. Providing a general account of the overall significance of Sellars' philosophy is not an easy task, for Sellars was, like Whitehead, an extremely "difficult" philosopher who articulated his ideas in highly elliptical ways. As one recent commentator has written, "he was not one of the most celebrated representatives of contemporary analytic philosophy: however original, diversified, and acute Sellars' writings are, throughout his lifetime he remained in the shadow of those who were able to impress more palpably by technical niceties or glamorous style." For some, his work suffered from an obscure style that has been termed "bewilfridgkeit"—see Seibt, "Analysis without Synopsis," 6.

13. Sellars, "Scientific Image, 1."

14. In order to incorporate the theoretical worlds of contemporary science into his synoptic metaphysical vision, Sellars' begins with the now familiar problematic of how to make sense of the "empirical meaningfulness" of theoretical statements about scientific "unobservables" (and the related problem of the ontological status of such theoretical entities). Sellars' solution to this problem is to grant a certain metaphysical primacy and autonomy to acts of theoretical postulation by ontologically "separating out" the worlds opened up by the "theorems of scientific theory" from those associated with the more immediate, "empirical," phenomenal events that support them in basic verifiable statements. In this way, he begins the process of separating questions of meaning from more important metaphysical questions (and ultimately, like Quine, he ends up rejecting the analytic problem of meaning *tout court*, focusing instead on the relationship between scientific knowledge and metaphysical truth). More specifically, the meaning of statements about theoretical unobservables does not, in Sellars' view, depend of their reducibility to the protocol statements of the observation language, because their meaning is given by their "explanatory role" in a much wider conceptual framework (what might be termed "the whole of science," conceived as a metaphysics). See Sellars, "Theories," 107.

on) not via the immediacy of empirical fact (or the givens of innate cognitive structures) but via two historical frameworks—one that we might term "traditional" and the other dynamically modern and "scientific." In this way, the key philosophical problem, according to Sellars, is that the late-modern philosopher is presented with two radically incompatible conceptualities, each expressive of a very different type of worldhood—an incompatibility that he believes obstructs the development of a single unified metaphysical language pertaining to the world as whole and an impediment to philosophy as a discourse about the real. More specifically, according to Sellars, these two accounts—what Sellars famously referred to as the "scientific image of the world" and the "manifest image of the world"—*clash,* in that each seems to assert at the most fundamental of level what the other denies (and there being no way to move from the ontology of one image to the other *salva veritate*).[15]

The scientific image, in Sellars' view, articulates the world as a complex assemblage of unobservable micro-entities, structures, and processes. As such, it is largely the world as represented in the current and most up-to-date theoretical discourses of the late-modern physicist (although, in this respect, Sellars' account may, arguably, need updating because in recent years biology has increasingly replaced physics as "the fundamental science" in both cultural and metaphysical terms. A version of the scientific image derived from biology, as we will see, is integral to Whitehead's alternative metaphysics of late-modernity).[16] Importantly, in Sellars' view, the scientific image must also be understood *historically*—that is, as an image that is still in the process of intellectual construction and conceptual refinement.[17] Moreover, for Sellars, the scientific image is ontologically

---

15. As has already been mentioned, Sellars claims that these two fundamental images of the world conflict—in what might be termed a conflict of "fundamental metaphysical interpretations." For him, this is essentially a conflict between the speculative *postulational* ontology of theoretical science (taken up by scientists when explaining particular phenomena) that posits micro-theoretical entities for explanatory purposes, and the *non-postulational* stance of common sense (taken by ordinary persons engaged in everyday forms of understanding). Sellars uses the famous example of the pink ice cube here to show how the non-postulational attitude implies an ontology, in being essentially continuous, that is radically at odds with the discontinuous ontology of that is the metaphysical consequence of all forms of theoretical postulation.

16. In this respect, I side with Sellars—physics, as it is tied to cosmology, continues to be the *ur*-science in many respects and remains for us (late-moderns) ontologically fundamental.

17. Sellars recognizes that generic terms such as "science" and especially "the scientific image" are clearly idealizations, perhaps even philosophical "ideal types," in that the latter is "a conception of a manifold, each of which is the application . . . of a

committed to the existence of a particulate realm comprised of abstract theoretical entities such as atoms, quarks, free radicals, and so on: what Sellars termed "a swirl of particles, forces, and fields."[18] In late-modernity this image is increasingly viewed as "ontologically fundamental"—as the true metaphysics—and the problem of its abstractness and its fundamental otherness with respect to everyday ontologies is only a problem for those who, because of their lack of knowledge, skills, or specialized instrumental means, are prevented from articulating the world in terms of scientific vocabularies.[19]

The manifest image, on the other hand, is a global representation of the world as seen from the perspective of what might be termed "enlightened everydayness." As such, this image, as Sellars recognizes, expresses the metaphysics through which individuals recognize themselves, as *themselves*—that is, as *persons*. For Sellars, as he makes clear in a later piece, persons in this image are essentially Aristotelian in nature, in that they are conceived as singular logical subjects that do not have subordinate individuals as parts.[20] Moreover, this image is, in historical terms,

---

framework of concepts that have a certain autonomy" (Sellars "Scientific Image," 20). As he puts it: "our contrast then is between two ideal constructs: (a) the correlational and categorical refinement of the 'original image,' which refinement I am calling the manifest image; (b) the image derived from the fruits of postulational theory construction which I am calling the scientific image." Sellars, "Scientific Image," 19. In this way, Sellars philosophy assumes that there is a metaphysical unity to all the natural sciences.

Although, post-Kuhn, it has become commonplace to deny this in a new sociological recognition of science as comprised by a multiplicity of competing paradigms, Sellars is surely right about this. For, from the vantage point of the contemporary metaphysician, all sciences clearly share a basic set of metaphysical assumptions; the most important being science's skepticism towards the epistemic worth of ordinary ontologies (something that is only possible because of the postulation by the scientist of *another world*, populated by theoretical entities and processes of various kinds).

18. Sellars, "Scientific Image," 20. In this respect, Sellars' ideas are similar to those of the twentieth-century physicist Arthur Eddington (see Stebbing, *Physicists,* for a discussion). For Eddington, when we are confronted by a familiar everyday object, such as a chair, we, unbeknownst to us, are not confronted by one object, but by two objects; one concrete and visible, the other abstract and unobservable.

19. But the important point to note here is that the cultural-metaphysics of science is not simply a specialized and esoteric metaphysics. In the twentieth century it increasingly found a role outside of scientific institutions and now plays something of a determining role in more everyday decisions: for example, in explaining why someone's car doesn't start. Consider, also, how scientists' proclamations about global warming are effecting changes in the patterns of consumption in Western societies.

20. See Sellars, "Concept of a Person," 216. This is the precise difference between Sellars' and Whitehead's metaphysical schemes.

*primordial* and therefore provides the historical ontological conditions for the emergence of the scientific image; an image that, in late modernity, is now claiming a certain autonomy with respect to it (bringing about the metaphysical problem that we are currently discussing).[21] Thus in combining these two aspects—the personalist and primordial—the manifest image is the framework through which the human being first came to be aware of himself as, what Sellars refers to as, "man-in-the-world"—that is, as the "folk-psychological" bearer of beliefs and desires, capable of rational agency and a capacity for conscious reflection and self-knowledge.[22] As such, it is the framework whose emergence made possible the moment of original human self-consciousness through which humans emerged, in the Hegelian/Sartrean sense, "for themselves," that is as ethical and political beings who view the world as there somehow "for them" in a way that renders both self and world as sites of existential significance.[23]

For Sellars, the world as conceived in terms of the scientific image is the Kantian noumenal world immanentized as sets of abstract microprocesses—not *causes*, as causality, for him, is of necessity a manifest concept—that science has, so far, understood to be comprised of "particles

---

21. However, for Sellars, it is important to grasp that this image has also evolved significantly since the moment of its primordial appearance, and that in its contemporary "developed" form the manifest image conceives of the world as populated by self-conscious persons (humans and higher mammals) surrounded by an "inanimate" nature. The latter conception was not present in this image in its original form (as then a crude animism held sway). In this way, the manifest image must be viewed as a self-rationalizing image (as its basic rationality is inductive in nature, although this mode of rationality only takes the manifest image "so far" in ontological terms). At present, the manifest world is primarily a world of personals (I) and collectives (we)—surrounded by a nature that it conceives as "inert stuff." Thus the scientists are, in metaphysical terms, right to suggest that the manifest image is, at stands, in need of "correction."

22. Again, it is important to point out that this image is not a static one but one that has undergone a constant process of conceptual refinement. More recently, this process of refinement has occurred in response to conceptual innovations in the scientific image. In this way, the manifest image is not subject to a process of elimination—à la contemporary eliminativism—but a process of revision and reformation, albeit one where its core conceptuality is largely left intact.

23. See Sellars, "Scientific Image," 6. For Sellars, there is a real sense in which we can only understand the manifest image as something that appears "all at once"—thus suggesting that initially it was a "revelation" more than a "discovery," perhaps even a "divine creation." Moreover, in Sellarsian terms the human, "as such," only appears in within a metaphysical scheme that itself can only have *appeared* as a matter of contingent fact. Here, we can see the rudiments of a theology in Sellars' metaphysics, as for Sellars the human is nothing without a prior revelation of the human as a site of significance; that is, as a person.

forming ever more complex systems of particles."[24] Thus in Sellars' metaphysics what is distinctive about the scientific image is precisely that it articulates the contents of a world that exists *beyond* all localized concrete phenomenologies, a world where the familiar substantialist and personalist metaphysics of the manifest image breaks down. As he puts it:

> the perceptual world is phenomenal in something like the Kantian sense, the key difference being that the real or "noumenal" world which supports the "world of appearances" is not a metaphysical world of unknowable things in themselves, but simply the world as construed by scientific theory.... To say that the [manifest] framework is phenomenal in a quasi-Kantian sense ... is to say that science is making available a more adequate framework of entities which *in principle*, at least, could serve all the functions of the framework that we actually employ in everyday life.[25]

How then to reconcile to the phenomenality of the manifest world with the noumenality of the scientific world, the "world beyond" that is "somehow" entirely immanent to the world as it ordinarily appears to us in the manifest image? What kind of scientific image is implied here? Here Sellars reflects on the metaphysics of an everyday object (rendered somewhat strange)—a pink ice cube. Sellars' philosophical reflections on the essence of this, perhaps deliberately aestheticized, object brings out the metaphysical problem of late-modernity in a highly illuminating way (one that shows the extent to which this problem is intimately related to the metaphysical problem of color). For Sellars, understanding the nature of the ontological commitments associated with our experience of pink ice cubes will demonstrate why all manifest objects must today be viewed in terms of his two, radically incompatible, metaphysical schemes; both of which, when viewed in this particular context, appear to be absolutely fundamental and primary. More specifically, when seen in terms of the scientific image, the pink ice cube is essentially a discontinuous and particulate agglomeration; whereas when viewed in terms of the manifest image the pink ice cube is a continuous and homogeneous three-dimensional color solid.[26] The incompatibility of these two conceptions is the

24. Sellars, "Scientific Image," 37
25. Ibid., "Phenomenalism," 97; original emphasis.
26. In this way, Sellars is a long way from the recent attempt by Alain Badiou (and his followers) to resolve this clash by reducing the manifest to the scientific—in Alain Badiou's case by viewing the realm of the manifest in terms of an "impressionistic metaphysics" of phenomenological atoms, "atoms of appearing." See Badiou, *Second*

*Neil Turnbull*                *Persons or Creatures?*

result of the fact that the former offers us an ontology of discontinuity, the latter one of continuity. As Sellars puts it, in contradistinction to the particulate conception, "[t]he manifest ice cube presents itself to us as something that is pink through and through, as a pink continuum, all the regions of which, however small, are pink."[27] In Sellars' view, this basic metaphysical difference can only be resolved by holding both together in a "stereoscopic focus" that places both images together—side-by-side, as it were—with a view to *fusing* them into a new, singular, metaphysics.[28] Thus, for Sellars, reflection on the philosophical significance of *phenomena* shows us that the philosopher today is met "not by one complex many dimensional picture, the unity of which he must come to appreciate; but by two pictures of essentially the same order of complexity, each of which purports to be a picture of man-in-the-world, and which . . . he must fuse into *one vision*."[29] This, for Sellars, is the important point for contemporary philosophy to grasp; that today the philosopher is faced with two rival metaphysical schemes that need to be speculatively resolved (fused) into an account of a new ontology that does philosophical justice to both by appealing to a more general, global, standard of rationality (the criterion of "explanatory adequacy" in Sellars' case, although this is clearly not the only criterion in this regard).

Therefore, the main problem here, as Sellars recognizes, is that any attempt to forge such a grand metaphysical synthesis in the crucible of late-modern philosophy is immediately undermined in the immediate recognition that the manifest image articulates the world in terms of things and qualities that have *no place at all* in the scientific image as it is currently conceived; things and qualities that are, more precisely, *redundant* from the scientific point of view (*eliminable* from the point of view of the scientific image, yet phenomenologically and ethically *primordial* from the

---

*Manifesto*, 55–56. Such moves grossly underestimate the depth of the metaphysical problem here. Sellars recognizes this in claiming that objects in the manifest realm are absolutely continuous—there are no particles of color from the manifest point of view—and hence Badiou's metaphysical impressionism misses the basic point of phenomenology of the manifest: its unity, its fundamental *oneness* (and in many ways Badiou's analysis proceeds *as if phenomenology had never occurred*).

27. Sellars, "Scientific Image," 26.

28. Sellars is thus essentially concerned with how to resolve the contradictions that exist between the two basic meaning-frameworks that have come to define the intellectual landscape of late-modernity.

29. See Sellars, "Scientific Image," 40–44; my emphasis. Thus, unlike Eddington, Sellars' overall aim was to forge a new articulation of the metaphysics of modern theoretical science with the "qualitative and value oriented" metaphysics of ordinary life.

point of view of the manifest image). Accordingly, Sellars believes that any synthesis of the images is impossible given the conceptualities integral to both images today; to the extent that any resolution to the clash will only be possible once the scientific image is rearticulated in terms of a scheme that allows the world that it posits in theory to be understood from the manifest point of view, in terms of "enlightened common sense"—and in his view this will mean that the scientific image of the world will have to understand its object domains in a way enriched by the language of community and intentions, something that he claims will require a new concept of process that retains some of the "psychic," personalist, forms of conceptuality that lie at the core of the manifest image of the world.[30]

Through Sellars' cogent analysis we can perceive, no doubt, the depth of the difficulty involved in providing a general philosophical solution to our current cultural-metaphysical problem.[31] For these two images of the world clearly give legitimacy to two radically different kinds of metaphysical truth: one supported by a metaphysics of personhood, the other supported by a metaphysics of "radical particulate abstraction," a metaphysics of essentially placeless particles and processes where ideas of persons—and substantial things more generally—gain no philosophical traction. As such, for Sellars, there is no easy relativist solution to the late-modern metaphysical problematic—which views both images "as true"—because authentic philosophical thought can never accept this as it will always give

---

30. See Sellars, "Scientific Image," 40. As such, Sellars is the chief prophet of the current era of philosophy where metaphysics has re-emerged from underneath the rubble of the post-modern.

31. Some, for example Dennett (see "Wondering," 103–4) have suggested that Sellars is mistaken about the significance of the clash here. The argument he offers, against Sellars, is that phenomenological experience, for example the experience of color, *can* be broken down in a principled way into various constituent "bits." These bits can then be handled in entirely non-revolutionary ways by the currently entrenched version of the scientific image (in our case, by the cognitive neurosciences). Thus, the bare non-eliminable unity and facticity of the phenomenological level of experience is far from obvious in Dennett's view. However, as with Badiou, it is hard to see how one could provide an account of, say, the experience of a pink ice cube in, say, neuro-computational terms and not be profoundly "unsatisfied." For although such explanations may suffice at the level of behavior—in terms of predictive adequacy and so forth—they clearly tell us very little about the quality of this experience as such; as the pinkness of pink, its "eternal aspect," is entirely missing in such accounts. For although the difference between pink and yellow is clearly computable, pink in itself, the immediate and direct experience of "occurrent pinkness," seems to sit rather uneasily within this paradigm and can only be conceived in terms of an alternative metaphysics that accounts for the existence of such "qualitative states" in a way that sees them as much than an "emergence from below."

rise to contradiction at the level of the manifest, the level of life as it is ordinarily lived.³² For Sellars, the clash of the images can only be resolved, *in the long intellectual durée*, by one of these frameworks finally "winning out" over the other (and in so doing replacing the defeated one, as the "historically superior" metaphysical account).³³ In Sellars' view, this implies, specifically, that the metaphysics of one image must be ultimately rejected as *false*. For him, as it is the scientific image that has proven, historically, to possess the greater "explanatory power," then it is the scientific image that is, in principle, the more adequate one and therefore should, in the final historical analysis, be accepted as *true* in the metaphysical sense of standing closer to the absolute, the world *an sich*.³⁴ As such, for Sellars, any resolution to late-modernity's metaphysical *aporia* will only ensue once science has been perfected to such an extent that—as he states in another key article, *Empiricism and the Philosophy of Mind*—"the scientific image of the world replaces the common sense picture; that is when the scientific account of what there is supersedes the descriptive manifest ontology of everyday life."³⁵ For Sellars, however, this will only occur once the core conceptual elements of the scientific image are synthetically appropriated and incorporated into a new metaphysics that recognizes the significance of the qualitative aspects of perceptual and conceptual modes of consciousness. In this way, for Sellars, any adequate late-modern metaphysics will only emerge once the philosopher finally gives ground and recognizes that "things as they are in themselves are things as an ideal science would find them to be."³⁶

---

32. For Sellars, we might say that the human demand for explanation takes thought beyond the manifest image and ultimately beyond the scientific image as well—for explanatory rationality seems to lead inexorably towards an account of the nature of everything, including an explanation of the possibility of explanation itself.

33. However, in Sellars' view this will only be possible if the "triumphant framework" has evolved in such a way as to produce a metaphysics that, in some sense, at least from the vantage point of the manifest image, *works*, that is, allows for the totality of fundamental human concerns, concerns that always require that concept of personhood, to play their part in how the world as a whole is understood. Or in other words, for Sellars, the resolution of the clash of the images requires that the demand for both ethical personal existence and general forms of theoretical explanation be accommodated into a new metaphysical scheme that gives theoretical support to the practical and practical significance to the theoretical.

34. Sellars, "Scientific Image," 36. This is Sellars' neo-Peircean aspect.

35. Ibid., "Philosophy of Mind," 302.

36. Ibid., "Concept of Person," 240.

## Sellars' Kantian Metaphysics of Science

Thus, according to Sellars, there is a route out from Kant that brings "the metaphysical" back into play through a recognition that it was he who first attempted to negotiate a more harmonious conceptual relationship between modern scientific and traditional metaphysical schemes. As Sellars puts it, "in their most general aspect both his problems and our perplexities spring from the attempt to take both man and science seriously."[37] Thus for Sellars, philosophers today need to again begin with Kant's most basic metaphysical problem—the problem of the precise nature of the relationship between the phenomenal and noumenal dimensions of reality—and understand that Kant could not have conceived of the way that modern science allows for "a theoretical understanding of the noumenon."[38] Thus for Sellars, Kant sets out the metaphysical problem that science poses vis-à-vis ordinary human life clearly, even though his "transcendental resolution" to this problem was metaphysically suspect. However, although Sellars urges contemporary philosophers to recognize "the astonishing extent to which in epistemology and metaphysics the fundamental themes of Kant's philosophy contain the truth of variations we now hear on every side," he also urges them to appreciate that the metaphysics of contemporary science demands that they take a step beyond Kant.[39] In this way, Sellars views Kant as the first modern philosopher to strive to preserve a strong metaphysical notion of personhood in a modernity increasingly dominated by scientific metaphysical facticity, but he is also a philosopher

---

37. Ibid., "Science and Metaphysics," 1. In Kant's case, the Newtonian world of forces and the ethical of world of persons; in our case, the post-Einstenian world of particles and processes and the social world of persons in communities.

38. For Sellars, if philosophy is to begin the necessary task of accounting for the ontological split in late-modern worldhood—a split that, as we have seen, "worlds the late modern world" in two mutually antagonistic ways—we are forced to set off on a what he terms a "slow climb back to Kant" with a view to re-appropriating and re-articulating his core problematic for a new, more theoretical, scientific age. See Sellars, "Science and Metaphysics," 29.

39. Sellars, "Science and Metaphysics," x. Sellars engages with Kantian philosophy with the avowed aim of amending and adjusting its basic philosophical vision in order to meet the demands of an intellectual landscape that has been radically altered by the "progress" of scientific modernity. Sellars' "quibble" with Kantianism is this: how can science correct the limitations of ordinary conceptualities if it remains, ontologically, tied to the same phenomenal realm that supports them? More specifically, how can the realities postulated by theoretical science trump those of more mundane "human" contexts if, epistemologically, the former presupposes the latter?

who misunderstood the metaphysical powers of modern science.⁴⁰ In this regard, Kant's separation of "the phenomenal" from "the noumenal" should be viewed as a (first) "defensive" philosophical move aimed at protecting the metaphysics of the manifest image from eliminative attack. For Sellars, however, the epistemic limits that Kant placed on the noumenal can no longer be sustained given that the scientific image, as a space of explanatory reason, has proved its historical metaphysical importance by an on-going and partially successful conceptualization the noumenal realm (of *ding an sich*).⁴¹ Thus today, both epistemologically and ontologically, modernity has undergone a profound entanglement of the noumenal within the phenomenal, because contemporary science has brought the noumenal "out into the open" of theoretical reflection. As such, for Sellars, every late-modern mode of theoretical explanation—and epistemology more generally—is now enmeshed within a set of deeper ontological questions; or as he put it "[e]pistemology cannot be severed from ontology as with a knife."⁴² Thus a key aspect of Sellars' metaphysics is that our basic

40. Some contemporary metaphysicians agree with the general tenor of this view—see Meillassoux, *After Finitude*—but view Kant as very much the historical villain of the history of modern metaphysics, in that he is seen as having given up the possibility of genuine metaphysical insight into the nature of the real in order to preserve the coherence and integrity of the early-modern epistemological project. Meillassoux, like Sellars, recognizes that in modernity philosophers need to acknowledge the importance of science's theoretical grasp on the absolute. However, Meillassoux argues for this in complete isolation from any appreciation of the need for philosophical personalism, something that he believes represents a form of wrong-headed "correlationism." As such, his philosophy amounts to an attempt to theologize science—something that may well be possible, but not without the necessary prior metaphysical work. Meillassoux needs to read Sellars and read him carefully in this regard.

41. As such, for Sellars, the manifest realm, the realm that continues to provide the forms of observational data deemed to be necessary for the development of scientific knowledge, is not simply a basic epistemological foundation for all knowledge claims—both manifest and scientific—but rather amounts to a distinct ontological realm in its own right; one whose foundational epistemic role is now being challenged because of the contemporary scientific theorist's ability to *posit* another, "epistemologically superior," ontological realm (often simply by theoretical fiat, that typically stands in only a very weak epistemic relation to the experiential immediacy of the manifest realm). However, I would argue, both Kant and Sellars were mistaken in equating noumena with "things in themselves." Their mistake stems from their rationalist philosophical sympathies and their commitment to an absolute conception of knowledge that led them to identify knowledge and truth. In this regard it is important today to distinguish questions of knowledge from questions of truth, but without succumbing to the temptation to conceive of the former in instrumentalist terms. Science deals with knowledge, philosophers and theologians deal with truth; we understand the truth; we grasp it and appreciate it. The same cannot be said of knowledge.

42. Sellars, "Being Known," 76. This clearly involves of rejection of Kant's scheme/

phenomenological access to the world, sensation and observation, can no longer function as the foundation for scientific knowledge, as scientific theory has now become uncoupled from them rendering the precise epistemological status of sensation and observation a matter of new *metaphysical* concern.[43] In other words, modern epistemologies must be seen not only as the expressions of a very particular metaphysics in their own right, but also of one now rendered increasingly anachronistic given the explanatory powers of the scientific image, an image that proceeds via ontological "posits" rather than epistemological "correlations" with empirical phenomena.[44] In other words, given the manifest explanatory successes of modern science's theoretical claims on the world, Sellars believes we must finally recognize that science articulates an alternative metaphysics in its own right, one that denies the ontological significance of everything "manifest" and is "much closer," in spirit if not in letter, to the world *an sich*.

---

content distinction. For Sellars, content is in part, although not in its entirety, given by the scheme itself. The metaphysical implications here should be apparent. For Sellars, the world *is itself* conceptual but the conceptual is not a product of "an individual mind." The barely submerged Hegelian content of Sellars' philosophy should be apparent here too.

43. In this way, Sellars' metaphysics provides us with a way beyond the recently fashionable, but ultimately philosophically trite, "post-modern" arguments referred to above that have concluded that modern science's epistemological project should be "unmasked" or "deconstructed" as simply another set of instrumental discourses or cultural practices. In Sellars' philosophy—given the rational evolution of science, from its primordial origins in an animistic conception of the "world as person" to its contemporary status as a "world of micro-physical processes" that is now striving to achieve a final cultural-metaphysical hegemony—the basic reality orientation of scientific metaphysics cannot be in doubt. It is simply that scientific metaphysics as it currently exists as a historical formation cannot be viewed in realist terms.

44. In this way, and against what has now become the received view of his work, I will argue that Sellars' philosophy rearticulates a philosophical concern that he shared with his "critical realist" father Roy Wood Sellars; the question of what it means to be human in the age when ontological forms of authority reside within paradigmatic theoretical claims made by institutionalized science. However, it is important to point out that Sellars was not a philosopher who believed that the older humanist culture could be trashed in the name of a newly ascendant scientific metaphysics. The view of Sellars as an "eliminative materialist," a view that has become something of an orthodox reading itself in recent years, is simply false. Sellars did *not* believe that scientific metaphysics could eliminate humanist metaphysics' cultural common sense at all; because the particulate metaphysics underpinning contemporary science was simply not up to the task of accounting for the qualitative character of first person phenomenological states and the necessity to posit the existence of persons in all matters of practical concern.

Thus for Sellars, the growing recognition of the ontological significance the worlds postulated by late-modern science demands that we *ontologize* Kant much more explicitly (and in so doing free him from the forms of skeptical empiricism and critical rationalism that tied him to the anti-metaphysical dispensation that went on to define much of the post-Kantian philosophical agenda).[45] For Sellars, with a nod here to Hegel, any resolution to Kant's metaphysical problem must be radically historicized—effectively deferred until the moment when an "ideal science" emerges with the requisite metaphysical vision and conceptual powers to explain the existence of the manifest *tout court*; that is, account for the existence of a baseline facticity of *both* persons *and* particles; practical *and* theoretical reason; qualitative consciousness *and* affective embodiment, and so on. More specifically, according to Sellars, it is only when the scientific image can explain not only why there are such things *as persons*, but also find room to explain why the world has to be seen from the *point of view of persons* if it is not to be deemed "fundamentally irrelevant," that we will be able to develop an adequate synoptic metaphysics of the late-modern whole. Or in other words, only when we develop a metaphysics of science from *the personal point of view* will the scientific image be in a position to replace the manifest image as a metaphysics that could both

---

45. More generally, what Sellars is offering us is a rather sophisticated neo-Kantian way of analyzing the metaphysical problem of late modernity in terms of two competing *worldviews*. In the twentieth century it seems as though the natural sciences broke away from the metaphysics of the manifest image in such a way that any orthodox Kantian is caught in a double bind—as science creates for itself a new and radical autonomy with respect to the phenomenal realm, then, in Kantian terms, it loses the conditions of possibility for its knowledge claims. In the twentieth century, science, when viewed in terms of Enlightenment philosophies, thus ceases to be knowledge! Defenders of Enlightenment could be tempted here to follow Habermas and the Frankfurt School and look for sources of "true rationality" elsewhere: in hermeneutics or in the aesthetic. However, as modern science represents the apotheosis of modern rationality, an orthodox Enlightenment rationalist (as in many ways Sellars remains) will feel uneasy about this. In response, we might say that Sellars wants to keep his Kantian cake and to eat it as well—but he does this by recognizing, quite rightly in my view, that what we have today are two radically different and probably incompatible rationalities. Modern reason, we can say, has essentially "split" in late-modernity—not into its dark dialectical other in the way of the Frankfurt School but rather *into two* equal but opposite rationalities: one a scientific rationality of dialectic of postulation and explanation, and the other a practical rationality of personal and social engagement. This splitting of reason into the theoretical and the practical-hermeneutic cannot, however, be resolved by viewing the former as merely an instrumental rationality of prediction and control. What is needed is new conception of reason (and reality) that combines both the theoretical and the practical, the experiential and the particulate.

explain and *guide* modern existence.[46] In this case, a new scientific metaphysics would have emerged, one that could allow for the development of a scientific conceptuality that dovetails with the wider democratic demand that scientific theories *make sense* at the level of both persons and communities. In short, for Sellars we will only be able to justify a full-fledged metaphysics once the scientific image *personalizes*—and socializes—itself so as to become comprehensible to both persons and communities.[47] Sellars puts this in this way:

> the conceptual framework of persons is not something that needs to be *reconciled* with the scientific image, but rather something to be *joined* to it. Thus to complete the scientific image we need to enrich it not with more ways of saying what is the case, but with the language of community and individual intentions, so that by construing the actions we intend to do and the circumstances in which we intend to do them in scientific terms, we directly relate the world as conceived by scientific theory to our purposes, and make it our world and no longer an alien appendage in which we do our living.[48]

Here, we can see the broad thrust of Sellars' reformist metaphysical project in clear relief. For him, if it is to fulfill its "historical destiny" as a

---

46. Sellars, like Hegel, understood modern philosophy to be a dynamic phenomenon determined in the last instance by specific kinds of conceptual contradiction. In this way, Hegelian influences are apparent throughout the entire corpus of Sellars' writing. In *Philosophy and the Scientific Image*, he develops a "Hegelianesque" account of the evolution of scientific objectivity from its origins in the animistic immediacy of an original and primordial "manifest" conceptual framework to its current position as a potential successor to that framework (and thus, Sellars' commitment to key themes in Hegelian philosophy transcends the similarity, noted by Sellars himself, that his critique of the attempt to found acts of knowing upon a conception of "the given" amounts to a "Hegelian meditation"). Moreover, in this way Sellars' thinking about science orbits around some very general phenomenological concerns. This is the direct result of biographical influences upon Sellars' thinking. Sellars studied in France in the 1930s and was exposed to the ideas of Hegel and Husserl during his time there. However, the biggest influence on his thinking was the work of his father, Roy Wood Sellars, the Marxist Humanist philosopher whose main concern was with reconciling the idea of science with the possibility of freedom—see Sellars, "Autobiographical Reflections." Thus although Sellars drew upon the insights of a varied selection of the ideas of different philosophers and philosophical traditions—phenomenology, Thomism, twentieth-century logical empiricism, American pragmatism, and Wittgensteinian philosophy of language to name but five—it is clear that Sellars conceived of himself as a metaphysician who straddles the old rationalist/empiricist divide.

47. "The social" being "the personal" expressed in a wider communicative mode.

48. Sellars, "Scientific Image," 40.

final and completed metaphysics, modern science requires a transformation of its basic conceptuality in way that could render theoretical discourses capable of hermeneutic appropriation in terms of the personalist (and communitarian) metaphysics of the manifest image—so that, in this way, the scientific image can begin to assist the lives of modern persons living together.[49] Late-modern forms of alienation from the worlds of science are thus, in Sellarsian philosophy, viewed as the result of the former's uncoupling from the traditional metaphysics of "persons in communities" implicit within all forms of ordinary action and interaction, to the extent that the task for the contemporary metaphysician is no longer that of an under-laborer to the modern scientific project, but one of facilitating a new entry into a new scientific language—one that allows science to be reincorporated back into, and understandable in terms of, the realm of everyday, "personalist," existence. For Sellars, we might say that scientific metaphysics must never be allowed to fully "colonize the lifeworld"—to lean on Habermas' perennially useful philosophical term of art—but rather the very reverse, in that it must find a way of "rationalizing the lifeworld" while at the same time retaining the manifest dimensions of objects, persons, and events. (Can we conceive, we might ask after Sellars, of a "rational animism"; one that gives "ontological priority" to the idea of the person in all interpretations, whatever the extension of this concept might be in a completed scientific image, but in way that avoids the errors of "primitive animism" that viewed *everything as intentional.*) Although it is difficult to conceive—at least from our contemporary vantage points—what such a version of the scientific image might look like, clearly it must, of metaphysical necessity, express a form of conceptuality that appears significantly re-enchanted and re-politicized from the point of view of our late-modern understanding of science. This suggests not only a less mathematicized science but also a science less hostile to the idea of the person and to "the personalist principle" that views all personal existence as *essentially* related to ethical and political concerns. Metaphysics, we might say, must begin to allow the world to be understood as a set of fundamental processes within which the personalist point of view is legitimated as primary, even if even this point of view is only applicable to a narrower range of entities.[50] This is not simply to call for a popular

---

49. It is important to point out that for Sellars the person is always a *socialized* person—it is not the individual of classical liberal theory, for example. There is a hidden dialectic of "I" and "We" in Sellars' philosophy to the extent that persons as such always exist collectively as well as individually.

50. That is, science must articulate itself at the level of an enlightened common

science, or for a changed public understanding of science, but rather amounts to a speculative demand for a *radically different conception of science itself*, a science that is able to *communicate its ontology* in relation to ordinary modes of conceptuality in ways that were formerly achieved only by religious discourses (with their historic commitment to a metaphysical personalism). In the end, this may mean the collapse of science back into "theology" and for theology to begin the process of accepting not only the utility but the essential truth of science.

## Whitehead's Organismic Resolution

This brings me to the second response to the metaphysical problem of late-modernity—that offered by the self-proclaimed "process metaphysician" A. N. Whitehead. In a series of books—but especially in his *magnum opus, Process and Reality*—Whitehead offers us a rather different metaphysical resolution to the clash of the images outlined by Sellars, one that asks for a radical reform to the metaphysics of the manifest image in the light of recent theoretical developments in physics, but more especially within theoretical biology. This metaphysics will, in his view, necessarily be "radically revisionary" with respect to the traditional personalist metaphysics of everyday life because, for Whitehead, the philosopher must recognize that when faced with the metaphysical significance of late-modern science a radical rejection of all forms of enlightened common sense is required in a "transcendence of what is obvious," especially of the subject-predicate logic that sustained traditional metaphysics. Thus, like Sellars, Whitehead recognizes that a clash of doctrines represents an opportunity for creative innovation at the level of concepts. However, in this regard, for Whitehead the clash of the images can only be resolved by means of an imaginative reworking of the basic conceptuality of the *manifest image* by using contemporary scientific theory as an analogy (and not, as with Sellars, a conceptual reworking of the scientific image using the manifest image as an analogy).[51] More specifically, for Whitehead, the bridging philosophy allows us to begin to fuse Sellars' images into a new synoptic metaphysical vision in what he terms a "philosophy of organism,"

---

sense that is always orientated towards a *phronesis*, a personalized way of living that allows individuals to achieve their shared projects through the incorporation of scientific ontologies into our folk-psychological and folk-sociological life (one immediately thinks here of the recent metaphysical innovations proposed recently by Bruno Latour in contemporary sociology).

51. See Whitehead, *Process*, xii.

*a universal metaphysics biology*. This is a philosophy that views all reality as creaturely and all experience as the basic product of the creaturely-affective existence (and here Whitehead attempts to resolve the clash of the images in terms three unifying biological concepts—creativity, energy, and affect). As such, Whitehead offers us a biological re-articulation of the manifest image in terms of a vitalist metaphysics within which the key manifest concept is shifted from "rational autonomous personhood" to "affective creaturely existence." In this way, in a shift from physics to physiology, Whitehead proposes a radical dissolution of the comfortable materialist metaphysical schemes that upheld the scientific materialism of the nineteenth century (and thus his metaphysics is not a version of "scientism," at least not as it has been traditionally conceived), especially those that associated materiality with "inert mechanism." As such, Whitehead stands opposed to Sellars in that his metaphysics is an attempt to revise the conceptuality of the manifest image *from within* in a way that allows the manifest to be understood *scientifically*; as much more than an array discrete subjects and substances, but as a bio-vital world of constantly created (concreted) creatures (even atoms must be viewed as creatures, according to Whitehead). Importantly, for Whitehead, the human creature, unlike a person, is not a logically unified subject at all, but rather a macro-event comprised of discrete micro-occasions, out of which the creature emerges as a "created concretion" of more fundamental creative processes. An idea of the personal is retained here, but only as an *effect*—as a human moment in "the shaped togetherness of things"—and thus here we have a much weaker conception of personhood that is much more closely tied to the body (and therefore Whitehead's understanding of the person is one that is significantly less autonomous, especially in contrast to the Kantian one. For this reason Whitehead's conception is more "early modern," more Spinozist).[52]

Thus in opposition to Sellars, Whitehead's is very much a metaphysics that advocates a biological recoding of the manifest image (supplemented by a quasi-theological metaphysics of creation) in way that significantly reduces the autonomy of personhood and redefines the person as an "ontological product" (rather than an active agentive producer). Here a particulate ontology and a scientific notion of process are retained, but in conjunction with a neo-vitalist idea where the basic atomic substrate possesses are the bio-affective powers and liabilities—what Whitehead terms "prehensions." It is these, he believes, that facilitate the coalescence of

---

52. Whitehead, *Adventures*, 216.

"primate" micro processes into "real" macroscopic entities (in Whitehead's case the key fundamental particle in this regard is the living cell and not the atom or sub-atom of twentieth-century physics; it is this that provides the primary analogy for all being). Thus for Whitehead, every manifest object is in fact more than an entity, it is an occasion that exhibits itself as process (a "becomingness") that operates according to an underlying vitalist principle of concretion and cosmic limitation.[53] For this reason, against Sellars' personalist metaphysics of "man-in-the-world," Whitehead offers us the much more limited metaphysical anthropology of "man in one moment."[54] Overall, we might say, the conceptual shift advocated by Whitehead is a shift from a manifest metaphysics of rational personhood to a quasi-scientific metaphysics of affective creatureliness, where the creature is conceived as a composite occasion "eventually emergent" out of wider sets of more basic bio-cosmic processes.[55] In a certain sense, creatureliness represents a radical diminution of the status of the human within the cosmological order (a diminution that is in line with the anti-humanist logic of modern science more generally). The manifest world is thoroughly colonized here, but not perniciously—as in contemporary eliminative materialism—in that a weaker image of the personhood is retained (as creature). But it must be pointed out, again, that creatures are not persons—there is a logical distinction to be made here, as one can be a creature but lack the qualities and virtues required on personhood.[56] Although all creatures must possess creatureliness and thus, in a way, a certain level of intentionality—and thus mindedness—clearly they need not possess the higher level forms of cognitive functioning, such as plans and dreams, that characterize persons (and thus creatures do not *necessarily* deserve entry into our ethical communities). Moreover, in Whitehead's account, as there is no existent as such apart from as an emergent epiphenomenon, the manifest image is, in the last analysis, reduced to the level of pure event-experience, something that, if read in strict metaphysical

53. Ibid., 218.

54. See Whitehead, *Symbolism*, 27. We might say the subject/person is reduced to series of cosmic affective events in Whitehead's philosophy.

55. In many ways, Whitehead's philosophy is a metaphysical variation on the old positivist idea that material objects are constructed out of "sense data," albeit here the process of construction is understood metaphysically rather than "logically."

56. The choice between these metaphysical schemes is not simply a matter for "logic"—it is also, ultimately, an ethical and a political one. For "creatureliness" in many ways implies passivity, a lack of political purpose and perhaps even an anti-intellectualism that would push thought in the direction of (reactionary) disavowal of both human freedom and the rational capacities associated with human agency.

terms, implies a Humean dissolution of the subjective point of view.[57] In its attempt to retain a strict empiricist starting point for thought, in Whitehead's metaphysics the manifest image is not preserved but reduced, relationally, to an emergent phenomenon that exists as only as a vitalist chaotic "ontological democracy" within a wider pre-personal creative process. As he states, the true reality of late modern life is that "we find ourselves in a buzzing world, amid a democracy of fellow creatures; whereas under some disguise or other, modern philosophy can only introduce us to solitary substances, each enjoying an illusory experience."[58]

Thus for Whitehead, everything, from atoms to persons, is essentially creaturely and creative and for him this is the answer to the metaphysical problem of late-modernity: a radically depersonalized conception of existence. In this regard, a key issue for Whitehead is how to understand what the ultimate fundamental creative processes—and the "fundamental creatures"—might be. What is the metaphysical cement that holds this creaturely universe together? Interestingly, the key concept here, in Whitehead's view, is "*energy*" (showing his debt to conceptual developments that followed in the wake Einsteinian theories of relativity in the twentieth century, and also revealing the extent to which the "philosophy of organism" is complicated by his attempt to reduce the manifest image to a metaphysics of the quantum). In this way, for Whitehead, in order to resolve the clash of the images contemporary philosophers will have to recognize that, in the end, both processes and persons, quanta and qualia, are manifestations of a more basic kind of bio-energy; or as he puts it, "the energetic activity considered in physics is the emotional intensity entertained in life."[59] Here the creature is simply the occasion through which the creative powers of cosmic bio-energy express themselves as a singular concrete objective manifestation. The metaphysics of everyday life, with its persons and things, thus becomes conceived as radical illusion—the only real at the level of the everyday is the reality of experience, a reality that is in many ways the thinnest of beer when conceived in metaphysical terms.

---

57. According to Whitehead, after the nineteenth century, science took charge of "materialistic nature," philosophy "cogitating minds." See Whitehead, *Modern World*, 180. Metaphysics today, however, needs to challenge this distinction; especially as it has supported the splitting of modern thought into psychology and epistemology. Psychology, the idea of a "science of the mind," is likely to be the first casualty of the new metaphysics, as the above analysis should have demonstrated.

58. Whitehead, *Process*, 78.

59. Ibid., *Modern World*, 96.

## Modernity, Science, and the Return to Kant

Thus for Whitehead, the late-modern absolute is understood in terms of a metaphysical energetics of "vibratory streaming" that binds everything together into something like a unity.[60] This may seem like a wild metaphysical claim, and one is tempted here to reach (again) for the Kantian scissors—but we should recognize that, in the end, this metaphysics is clearly the logical consequence of contemporary theoretical physics. Although philosophers have had very little to say about the status of energy as a philosophical concept, there is clearly significant mileage to the idea that both manifest quanta and qualia are manifestations of cosmic energy (as some aspects of psychoanalytic theory, especially those of a Reichian variety, have also claimed).[61] Could this very simple move resolve the clash of the images—and resolve the problem of the metaphysical problem of later modernity? Clearly, any metaphysics of energy represents a radical rejection of Kantianism, in that for Kant the basis of true understanding was the personalist notion of "I think" (and not "it vibrates").[62] Whatever we make of this claim, in one way it must be acknowledged that it is Whitehead who allows philosophy to begin the process of finally engaging with the metaphysics of the post-Einsteinian world. This has yet to happen, and so Whitehead's is a philosophy that speaks to late-modern metaphysical problem in a highly pertinent way.

However, things are not so simple. Overall, bringing Sellars back into play here, it seems that what we have before us today are two resolutions to the metaphysical problem of late-modernity: one, a "personalist science," where metaphysics becomes a revisionary instrument through which philosophy renders science livable for both persons and communities; and the other, a more radical revision to the manifest image that allows for a cosmological resolution to the clash in a universal and creative bio-energetics. We might think that theologians would prefer the latter route; after all, it works with an idea of creation, as well as the inherent creative power of all forms of life (and amounts, as Whitehead himself recognized, to a call for a new religious reformation). There are many theological Whiteheadians, but no—at least to my knowledge, speculative materialism not

---

60. Ibid., 46.

61. See Caygill, "Life and Energy."

62. Reichian new age energy mysticism aside, it is hard to understand how thought could be an expression of vibrations ("desire" could be accounted for in this way, but not "belief" as beliefs possess content in a way that desires do not).

withstanding—theological Sellarsians.[63] Moreover, Whitehead's essentially Platonic vision may suggest that he is the quintessential modern Christian metaphysician, especially through his advocacy of a "metaphysics of harmony" where everything participates in a modern cosmological drama of divine creative compassion

However, in many ways, Sellars' Kantian resolution might prove to be a more attractive proposition for both the contemporary philosopher and the contemporary theologian—not only because of its commitment to metaphysics of agency, but also, more importantly, because it represents an attempt to resolve the clash of the images through a personalist recalibration of science, showing the extent to which the personalist principle, the metaphysical basis of Judeo-Christian religious theory and practice, although redundant when viewed in purely scientific terms, is *practically* ineliminable from the point of view of *life*, even for the theoretical scientist, whose reflections are necessarily the result of the practical engagements of (experimenting) persons.[64] Moreover, from a Christian point of view, if we accept, with Robert Spaemann, that the main problem with late-modernity's intellectual cultures is that they have denigrated the notion of the person, to the extent that the main philosophical task today is to reclaim and defend notions of personhood as both intrinsically valuable and as the highest mode of earthly existence, then it is Sellars and not Whitehead who speaks most directly to those with orthodox Christian interests and concerns. For if we are, as Christianity proclaims, born as creatures who are "not yet fully persons," to the extent that the achievement of personhood becomes the ultimate task of the human creature,

---

63. When seen in terms of a metaphysics of creation, we could view the manifest world as a "created concretion" that allows itself to be understood as such to at least one type of creature (to the extent that we might say that creation allows itself to be known, but only to those who belong to it most intimately). In this way, Christ could be viewed as the essential "personification" of the manifest image itself—the metaphysics of the manifest made flesh; *the true (most real) person*. I will leave it to others more knowledgeable than me to tease out the appropriate theological connections here.

64. Creatureliness may prove to be the more useful concept if theologians wish to wrestle with the philosophy and wider intellectual significance of Darwinism (and maybe, with Whitehead, biology more generally); but it provides little guidance when it comes to questions of history and politics (and the way that we should engage with modernity itself). Here, a very different metaphysics comes into play. Although progress can easily be read in terms of creative providence, it is not clear how we can engage in the "drama of the modern" without conceiving of ourselves as "self-conscious persons." Moreover, Whitehead's philosophy, in political terms, represents a pagan cosmo-political response to modernity that is in many ways at odds with the Judeo-Christian politics of emancipation.

then we are forced to accept that, metaphysically, there is more to the human than "mere creature." If this is accepted, then in the context of late modernity, the theologian needs to find a way towards an acceptance of the "truth" of the scientific image while continuing to defend the claim that personhood is metaphysically ineliminable, at least if we want to a retain an idea of a significant and livable life. Therefore, in a certain sense it is the Sellarsian option that lends itself to an orthodox Christian project of finding "another modernity," one that preserves the idea of "primordial personality" in upholding the significance of personhood in the conceptuality in and through which we have traditionally lived, but without rejecting the scientific image as the mere instrument of personhood. This is a modernity that must now proceed via a *rapprochement* of philosophy and science in a way that allows the discourse of both to converge on a new metaphysics. By these lights, Whitehead's metaphysics, in the end, does little to help us deal with the clash of the images as a real and pressing late-modern issue—and, we might even say, *lived* problem—and therefore it is the Sellarsian route that offers philosophy, theology, and everything else with a personalist leaning a way back to a sympathetic re-engagement with the metaphysics of the scientific image itself. As a result it is perhaps Sellars who provides us with an intellectual pointer towards a theologically informed and reformed metaphysics of science (a conception of science that is needed now, as we stand on the cusp of a new positivist era, more than ever). For contemporary theoretical science, it seems, has again forced upon us a Kantian recognition that, with respect to scientific modernity, there is always going to be a radical and rival metaphysics to that espoused by today's scientists: the ancient one associated with the autonomous actions of persons—a metaphysics that cannot be ignored on pain of thought's and life's irrelevance.[65]

## Bibliography

Apel, Karl O. *Towards a Transformation of Philosophy*. London: Routledge and Kegan Paul, 1972.
Brassier, Ray. *Nihil Unbound: Enlightenment and Extinction*. London: Palgrave Macmillan, 2008.
Caygill, Howard. "Life and Energy." *Theory, Culture and Society* 24.6 (2007) 19–28.
Dennett, Daniel. "Wondering Where the Yellow Went." *The Monist* 64 (1981) 102–8.
Eddington, Arthur. *The Nature of the Physical World*. New York: University Press, 1929.

---

65. We might say that for us it is a "scientized" Kant that speaks to us more directly than a "positivist Plato."

———. *The Philosophy of Physical Science*. Cambridge: Cambridge University Press, 1939.

Meillassoux, Quentin. *After Finitude: An Essay in the Necessity of Contingency*. London: Continuum, 2009.

Olafson, Frederick, A. *Naturalism and the Human Condition: Against Scientism*. London: Routledge, 2001.

Seibt, Joanna. "Analysis without Synopsis Must be Blind: Obituary for Wilfred Sellars." *Erkenntnis* 33 (1990) 5–8.

Sellars, Wilfred. "Autobiographical Reflections." In *Action, Knowledge and Reality: Critical Studies in Honor of Wilfred Sellars*, edited by Hector-Neri Casteneda, 277–93. Indianapolis: Bobbs-Merril, 1975.

———. "Being and Being Known." In *Science, Perception and Reality*, 41–59. London: Routledge, Kegan and Paul, 1963.

———. "Empiricism and the Philosophy of Mind." In *Science, Perception and Reality*, 127–96. London: Routledge, Kegan and Paul, 1963.

———. "The Language of Theories." In *Science Perception and Reality*, 106–26. London: Routledge, Kegan and Paul, 1963.

———. "Metaphysics and the Concept of a Person." In *Essays in Philosophy and Its History*, 214–44. Dordrecht, Holland: Reidel, 1974.

———. "Phenomenalism." In *Science Perception and Reality*, 60–105. London: Routledge, Kegan and Paul, 1963.

———. "Philosophy and the Scientific Image of Man." In *Science, Perception and Reality*, 1–40. London: Routledge, Kegan and Paul, 1963.

———. *Science and Metaphysics: Variations on Kantian Themes*. Atascadero, CA: Ridgeview, 1992.

Stebbing, Susan, L. *Philosophy and the Physicists*. London: Methuen, 1937.

Whitehead, Alfred. N. *Adventures of Ideas*. New York: Free, 1934.

———. *Process and Reality*. New York: Harper and Row, 1929.

———. *Science and the Modern World*. London: Free Association, 1985.

———. *Symbolism: Its Meaning and Effect*. 1927. Reprint. New York: Fordham University Press, 1985.

# 8

## Taking Life out of Nature
### Jewish Messianic Vitalism and the Problem of Denaturalization

*Agata Bielik-Robson*

~

"Living according to Nature" means actually the same as "living according to Life"—how could you do differently? ... Let us beware of saying that death is opposed to life. The living is only a form of what is dead, and a very rare form.

NIETZSCHE, *BEYOND GOOD AND EVIL*, 7

I have set before you life and death: choose life.

DEUTERONOMY 30:19

THE AIM OF MY essay will be to focus on the problem of denaturalization as the main conceptual axis that organizes the crucial difference between *Shem* and *Yafet*, Jewish and Greek thought. While the Jewish mode of thinking relies on the affirmation of the denaturalizing process that constitutes the very gist of exodus, the progressive exit of man out of the house of natural bondage—the Greek paradigm, which, paraphrasing Rosenzweig, spreads from "Ionia to Jena, and beyond," approaches the idea of man's maladaptation to nature (*phusis*) with suspicion and appears to be driven by a nostalgic, regressive ideal of renaturalization.

Yet, the issue becomes more complex and the differences more dialectically intertwined when we juxtapose these two attitudes toward denaturalization with two, Jewish and Greek, concepts of life and attempt to translate this relation into the idiom of modern vitalism. The case of Nietzsche is particularly interesting here, for his ultimately modern "philosophy of life" is visibly torn between two irreconcilable perspectives: the tragic and the messianic. While the tragic perspective encapsulates life within the natural cycle of life-towards-death, where two powers—of becoming and perishing—check themselves in a perfect balance, the messianic perspective, operating with the promise of "more life," sports an image of a denaturalized life-against-death, which manages to escape the natural equilibrium and create (I emphasize the word *create*) a new form of living that no longer obeys the laws of nature.

According to the classical definition of Aristotle, *phusis* is a system of all beings that fall under the inexorable rule of cyclical alternation between *genesis* and *phtora*, generation and corruption: the rule which knows no exception. And while the conception of nature and natural laws will be changing during the intellectual history of the West, one general criterion defining the natural mode of existence will always remain: the idea of "natural necessity" which links birth and death in form of an insoluble knot. Whether as pre-Socratic *phusis* or as scholastic *natura*, nature is always defined in the light of this mysterious ambivalence: "What causes birth tends to cause death too."[1]

This necessitarian "secret" of nature is made absolutely clear in Nietzsche's vision of the eternal return of the same. Nietzsche indeed puts his finger on the natural *transcendentale*, when in *Gay Science* he openly opposes the changeable laws of nature and the unchangeable necessities of nature, and says that we must "beware of saying that there are laws in nature. There are only necessities."[2] It is the same fundamental necessity, as opposed to minor laws, that underlies the vision of life as an inexorable

1. The best speculative account of the history of the concept of *phusis* is given by Pierre Hadot in his book *The Veil of Isis*, where he begins with Heraclitus, goes through Schiller and Nietzsche, and ends with Merleau-Ponty. The main subject of the essay is the "secret of nature" which "loves to hide." See Hadot, *Veil* , 1; i.e., the mysterious bond of inner natural necessities that organize every individual "growth" into a system of becoming and perishing. Hadot thus interprets the famous aphorism of Heraclitus—*phusis kruptesthai philei*—as "what is born tends to disappear" or "what is born wants to die." Hadot, *Veil*, 11.

2. Nietzsche, *Gay Science*, 110.

*Sein-zum-Tode*, first in German *Lebensphilosophie* and then in Heidegger, who will explicitly resume the pre-Socratic notion of *phusis* in his metaphor of *die Erde*, the power of Being responsible for ruling the cyclical movement of beings, emerging from and disappearing into the dark abyss of *Seyn*. This natural *transcendentale* always implies cycle, repetition, immanent self-enclosure, and—last, but not least—the guiding role of death, which, in Anaximandrian formulation, constitutes the "just measure" of every life, and as such runs the timing of its sequence from birth to decay. It doesn't matter, therefore, if the post-Nietzschean Deleuze declares nature to be a "lawless" realm of the spontaneous hylozoic generation of beings, because Nietzsche himself had already very soberly set the limits for such a dubious emancipatory enterprise by laying bare the ultimately necessitarian form of all possible immanence; nature may not have well defined laws, but it nonetheless is governed by necessity.[3]

This transcendental concept of *phusis* designates a paradigmatic point of reference for the whole Western philosophical tradition. But it is also a paradigmatic point of reference for the Jewish critique of this tradition, which they rightly perceive as the very gist of *Hokhmah Yevanit*, "the wisdom of the Greeks": indeed, as Rosenzweig put it, spreading "from Ionia to Jena." The fateful infatuation of philosophy with nature becomes a frequent target of many polemical interventions of Jewish modern thinkers who tend to perceive nature as a homeostatic isolated system operating with the economic minimum of energy, where all powers keep themselves in mutual check. For Scholem, Taubes, Benjamin, Adorno, and (last but not least) Harold Bloom—nature is simply "boring": it is a dullest and least inventive form of minimal existence that merely "piles life upon life" and allows for no true creation, stifled in advance by the principle of balance

---

3. The rest of Nietzsche's anti-theological diatribe from *Gay Science* goes as follows: "there is no one who commands, no one who obeys, no one who transgresses. Once you know that there are no purposes, you also now that there is no accident; for only against a world of purpose does the word 'accident' have a meaning. *Let us beware of saying that death is opposed to life.* The living is only a form of what is dead, and a very rare form. *Let us beware of thinking that the world eternally creates new things.* . . . When will all these shadows of god no longer darken us? When will we have completely de-deified nature? When may we begin to naturalize humanity with a pure, newly discovered, newly redeemed nature?" (ibid., my emphasis). Needless to say, this *de-deified* nature, deprived of all features of "creatureliness," becomes immediately once again *divinized* and turned into a necessitarian goddess who rules everything with iron hand of death; this elevation of death to the only "natural necessity" and its instant sacralization is confirmed by Hadot as one of the most ancient religious views of *phusis*, which "loves to cover itself with the veil of death." Hadot, *Veil*, 7.

and compensation.[4] But they do not criticize nature as "enemies of life" or "priestly vengeful spirits," as Nietzsche, Heidegger, or Deleuze would like to dismiss them. Quite the contrary, they criticize nature and praise anti-natural revelation not against, but for the sake of life. For all of them, revelation constitutes a welcome denaturalizing shock that breaks the homeostatic balance of the closed natural system and sets living beings on the move—making thus a much more dynamic use of life, closer to the intent of the initial act of creation. They all depart from the passage from Deuteronomy where God, deceptively simply, says: "I have set before you life and death: choose life."[5] *Choosing life* means here more than just taking the side life in its opposition to death. It means taking life out of the context where life and death lie bound with each other in the secret bond of *phusis*; it means taking life out of nature.[6]

4. The hostility to nature as the least inventive system of beings, deprived of true ethical laws and purpose—just "sitting there," hopelessly and aimlessly—is such a frequent motif in Jewish writings of all ages, from Mishna to Derrida, that it is impossible to give a full account of this position here. I will just illustrate it by two examples of modern Jewish philosophy, especially concerned with the issue of life, namely: Henri Bergson and Hans Jonas. In their philosophy of biology, they both build a clear opposition between two forces of life: the conservative, self-repeating, and inertial system of preservation (which tends towards necessities and laws) and the progressive, innovative force of ongoing creation (which is creation proper, i.e., capable of creating truly new forms, not just forms potentially preexisting). But there is no lofty secret hidden in the former that only sustains the circulation of birth and decay; the mystery now travels on the other side, where the proper *creative evolution* takes place. On this understanding, "nature" as a self-preserving system is nothing but a *tautology*, a boring and not at all mysterious self-evidence of being which, in order to be, must preserve itself in a form of repetition. Hans Jonas says: "The foundation of all order in nature, of any nature at all, lies in the laws of conservation. But these have come to govern because it is only self-conserving reality that conserves itself. This tautology explains the lawfulness of nature as it is given to us: nature itself is already a result of selection, a universal result which then posits rules for further, more specific, and local selections"; Jonas, *Mortality and Morality*, 168.

5. Deut 30:19.

6. This is precisely why in *Occidental Eschatology* Jacob Taubes can define revelation as most of all a "reminder of creation," which throws the human subject out of the rails of his natural slumber, and, accordingly, defines nature as the state of forgetfulness of the creative and revolutionary principle of the beginnings. The same motif can be found in Erich Gutkind, who in his book *Choose Life* nicely summarizes the discursive atmosphere of the group of the German Jewry in between the wars (Landauer, Buber, Bloch, Benjamin) that decided to redefine "philosophically" the main points of the Hebrew Bible, thus steering away from both the Greek conceptuality and the Rabbinic form of Judaism: "The Jewish revolution restores the growth, man's neverending transcendence of himself. Revolution and transcendence are very much akin. The equation: transcendence-revolution may restore both terms to their fullest

## Nietzsche's Modernity

I say that Nietzsche's *Lebensphilosophie* is ultimately modern because it draws on all metaphors of life operative in Western modernity by causing them to clash with one another. What makes Nietzsche paradigmatically modern is precisely this muddled mixture of idioms, which reveals *modernitas* as an epoch in transition, an era of a constant *self-overcoming* (*Selbstüberwindung*). In Nietzsche, we can thus see in its clearest form the modern infatuation with nature as the newly recovered divinity of the benevolent balance of powers, which Enlightenment restored to her cult against the capricious and imbalanced God of Christian nominalism—but we can also see an impatience with this system of natural self-regulation, which leaves no room for life's truly artistic inventiveness, by condemning it to the eternal return of the same. Nature, Life in general, written capital L, is for Nietzsche a goddess of the sacred life-cycle, presiding over the constant hecatomb and renewal in the abundance of generation—but it is also a limit, an impossibility of a true creation, in which Nietzsche, as an Artist, locates his vision of a life properly individuated and fulfilled.

Nietzsche's overinvested, self-contradictory love of nature wants nature to deliver what she cannot deliver: *creation instead of generation*. Where Nietzsche fails most is precisely in his attempt to substitute generative abundance (where life always copies the same, ever recurring paradigm of birth and decay) for creativity (where something truly new appears, discontinuous with the previous set of conditions). Thus, when he makes nature say in *The Zarathustra*—"And this secret did Life herself tell to me. 'Behold,' she said, 'I am *that which must always overcome itself.*'"[7]—he only apparently makes a room for an artistic "invention of the other." In fact, what Nietzsche implies is a typically tragic praise of the *untergehen*, the self-sacrificial dying in the right time—for the sake of Life's allegedly creative force (*schaffende Kraft*) of spitting out new beings: "I would rather go under than renounce this one thing: and verily, where there is going-under and falling of leaves, behold, there life sacrifices itself—for power!"[8] Yet, this *schaffende Kraft* and its vital power is nothing but a generative waste, the same terrible idle squander that abhorred Schopenhauer, and no rhetorical twist on the Schopenhauerian diagnosis, performed by Nietzsche, can disguise its meaningless futility and horror.

---

efficacy; it is a mutual reevaluation"; Gutkind, *Choose Life*, 74.

7. Nietzsche, *Zarathustra*, 99
8. Ibid., 100.

But Nietzsche himself is often more than aware that he is failing in the contest with his teacher, Schopenhauer; especially when he dreams of life's other, more radically creative possibilities: "To live"—he asks dramatically in *Beyond Good and Evil*—"is not that just endeavoring to be otherwise than *this* Nature?"[9] Even Nietzsche, the greatest self-professed naturalist of all times, grants himself the messianic *Schwärmerei* of taking life out of nature, of breaking the iron cage of natural necessities—not against life as such, but for life's sake, for augmenting its vital powers. Yet, his freely chosen "Greek" idiom does not allow him to see this clearly; its gravitational force tends towards seeing life as necessarily coextensive with nature only (*"Living according to Nature* means actually the same as *living according to Life*—how could you do differently?"[10]), and, accordingly, towards seeing every effort of denaturalization (i.e., of taking human existence out of nature) as the act of an ascetic renunciation of life. Either one says Yeah to both powers and necessities of nature ("the power of indifference"[11]), which makes him a vitalist—or one says No to life in its natural form, which immediately makes him an anti-vitalist, a Thanatic "life-denier," or, in Nietzschen words, the "greatest enemy of life, the ascetic priest."

It was precisely against this staple double association of life with nature and denaturalization with life-negating askesis that Jewish thinkers made their greatest critical contribution to late modern thought. Absolutely pioneering in this respect is the work of Walter Benjamin, who openly criticized German followers of Nietzsche, coming under the heading of *Lebensphilosophie*, for their misconception of life and its creative powers. Benjamin's critique of Dilthey—constituting one of the leading motifs of *The Origins of German Tragic Drama*, as well as his early essay "Critique of Violence"—reproaches him for depicting "the creative force of history" (*die Schaffende Kraft der Geschichte*) as nothing else than "the generative force of nature," and thus for deepening the Nietzschean confusion that obfuscates this essential distinction. In championing a different, less naturalistic concept of life, Benjamin draws on the Hebrew sources and introduces a notion alternative to that of nature, namely "creatureliness" (*Kreatürlichkeit*) as a category denoting a special condition of a created, not just generated, life. Contrary to the Greek understanding of *phusis* as the self-regulating totality of "becoming and disappearing," creatureliness is a wider category that allows us to speculate about life outside the

---

9. Nietzsche, *Beyond Good and Evil*, 7.
10. Ibid.
11. Ibid.

confines of the restraining totality nature and under a new light of revelation. But it also allows us to rethink the position of a denaturalized human being, conceived no longer as an "outcast of nature," a "life-denying" being diminished in natural vitality, but rather as, in Benjamin's words, *ein Fürsprech der Kreatur*, a "spokesman of creation," representing for the whole of the living a possibility of another—better, freer, blessed—life.[12] A life according not to the principle of natural generation, but a life according to the principle of creation: the double bind of the creaturely existence, destined not just to be created, but also—to create.

Perhaps, the best way to approach this creaturely concept of life, which struggles against the confines of mere *physicality* and tries to emancipate life from the naturalistic biologism, is to refer to one of the more enigmatic but also potentially very fertile passages in Derrida, who in his commentary on Benjamin's essay "Critique of Violence," defines it as follows:

> This critique of vitalism or biologism . . . —says Derrida in "Force of Law" a propos Benjamin's vehement rejection of German *Lebensphilosophie*—here proceeds like the awakening of a Judaic tradition. And it does so in the name of life, of the most living of life, of the value of life that is worth more than life (pure and simple, if such exist and that one could call natural and biological), but that is worth more than life because it is life itself, insofar as life prefers itself. *It is life beyond life, life against life, but always in life and for life.*[13]

This highly dialectical notion of life, struggling against its merely natural manifestation, but always for the sake of its redeemed, intensified form, can become a motto to my reflections here. Using Nietzsche's paradigmatically modern philosophy as the battlefield of two contradictory visions of life, I would like to propose the notion of the *messianic vitalism*, which confirms the process of denaturalization as a positive possibility of "life-enhancement"—against the Greek prejudice, which insists on perceiving denaturalization as the "ascetic" moment of life-negation. In doing so, I will focus on the latest follower of the Benjaminian line, Harold Bloom. In *The Book of J*, Bloom offers highly original interpretation of the earliest texts of the Hebrew Bible, but he also offers an intriguing—Jewish and psychoanalytic at the same time—reading of Nietzsche. In Bloom's critique, Nietzsche comes out as a typically modern thinker:

---

12. Benjamin, "Der Erzähler. Betrachtungen zum Werk Nikolai Lesskows," 463.
13. Derrida, *Acts of Religion*, 289; my emphasis.

self-contradictory, baffled, reluctant, and altogether unaware, but still an *ally* of the denaturalized creaturely life that lives in the state of deviation—Bloom says: *clinamen*—from everything natural.[14]

## Exodus from Tragedy

A more detailed discussion of Nietzsche is inevitable here, mainly for the reason that Bloom, although a self-declared Jewish thinker, has blinded his sight by sticking to Nietzschean arguments for much too long. For a very long time, remaining both a Jew and a vitalist simultaneously appeared to Bloom as impossible as squaring the circle: while reading his middle period works (as *Anxiety of Influence, Map of Misreading*, or *Kabbalah and Criticism*) we can see how he palpably struggles to keep both these strains of thought within one theory and how he nonetheless fails every time. It is only later, in the eighties, that Bloom begins to work on the different, "early Hebrew" notion of vitalism that will finally say farewell to the Nietzschean concept of life based solely on natural power—yet, the retrospective projection we propose here is not completely unjustified. Bloom's growing impatience with Nietzsche, which culminates in "Freud and Beyond," the famous essay from *Ruin the Sacred Truths!*, is mainly due to the *aporias* created by his own antithetical criticism that could not be resolved on the ground of purely Nietzschean vitalism. Thus, although in *The Anxiety of Influence* Bloom continues to use Nietzsche's distinction of active and passive sin, coined by him in *The Birth of Tragedy*, he already implicitly disagrees with him and perceives "the Semitic sin" as a refined and in consequence far more militant version of the agonistic stance in which man is capable of expressing his "vital powers." In one of the most controversial fragments of *The Birth of Tragedy* Nietzsche proposes to distinguish the Greek wisdom on life against the Jewish unwisdom on life in the following way:

> The legend of Prometheus is indigenous to the entire community of Aryan races and attests to their prevailing talent for profound and tragic vision. In fact, it is not improbable that this myth has the same characteristic importance for the Aryan

14. Nietzsche, both a precursor and an antagonist, figures in all theoretical writings of Harold Bloom, but the most spectacular appropriation of his thought appears in *The Book of J*, where Bloom takes up the Nietzschean notion of "God as an artist" and projects it on the early Hebrew image of divinity. It is also in this book where Bloom offers his interpretation of the Jewish blessing, *l'chaim*, as "the promise of more life"; Bloom, *The Book of J*, 2.

mind as the myth of the Fall has for the Semitic, and that the two myths are related as brother and sister.... Man's highest good must be bought with a crime and paid by the flood of grief and suffering which the offended divinities visit upon the human race in its noble ambition. An austere notion, this, which by the dignity it confers on crime presents a strange contrast to the Semitic myth of the Fall—a myth that exhibits curiosity, deception, suggestibility, concupiscence, in short a whole series of principally feminine frailties, as the root of all evil. What distinguishes the Aryan conception is an exalted notion of active sin as the properly Promethean virtue.... The Aryan nations assign to crime the male, the Semites to sin the female gender; and it is quite consistent with these nations that the original act of *hubris* should be attributed to a man, original sin to a woman.[15]

Putting aside all the sexist and anti-Semitic innuendos, this passage tells us about two kinds of primal sin that begin the human odyssey. The Greek version of disobedience differs from the Jewish one in its tragic clarity: gods were cheated, gods want their revenge, and humans have to suffer either way, with or without the stolen fire. Whereas the Hebrew "passive sin" is "reactive" in creating a halo of mysterious, no longer conscious anxiety: the contradicted God, far from being the transparent agent of Greek tragedy, becomes internalized as a figure of a pressing moral commandment. Greek manliness, therefore, consists in brave fidelity to Prometheus: given the chance to repeat his sin, Aryans would have done it again and would bravely accept the fateful necessity of punishment. While Semitic cowardice lies in the repentance that their passive, weak sin had created: if only they could, Jews would have piously revoked their trespass, but would also plead, in a feminine way, for the alleviation of the punishing verdict.

This is hardly an alliance for Harold Bloom. Everything Bloom tells us in *The Book of J*, which constitutes his highly original reading of the earliest texts of the Hebrew Bible, blandly contradicts Nietzsche's flippant dismissal of the non-Aryan, female passivity of "Jewish sin." In Bloom's account (which closely mirrors the traditional midrashic approach, very far removed from the Paulian-Augustinian insinuation into this biblical story an original sin of mankind) it isn't even a *sin*: first, it is a childish misbehavior of defiance, which slowly and gradually matures into an agonistic attitude that finally surpasses everything the Greek *hubris* ever produced. Such a mature, agonistic attitude is best represented by the

15. Nietzsche, *The Birth of Tragedy*, 63–64.

figure of Jacob, Bloom's favorite Hebrew hero. Jacob's determination to cheat his own natural fate, which destined him to be only the second son, forms an image of a high-willed pride preparing itself to crush the forces of destiny, and thus to *get out* of the tragic condition, this Greek predicament of ultimate restriction, which builds a sublime halo around nature's bare necessities. The Greek active sin may therefore consist in triggering the tragic course, in which the singular outburst of life clashes with its inevitable limitation, yet the Hebrew sin aims at something else: it may consent to diminish the eruption of vitality by a sense of guilt and anxiety, created by the supernatural superego, but always in order *to cross a limit*, and to "pass forth." The Greek sin inaugurates the tragic scene where the same drama is played over and over again: the unrepressed life meets its inevitable doom in the blind, all-leveling verdict of *Ananke*. Whenever it says Yes to life, it is always in the same, repeatable form: birth, hubris, retaliation of fate; hence the Greek, "manly" *Ja-Sagen* lies in its power of endurance, in accepting the tragic predicament of life which inevitably closes itself in the naturalistic circle of *genesis* and *phtora*, becoming and corruption. Whereas the Jewish sin internalizes punishment, saying No to life in its immediate natural form, and thus changes the idea of life itself, by producing a whole new sphere of denaturalized possibilities Nietzsche himself—although later, in *The Genealogy of Morals*—calls very aptly "an abundance of tender Yeses":

> One already understands me: this ascetic priest, this apparent enemy of life, this denier—precisely he belongs to the altogether great conserving and Yes-creating forces of life. . . . The No he says to life, his No, brings to light, as if by magic, an *abundance of tender Yeses*; yes indeed, even when he wounds himself, this master of destruction, of self-destruction—*it is henceforth the wound itself that compels him to live.*[16]

16. Nietzsche, *Genealogy*, 120–21; my emphasis. This salient difference between *Shem* and *Yaphet* has been well analyzed by Michael Walzer in *Exodus and Revolution* where he compares the notion of bondage in Hebrew and Greek thought. Greek mentality is tragic in a sense that it sees no escape from the bondage of fate and the only liberating feeling comes with cathartic recognition of this ultimate truth. Hebrews, on the other hand, created a paradigm of liberation that leads out of the house of bondage and thus forms a basic narrative of all revolutionary upheavals: "God's promise—says Walzer—generates a sense of possibility: *the world is not all Egypt*. Without that sense of possibility, oppression would be experienced as an inescapable condition, a matter of personal or collective bad luck, a stroke of fate. . . . Anger and hope, not resignation, are the appropriate responses to the Egyptian house of bondage." Walzer contrasts the story of Exodus with Eurypides' *Women of Troy*, which "describes a 'going out' that leads to slavery rather than to freedom": "Eurypides," he says, "makes no moral

## Vitality of Tender Yeses

"The wound that compels him to live" is, as Nietzsche rather helplessly attests, the most "striking effect," which, instead of issuing in one decisive No thrown against the whole world of the living, produces the halo of mysterious "tender Yeses." It is a trauma that breaks the cycle of natural existence, but it is not purely destructive or deadening; to the contrary, its repressiveness, directed against natural form of life, brings a paradoxical intensification of life that only then becomes truly "compelling": both exciting and imperative. This notion of enlivening and revelatory trauma (see again Taubes on the traumatic aspects of Jewish revelation!) requires a substantial revision of Nietzsche's notion of vitalism, but also a serious modification of Freud's necessitarian economy of drives: the two sources Bloom wrestles with but still "props himself up on" in *The Anxiety of Influence*. If we are to believe that *askesis* and vitalism, negation and affirmation, may go hand in hand in order to create a new, denaturalized notion of life—the life called by Derrida *life beyond life, life against life, but always in life and for life*, strongly associated by him with the Judaic tradition—we have to cross beyond Nietzsche and Freud or, at least, submit them to powerful non-dogmatic misreadings.

For *unlike* Nietzsche, who divides powers into active and reactive and calls only the former life-enhancing, Bloom does not hesitate to see more life where Nietzsche would see merely passivity of decadence. With a sole exception, however; and this exception is very significant for Bloom's implicit revision. In *The Genealogy of Morals* Nietzsche cannot but reluctantly admire the resoluteness with which the Hebrew priests turned the active power onto itself in order to *create*, as true artists indeed, consciousness and conscience:

> Whatever else has been done to damage the powerful and great of this earth—writes Nietzsche—seems trivial compared with what the Jews had done, that priestly people who succeeded in avenging themselves on their enemies and oppressors by radically inverting all their values, that is, by an act of the most spiritual vengeance. This was the strategy entirely appropriate to a priestly people in whom vindictiveness had gone most deeply underground. . . . It [the ascetic ideal] signifies, let us have a courage to face it, a will to nothingness, a revulsion from life,

---

judgment; at least, he makes no judgment of the slavery into which the women are led. The feeling that he means to evoke is pity, not anger or indignation"; Walzer, "Exodus and Revolution," 83–84; my emphasis.

a rebellion against the principal conditions of living. And yet, despite everything, it is and remains a *will*.[17]

Bloom's revision begins with dialectical completion of Nietzsche's ambivalent and aporetic fascination with this strange kind of will, which—"despite everything" he believes about health, power, and beauty—stubbornly remains what it is: forceful, high-willed, and distinctive in its wish to create "something truly new,"[18] boldly oblivious to natural constraints of health and sickness. Nietzsche's genealogical rhetoric is unstable and clearly demands such completion: stuck with his dogmatic naturalism, Nietzsche cannot find categories that would descriptively follow his inexplicable attraction to this weird, non-natural kind of will that refuses to say Yes to the circular logic of *phusis*, "the principal conditions of living." It should be nothing but "sick" and "morbid," yet, at the same time, it somehow strangely *transcends* the naturalistic opposition of sickness and health:

> But what about the sources of man's morbidity?—asks Nietzsche in one of the most hesitant passages in *Genealogy*.—For certainly man is sicker, less secure, less stable, less firmly anchored than any other animal; he is the *sick* animal. But has he not also been more daring, more defiant, more inventive than all other animals together?—man, the great experimenter on himself, eternally unsatisfied, vying with gods, the beasts, and with nature for final supremacy; man, unconquered to this day, still unrealized, so agitated by his own teeming energy that his future digs like spurs into the flesh of every present moment...[19]

In Bloom's interpretation, Freud's notion of the superego derives precisely from the same indeterminacy between the active and the reactive, the same ambivalence of sickness and health, life and death, when perceived from the naturalistic point of view, which we try to abandon here. On the surface it might seem that it simply uses life against life in order to reach a self-cancelling effect; yet, in fact, the superego uses life

---

17. Nietzsche, *Genealogy*, 299. And although *The Genealogy of Morals* is peppered with unkind remarks about Jewish rancor, which managed to overthrow the natural hierarchy of beauty and health, it is done in a "noble" spirit, i.e., with what the sublime Greeks used to call "agonistic respect" for a major enemy. In the conclusion of his essay Nietzsche says: "The Old Testament is another story. I have the highest respect for that book. I find in it great men, a heroic landscape, and one the rarest things on earth, the naivete of a strong heart. What is more, I find a *people*." Ibid., 281.

18. Ibid.

19. Ibid., 257.

in order to achieve a *different kind of life*, not the one associated with the id's spontaneous yet general *demands*, but the one enriched by the higher idea of *will*, teeming with future-oriented, proleptic energy and its infinite, singularized *desire*. This is why Bloom in *The Book of J* bases his "psychology of Yahweh" and his relentless vitalism not on the Nietzschean id but on the early Freudian paradigm of superego: "And it is precisely here, in one of the greatest ironies, Freud is J's descendant and is haunted by J's Yahweh in the figure of Superego ... the personality of Yahweh is one with the daemonic intensity of the Superego."[20]

This is precisely the gist of this *different* kind of vitalism that is offered by Bloom's misprision of *The Book of J*. Renouncing one's spontaneous needs for the sake of higher will is not exactly the Nietzschean version of crippling morality in which one abandons one's desires for the sake of obedience to norms. Superego appears here not as a Thanatic exercise of reactivity and asketic mortification, but as a manifestation of life that has traveled—or, in Jacob's way, "passed forth"—far beyond the barbarian vitality of the Nietzschean blond beasts. Vitality, therefore, may also lie in the power of repression, just as Jacob's high-willed vitality lies in his lameness, which signifies the cost of "mere life"—and the vitality of his descendants lies in the way they work hard to model the chaotic realm of their natural wants (*yezer* being the Hebrew equivalent of the yet untransformed id), as symbolized by the loss of their foreskins, the curtailment of the primitive phallic power. It would seem, therefore, that once we shift from Nietzsche and his fascination with barbarian, naturalistic liveliness to early Hebrew vitalism with its "new version of the id," then the paradox of a denaturalized life—which troubled Bloom's writings in the beginning—can be, at least partly, resolved. The simple Yes of the Nietzschean *Ja-Sagen* to the "physical" cycle of birth and death, shot through the prohibition to participate in the repetitive "ring of being," does not produce an equally simple negating effect; rather, it dialectically dissolves into a subtler halo of "tender Yeses." It is, therefore, not life itself that gets negated, but only its natural, ring-like, hopelessly cyclical manifestation, which binds its energy in a deadening compulsive repetition of *phusis*, the very model of the Freudian *Wiederholungszwang*. It is not life itself that is "damned" or "wicked," but merely this mechanical form of the eternal return of the same that constitutes the rhythm of nature.[21]

20. Bloom, *The Book of J*, 305–6.

21. This is precisely why Karl Löwith, in his *Meaning in History*, insists on an alternative translation of Psalm 12:9 which contains the word "ring"; instead of rendering it as "On every side the wicked roam" (as in JPS Hebrew-English Tanakh) he

And this abundance of tender affirmations is precisely the goal of Bloom's antithetical vitalism, drawn "out of the sources of Hebraism."[22] Bloom deliberately collates two ideals Nietzsche himself kept apart (the ascetic and the antithetical), knowing well that this separation is the very source of Nietzsche's insoluble antinomies. In the following fragment from *Kabbalah and Criticism*, which looks deceptively like a simple borrowing from Nietzsche, Bloom bridges this gap in one, seemingly innocuous maneuver:

> The ascetic ideal had kept man from nihilism, saving the will but at the expense of guilt, a guilt involving hatred of common humanity (with all natural pleasure). For the ascetic ideal is an interpretation, one that in turn inspires a change in the process of willing. This change signifies "a will to nothingness, a revulsion from life," yet still *a purposefulness. Life thus uses asceticism in a struggle against death*. Nietzsche, magnificently contrapuntal, attains a triumph in antithetical thought by declaring that to be ascetic is thus to be life-affirming.[23]

What Bloom calls here Nietzsche's magnificent contrapuntality, allowing him to jump in one rhetorical move from the ascetic to the antithetical ideal, is, in fact, nothing more than Nietzsche's major contradiction that he himself could not resolve, getting stuck, rather unproductively, with the traditional vitalistic notion of life as "natural life" (with all its natural, instinctual pleasures). The idea that "life uses asceticism in a struggle against death" and that "to be ascetic is to be life-affirming" is Bloom's (or, simply Jewish), but not Nietzsche's who, despite his inconsequential admiration for Hebrew priests, would always tend to maintain that asceticism is the struggle of death against life, even to the detriment of his own theory. But *when askesis becomes antithesis*, the image of life torn between natural instincts and the artificial superegoic demands, suddenly gains clarity:

---

proposes "The wicked move around in a circle" in order to emphasize the "futility and indignity" of such movement. It is also important here that the Hebrew word for "nature"—*teva*—shares the same root as the word "ring"—*taba'at*.

22. If not exactly the later, Talmudic Judaism, which might have some problems with such concept of unbridled vitality; *vide* Levinas! Yet, the fascinating topic of the relation between these two strains of Jewish thought—messianic vitalism, which invests in the "blessing of more life," and ethical Judaism, which concentrates on the teaching of the Law—goes beyond the scope of this essay. Suffice it to say, that I don't find this relation as antagonistic as it may seem *prima facie*; messianic vitalism, as I try to show it here, does not reject Law; it merely does not use it as an ascetic device, but rather as a "ruse of life" which in the end turns out to be "life-affirming."

23. Bloom, *Kabbalah and Criticism*, 51–52; my emphasis.

what initially (i.e., in the Greek eyes) appeared as an oppression of natural life by the constraints of morals, turns into a Jewish vision of liberation of life from the oppressive bondage of nature. It is precisely this radical *Gestaltswitch* of perspectives that allows Bloom to transform Nietzsche's incoherent notion of the ascetic ideal into an antithetical life-affirming vehicle of restless "passing forth," which produces "the wish to be elsewhere"—rather in the desert than in the fake fullness of *phusis*—the *exodic* desire of displacement. From the point of view of this liberated "more life," which initiated a "change in the process of willing," the natural existence, which lacks this sort of vitalistic inventiveness, seems nothing more than just a contemptible "mere life," unworthy of any nostalgic glorification.

## The Agon with the Vital Order: Revision of Freud

But this revision of Nietzsche cannot be complete without a thorough misreading of Freud. Since in his interpretation of *The Book of J*, Bloom relies heavily on Freudian notions (like superego), he must also twist Freud's metapsychology, so it fits better his revisionistic attempt to conceptualize the Jewish version of vitalism.

It is thus clear from the start that the concept of "more life" Bloom has in mind differs fundamentally from what Freud in his *Three Essays on the Theory of Sexuality* calls "the vital order" (i.e., the most basic natural system of the instincts of self-preservation); it appears much closer to the originally indeterminate and anarchic energy of libido, which cannot be contained within a well-defined, homeostatic system of needs and gratifications.[24] From Freud's speculation in *Three Essays* it follows that libido (i.e., human sexuality), precisely because of its indeterminacy, is always in danger of falling under the rule of the better organized vital order—but, at the same time, it can also use its original indefiniteness to free itself from the latter's mechanical functionality. Human sexual drive may thus be inchoate, premature, and deficient when compared to well-determined self-preservatory instincts—yet, this can also be seen as its advantage.

The story told by Freud in *Three Essays* goes as follows. In the first stage of development, libido has to learn from the better-formed self-preservatory instincts and *lean on* (*anaclisis, Anlehnung*) on their vital functions, like feeding or defecating, to use their objects for autoerotic purposes. Soon, however, this seemingly subservient "propping" turns into "wrestling," and *anaclisis* takes on the form of *agon*. In one of his

---

24. See Sigmund Freud, *Essays on the Theory of Sexuality*.

best pieces, "Wrestling Sigmund" from *Breaking of the Vessels*, Bloom boldly juxtaposes the story of wrestling Jacob from the biblical writer J with Freud's account of the beginning of human sexuality, thus giving a peculiar agonistic twist to the Freudian notion of *Anlehnung*. The picture that emerges out of the ingenious interference of two images—Jacob wrestling with the Angel of Death and human infant sucking maternal breast—presents human sexuality as a drive that fights with the vital order in refusing to be imprisoned by its mere natural functionality, the inexorable homeostasis of *phusis*. Using our concepts, we could say that here life fights against life, or, to be more precise, that human sexuality, forming the daring figure of "more life," opposes the system of self-preservation, which forms a humble figure of "mere life." It may thus seem that "wrestling a divine angel is rather a contrast to sucking one's mother breast, and achieving the name Israel is pretty unrelated to the inauguration of the sexual drive,"[25] yet, Bloom insists, these two narratives tell the same story:

> *All human sexuality is tropological*, whereas we all of us desperately need and long for it to be literal. . . . As Laplanche says, expounding Freud: "Sexuality in its entirety is in the slight deviation, the *clinamen* from the function. Or as I would phrase it, *our sexuality is in its very origins a misprision, a strong misreading*, on the infant's part, of the vital order . . . I call Freud . . . Wrestling Sigmund, because again he is a poet of Sublime agon, here an agon between sexuality and the vital order. Our sexuality is like Jacob, and the vital order is like that among the Elohim with whom our wily and heroic ancestor wrestled, until he had won the great name of Israel. Sexuality and Jacob triumph, but at the terrible expense of a crippling. All our lives long we search in vain, unknowingly, for the lost object, when even that object was a *clinamen* away from the true aim. And yet we search incessantly, do experience satisfactions, however marginal, and win our real if limited triumph over the vital order. Like Jacob, we keep passing Penuel, limping on our hips.[26]

25. Bloom, *Breaking of the Vessels*, 69–70.

26. In *Life and Death in Psychoanalysis* Laplanche distinguishes very clearly between *drive* and *function*: "*function, need*, and *instinct* characterize generally the vital register of self-preservation in opposition to the sexual register"; Laplanche, *Life and Death*, 16. "Thus the sexual object is not identical to the object of the function, but is displaced in relation to it; they are in a relation of essential *contiguity* which leads us to slide almost indifferently from one to the other, from the milk to the breast as its symbol" (ibid., 20). And further: "Sexuality in its entirety is in the slight deviation, the *clinamen* from the function. It is in the *clinamen* insofar as the latter results in an autoerotic internalization" (ibid., 22). The drive "mimics, displaces, and *denatures the*

Bloom offers here a Jewish version of sublimation that differs considerably from the teachings of "divine Plato" (as Freud calls him in the introduction to *Three Essays*). Instead of a winged Eros that flies above its abandoned, material objects to become unencumbered and purely spiritual, we get an image of an impaired, limping hero who managed to detach himself from the lethal embrace with the vital order and thus restlessly "passes forth," though severely damaged in his natural vitality. Instead of a Spirit that rises above matter in a triumphant ascension towards the supranatural sun, we see an anxious quester, walking through a horizontal desert away from the Egypt of nature, but always "limping," always endangered by the fall into the snares of the "vital order."

In this version of sublimating antithesis, nature is not so easily abandoned. The exodus from nature, from the seduction of "propping" (*Anlehnung*) on the certainties of the vital order, is a hard won victory that agrees with the fundamental dissatisfaction of the sexual drive: in not being able to find its true object (which, in fact, does not exist), it transforms everything natural into something figurative, i.e., something else that it actually is, an eternally vague object of desire (it is thus also a moment of the birth of language). *Anaclisis*, therefore, is a critical phase both of the greatest danger and the greatest chance: it is an agon that may be either won or lost. It may either bow down the sexual drive and turn it into a quasi-natural force imitating animal instincts, condemned to their naturalistic model of homeostasis and "health" ("to move around in a circle")—or, to the contrary, surrender the vital order to libido and allow vital instincts to be "troped" beyond its boringly "healthy" and literal mere functionality into the realm of more tender and more transgressive Yeses. The drive may thus either fall into embrace with nature, or, due to the superegoic repression, give up on its early fixations, renounce all (dis)satisfactions offered by natural objects, and expand into a figurative force, creating a desire for meaning in the domain where previously there was nothing but pure, senseless functionality.

This agonistic Eros, therefore, is not just an instinct of life as opposed to the instinct of death, closed within the repetitive circle of *phusis*, but a power of figuration wrestling both with life and death as a cycle of mere

---

*instinct*" (ibid., 22; my emphasis). This is why, in the end, "The whole of sexuality, or at least the whole of infantile sexuality, *ends up by becoming perversion*" (ibid., 23; my emphasis). "Now sexuality, in its entirety, in the human infant, lies in a movement which *deflects* the instinct, *metaphorizes* its aim, *displaces* and *internalizes* its object, and concentrates its source on what is ultimately a minimal zone, the erotogenic zone" (ibid., 23; my emphasis).

functions. It is no longer sexuality forced to conform with the natural need of self-preservation, but an *Erros*, eros and error combined: an energy of primordial *libido* that regains its original "erring" indeterminacy, which now serves not as its default but as its main asset and advantage. For, once it detaches itself from the vital order, it immediately begins to *err*: it crosses the limits of the functional system of *phusis* and wanders out from the Egypt of nature into the desert of open possibilities. *Erros* refuses to be closed within boredom of natural life, which just "piles life upon life," unable by itself to produce a single grain of meaning, but, unlike in the more traditional, Greek influenced teaching on sublimation and askesis, it does not reject life altogether. Quite to the contrary, instead of negating life, it regains its original anarchic libidinal form and, by liberating it from the confines of natural repetition, transforms life into an exciting "quest romance" of continuous "crossing" and "passing forth" that began with the most paradigmatic of all *Shem* heroes, Jacob at Penuel.

*Erros*, therefore, is precisely what Derrida calls "the most living in life itself" that cannot be confused with the natural, "physical" and functional, appearance of "mere life." It denounces *phusis* as a primordial site of the living, by exposing it as life's fallen, secondary manifestation, from which life as such can be saved—rescued from the creaturely fall, where it is forced to repeat the functional and necessitarian path of "mere life," and elevated to the messianic and creative level of "more life." And if I am right in my interpretation of Bloom's messianic vitalism, this redemption can only be anticipated in the denaturalized vitality of a human being, who, as such, becomes the true *Fürsprech der Kreatur*: the bearer of hope for all creaturely existence, who "chooses life" by taking it out from the natural ambivalence of "life-and-death."

## Bibliography

Benjamin, Walter. "Der Erzähler. Betrachtungen zum Werk Nikolai Lesskows." In *Gesammelte Schriften*, Bd. II, 2. Frankfurt am Main: Suhrkamp, 1977.

Bloom, Harold. *The Book of J*. New York: Harper, 1990.

———. *The Breaking of the Vessels: The Wellek Library Lectures at the University of California*. Edited by F. Lentricchia. Chicago: The University of Chicago Press, 1982.

———. *Kabbalah and Criticism*. New York: Continuum, 1975.

Derrida, Jacques. *Acts of Religion*. Edited by Gil Anidjar. London: Routledge, 2002.

Freud, Sigmund. *Three Essays on the Theory of Sexuality*. Translated by James Strachey. New York: Basic, 1962.

Gutkind, Erich. *Choose Life: The Biblical Call to Revolt*. New York: Shuman, 1952.

Hadot, Pierre. *The Veil of Isis: An Essay on the History of the Idea of Nature.* Translated by Michael Chase. Cambridge, MA: Bellknap, 2006.

Jonas, Hans. *Mortality and Morality: Search for God after Auschwitz.* Translated by Lawrence Vogel. Evanston, IL: Northwestern University Press, 1996.

Laplanche, Jean. *Life and Death in Psychoanalysis.* Translated by Jeffrey Melham. Baltimore: The John Hopkins University Press, 1976.

Löwith, Karl. *Meaning in History: The Theological Implications of the Philosophy of History.* Chicago: Chicago University Press, 1957.

Nietzsche, Friedrich Wilhelm. *Beyond Good and Evil: Prelude to a Philosophy of the Future.* Translated by Helen Zimmern. 1906. Reprint. No location: Forgotten Books, 2008.

———. *The Gay Science.* Translated by Bernard Arthur Owen Williams and Josefine Nauckhoff. Cambridge: Cambridge University Press, 2001.

———. *The Genealogy of Morals: The Birth of Tragedy.* Translated by Francis Golffing. New York: Doubleday, 1956.

———. *Thus Spoke Zarathustra.* Translated by Graham Parkes. Oxford: Oxford World Classic, 2008.

Taubes, Jacob. *Occidental Eschatology.* Translated by David Ratmoko. Stanford: Stanford University Press, 2009.

Walzer, Michael. "Exodus and Revolution." In *Exodus: Modern Critical Interpretations*, edited by Harold Bloom, 83–84. New York: Chelsea House, 1987.

# 9

# Reason and Church Social Doctrine

Benedict XVI and the Renewal of Tradition (2005–2008)*

*Evandro Botto*

---

## The Church's Social Doctrine: Between Philosophy and Theology

IN FORMULATING THE TITLE of this paper, I have considered that passage from the first Encyclical letter by Benedict XVI, *Deus caritas est*, in which the Pope underlined that "the Church's social teaching argues on the basis of reason and natural law, namely, on the basis of what is in accord with the nature of every human being."[1] Some have, worryingly, seen in this statement the symptom of a regressive aspect in church social teaching, back to positions now considered fundamentally passé. Those positions were typical of the time in which Church social teaching was treated as essentially a philosophical discipline—more precisely as a *social ethic*. It is important to remember that Pius XI considering, specifically, the doctrines formulated by Leo XIII in the Encyclical *Rerum novarum*, referred to a "new social philosophy"[2] and even to "Catholic principles on the

---

* This paper was presented at the Conference *The Grandeur of Reason: Religion, Tradition, and Universalism*, Rome, September 1–4, 2008. For this reason the present contribution does not consider the further documents published by the Pope on the same topic, and in particular his Encyclical letter *Caritas in Veritate*.

1. Benedict XVI, *Deus caritas est*, n. 28.
2. Pius XI, *Quadragesimo anno*, n. 14.

social question."[3] Throughout recent decades, one could say, in relation to this attitude Church social doctrine eventually resolved the problem both of its nature and of its epistemological status by abandoning its traditional position—a position that Benedict XVI is now accused to have retrieved. More specifically, Benedict XVI is accused of bringing the Church's social doctrine back to the field of philosophical ethics, to a purely "rational" ethics centered on the notion of natural law and separated from theology, which is now considered as a purely "supernatural" or "revealed" wisdom. The same attitude—as has been noted elsewhere[4]—was still visible and organically theorized by John XXIII in the Encyclical letter *Mater et magistra* (15th May 1961), as well as in the coeval program for the teaching of Church social doctrine formulated by the Congregation of Seminaries (25th May 1961). In 1975 Paul VI, with his *Evangelii nuntiandi* (the apostolic exhortation which followed the Synod of Bishops on the evangelization of contemporary world), abandoned or, at least, went beyond that attitude. "The resolutive text by Paul VI refused two extremist positions: the bourgeois one, which severs the evangelical message from social justice (denying any relationship between them); and the pro-third world one, which reduces the evangelical message to social justice. On the contrary it affirms the pertinence (in the sense of "belonging to") of social justice to the evangelical message: in different words it considers social questions as placed in the sphere of Revelation."[5]

The process of redefining the epistemological status of Church social doctrine comes to end with John Paul II's Encyclical *Sollicitudo rei socialis*, where it is presented as "a theological reading of modern problems." As such, "it therefore belongs to the field, not of ideology, but of theology and particularly of moral theology."[6] The Encyclical letter, published in 1987, refers controversially to that cultural context typical of the 1960s and 1970s (at that time already considered as almost historical), which was particularly hostile to Church social doctrine. Such hostility was encapsulated in the well-known essay *La doctrine sociale de l'Église comme idéologie* published in 1979 by the pre-eminent intellectual Marie-Dominique Chenu. This essay is proof of the "bad press" from which Church social doctrine suffered at end of the 1970s; not only within general public opinion, but also among many intellectuals and even among theologians

---

3. Ibid., n. 21.
4. Cf. Colombo, *Il compito della teologia*, 23–34.
5. Ibid., 31.
6. John Paul II, *Sollicitudo rei socialis*, n. 41.

(sometimes the expression *Church social doctrine* was even considered unpronounceable). Nowadays, however, Papal teaching explicitly recognizes that Church social doctrine belongs to the field of theology, and in particular to moral theology (as it was recognized, by many after the publication of *Sollicitudo rei socialis*). Therefore, the long period in which Church social doctrine was considered rooted in philosophical ethics or social philosophy has definitely come to end. The attitude that found in the domain of pure reason and in the theory of natural rights its favorite theoretical reference is now viewed as running the fatal risk of embracing a pure rationalistic model and an "ideological" reductionism.

One could say that Benedict XVI, maintaining that the social doctrine of the church is founded on the basis of reason and natural right, seems to be advocating a similar perspective. On the contrary; his proposal—and this is what I intend to show in what follows—is not simply to go back to the idea of Church social doctrine as an expression of a philosophical ethic or a "natural morality." In opposition to this, I want to claim that Benedict XVI, in "rehabilitating" the link between doctrine, on one side, and reason and natural right (understood as to what is adequate to the human nature), on the other, wants to provide Church social doctrine with a more solid basis as well as with a legitimacy beyond the boundaries of both the ecclesial community and the Christian world. This is crucial if the "sympathetic" attitude towards Church social doctrine, now shared by many scholars, is not to be reduced to a contingent knee-jerk reaction to the collapse of contemporary ideologies—based as they were on the hope for an imminent advent of an entirely new and better world; in particular in response to the retreat of Marxism, the major historical and theoretical parable of the last century. Once it is recognized that "this dream has disappeared" in *Deus caritas est*, the Pope says: "In today's complex situation, not least because of the growth of a globalized economy, the Church's social doctrine has become a set of fundamental guidelines offering approaches that are valid even beyond the confines of the Church: in the face of ongoing development these guidelines need to be addressed in the context of dialogue with all those seriously concerned for humanity and for the world in which we live."[7]

In what follows, I would like to show how the concept of reason envisaged by Benedict XVI as starting point for the arguments proposed by Church social doctrine is *not* reason severed from faith and resistant to it; it is *not* a "mutilated" reason, but rather it is a reason capable of recognizing

---

7. Benedict XVI, *Deus caritas est*, n. 27.

the essential contribution that comes from faith in order to enable the former to be authentic. "Faith by its specific nature is an encounter with the living God"—says Benedict XVI—"an encounter opening up new horizons extending beyond the sphere of reason. But it is also a purifying force for reason itself. From God's standpoint, faith liberates reason from its blind spots and therefore helps it to be ever more fully itself."[8]

## To Free the Reason from Its Blindness
## (and the Faith from Its Ideological Constraints)

From what does reason need to be purified? What is the blindness from which it needs to be freed? The Pope formulates a synthesis in answer to these questions (typical of his literary style), which is profoundly articulated. Considering not only the lecture given at the University of Regensburg, but also many other crucial texts concerning similar topics (among them his address in Verona in 2006 and the one prepared—but never delivered—for his visit to the University *La Sapienza* in Rome), it seems to me appropriate to interpret "the blindness from which reason has to be freed" (and for which faith can give its contribution) in the following way.

In the first place there is what we call the "positivist" or "scientistic blindness." According to the perspective of positivist scientism the concept of rationality is confined to the sphere of what, on one side, can be calculated through processes of measurement and, on the other, to the sphere of "what can be proven through experiments."[9] When this concept of a "self-limiting" reason is used to investigate the natural world it is not only right, it is even necessary, and can lead to highly profitable and otherwise unobtainable results, as happened often during the modern era. "It is the new correlation of experiment and method"—Benedict XVI says in his second Encyclical letter, *Spe salvi*—"that enables man to arrive at an interpretation of nature in conformity with its laws and thus finally to achieve"—and here the Pope quotes Francis Bacon—"'the triumph of art over nature' (*victoria cursus artis super naturam*)."[10] However, it would be wrong to pretend, as the different kinds of positivism that characterize the contemporary culture tend to do, that technical and scientific rationality (which is a rationality reduced to what can be calculated and experienced) can stand in itself as the entirety of reason and provide the basis of a new

8. Ibid., n. 28.
9. Ratzinger, *L'Europa di Benedetto*, 36.
10. Benedict XVI, *Spe salvi*, n. 16.

kind of universalism capable of presenting itself as the philosophy of the future. As the Pope says, "[t]his philosophy does not express a fulfilled human reason, but only a part of it, and because of that mutilation it cannot be considered rational at all."[11]

More radically, but not without a precise connection to what has just been emphasized, according to Benedict XVI the blindness from which reason suffers in our post-modern era is characterized by three aspects: firstly, a mistrust about the capacities of human reason to have access to the truth; secondly, by a mistrust nurtured by the fear that faith in truth necessarily involves intolerance and the use of violence, and finally by a mistrust that can lead to the denial of the need for truth and of the will to reach it. Concerning the first aspect, the Pope says: "In fact, our faith is decisively opposed to the attitude of resignation that considers man incapable of truth—as if this were more than he could cope with. This attitude of resignation with regard to truth, I am convinced, lies at the heart of the crisis of the West, the crisis of Europe. If truth does not exist for man, then neither can he ultimately distinguish between good and evil. And then the great and wonderful discoveries of science become double-edged: they can open up significant possibilities for good, for the benefit of mankind, but also, as we see only too clearly, they can pose a terrible threat, involving the destruction of man and the world."[12] As for the second aspect, Benedict XVI recognizes that, if it is true that "we need truth," it is equally indubitable that "in the light of our history we are fearful that faith in the truth might entail intolerance." At the same time, the Pope does not hesitate to say that even if faith has sometimes degenerated into intolerance, this is not attributable to that God who is "the same Truth," "the living God," "the God who has shown us his face and opened his heart to us: Jesus Christ," but to "the ideological constrictions" of faith caused by human beings or to "abuse of religion and reason for imperialistic purposes."[13] Whenever we are afraid of affirming the existence and the possibility of knowing that ultimate truth because it is seen as implying intolerance, "it is time to look towards Jesus as we see him in the shrine at Mariazell"—the Pope said during his apostolic journey in Austria. "We see him here in two images: as the child in his Mother's arms, and above the high altar of the Basilica as the Crucified. These two images in the Basilica tell us this: truth prevails not through external force, but it is humble and it yields itself to

---

11. Ratzinger, *L'Europa di Benedetto*, 52.
12. Benedict XVI, *Apostolic journey to Austria, Eucharistic Celebration, Homily*.
13. Ibid., *Apostolic journey to Austria, Meeting with the authorities*.

man only via the inner force of its veracity. Truth proves itself in love. It is never our property, never our product, just as love can never be produced, but only received and handed on as a gift. We need this inner force of truth. As Christians we trust this force of truth. We are its witnesses. We must hand it on as a gift in the same way as we have received it, as it has given itself to us."[14]

It emerges from these statements that the Pope invites us to look not only at the capacity, typical of the human reason, to recognize the truth against the constrictions of a modern understanding of reason, but also at the liberation of faith from an attitude characterized by voluntarism, irrationalism, and fideism, which—separating truth from love—have sometimes promoted the degeneration of faith into violent imposition or hegemonic demands. Only the living witness of an "enlarged" use of reason, capable of truth, and of a faith that is "a friend of intelligence" can reawaken the need for truth (which is proved by love) and for all essential human needs, needs that tend to be dissolved by the nihilism permeating our contemporary culture.

In front of a world in which sometimes the human heart seems to have suspended its search and human reason seems to have set aside the need for truth (through which it is constituted), the Pope underlines the fact that "the awakening of the Christian faith, the dawning of the Church of Jesus Christ was made possible, because there were people in Israel whose hearts were searching—people who did not rest content with custom, but who looked further ahead, in search of something greater . . . ; expectant people who were not satisfied by what everyone around them was doing and thinking, but who were seeking the star which could show them the way towards Truth itself, towards the living God." "We too need an open and restless heart like theirs"—Benedict XVI says—"in order to be able to face the future with confidence; . . . yet the earth will be deprived of a future only when the forces of the human heart and of reason illuminated by the heart are extinguished—when the face of God no longer shines upon the earth."[15]

It seems to me that Benedict XVI's fundamental thought on the relationship between reason, truth, and faith has been expressed most

---

14. Ibid., *Apostolic journey to Austria, Eucharistic Celebration, Homily.*

15. Ibid. The same concern is the basis of Benedict's interest towards education, considered by him as a real "emergency." The authentic educator is the one who is able to reawaken great questions, such as the human need for love, and the desire for truth among human beings (cf. Benedict XVI, *Address to the Participants at the Ecclesial Convention of the Diocese of Rome*).

emblematically in his visit in Austria, especially during a meeting with the authorities and the diplomatic corps. There he stated that beyond the kinds of reductionism, exclusivism, and one-sided perspectives that have characterized the modern understanding of reason (and of faith), "another part of the European heritage is a tradition of thought which considers as essential a substantial correspondence between faith, truth and reason."[16] Thus reason is not only and first of all the human capacity to know the truth (as considered from the perspective of gnoseology), but the essence of everything when seen from the vantage point of ontology. When considering a series of references pertaining to this topic, made explicit in Regensburg (but not only there), this constitutes the possibility for Christianity to be "re-Hellenized." Specifically, the Pope wants to clarify that "here the issue is clearly whether or not reason stands at the beginning and foundation of all things. The issue is whether reality originates by chance and necessity, and thus whether reason is merely a chance by-product of the irrational and, in an ocean of irrationality, it too, in the end, is meaningless, or whether instead the underlying conviction of Christian faith remains true: *In principio erat Verbum*—in the beginning was the Word; at the origin of everything is the creative reason of God who decided to make himself known to us human beings."[17]

## State and Politics: Justice and Rights

Above, I have analyzed the fundamental idea of reason as shaped by the teaching of Benedict XVI and in particular the point at which reason is called to combine itself with faith and faith is called to meet reason. Reason needs faith, as we have considered, in order to be authentic, to keep and recover its primal broadness—its capacity for truth—and in order to exercise it fruitfully. Faith, in turn, needs reason, to avoid the always-present risk of ideological constrictions and abuses operated for sectarian interests or desire of power. In the third and final section of this contribution I would like to present a synthetic (but as much as possible inclusive) reflection on the renewal of the tradition of Church social doctrine as it has been envisaged by Benedict XVI. Pope Benedict wants to focus on the contribution offered by Church social doctrine in order to re-define the nature and the tasks of the State and of politics, as he says: "justice is both the aim and the intrinsic criterion of all politics. Politics is more than a

16. Benedict XVI, *Apostolic journey to Austria, Meeting with authorities*.
17. Ibid.

mere mechanism for defining the rules of public life: its origin and its goal are found in justice."[18] The question of how justice can be achieved here and now—a question that the State always has to face and to answer—presupposes "an even more radical question: what is justice? The problem is one of practical reason; but if reason is to be exercised properly, it must undergo constant purification, since it can never be completely free of the danger of a certain ethical blindness caused by the dazzling effect of power and special interests." "Here politics and faith meet," Benedict XVI says, suggesting—in order to face the problem of the right order of society and State (once again the dynamic of reciprocal implication between reason and faith, as we have considered above). According to the Pope, it is exactly where political reason (intended as that reason capable of enlightening the origin, the need, and the criteria of good politics) and faith meet each other that "Catholic social doctrine has its place." The latter, as I have said at the beginning of this paper, "argues on the basis of reason and natural law, namely, on the basis of what is in accord with the nature of every human being." The concept of reason and of human nature that I am now considering, however, does not involve a reason folded in on itself, reduced and identified with just one of its dimensions, but a concept of reason that, in order to be fully itself, is aware of its need for the purifying and releasing power of faith. If this is the "statute" of Church social doctrine—which is a doctrine of reason and faith, philosophical and theological knowledge—what are the most fundamental directions suggested by Benedict XVI for "the actual human and cultural context" that derive from such an original understanding of the traditional structure of Church social doctrine? First of all, it requires a renewed consideration of the tasks of the church and the Christians in the sphere of politics. The church recognizes the autonomy of the political sphere: she is aware of the fact that a direct political involvement is not her proper mission. Instead of replacing the State in its effort to realize justice she entrusts "the lay faithful" with the immediate task to "take part in public life in a personal capacity." The church offers to politics a contribution that is not immediately political, but it has more to do with a capacity to understand politics properly and to act according to an enlarged use of reason. This is a contribution that enables people to recognize—and therefore to realize—the proper sense of politics, that is justice; it is a "help ... to contribute, here and now, to the acknowledgment and attainment of what is just"; and "to help form consciences in political

---

18. Ibid., *Deus caritas est*, n. 28; the other quotations in this paragraph also come from this.

life and to stimulate greater insight into the authentic requirements of justice as well as greater readiness to act accordingly, even when this might involve conflict with situations of personal interest."

The State, in turn, cannot pretend to transform itself in a kind of church, "The State may not impose religion, yet it must guarantee religious freedom and harmony between the followers of different religions." "For her part, the Church, as the social expression of Christian faith, has a proper independence and is structured on the basis of her faith as a community which the State must recognize": this involves State's capacity of respecting and valuing not only freedom of worship and the teaching of that doctrine, but also the social works (cultural, educative, welfare practices) realized by the church, as well as by any other social "living force." "We do not need a State which regulates and controls everything, but a State which, in accordance with the principle of subsidiarity, generously acknowledges and supports initiatives arising from the different social forces and combines spontaneity with closeness to those in need."[19]

Let us now focus our attention, in particular, on what Benedict XVI indicates as the specific task of a concept of reason "purified" by faith in front of a permanently changing scenario of society and politics; that is to help understand "what is right" so that it can be realized. The Pope does not present an organic reflection on the topic of justice and he is not even interested in formulating definitions of this term. On the contrary, in his lecture prepared for the University *La Sapienza*[20] (and which prepares what I consider the ground for one of his most interesting contributions on Church social doctrine) he investigates "how is it possible to identify criteria of justice that make shared freedom possible—as "human freedom" is always "freedom within reciprocal communion" and not an isolated and individual freedom—in order to "help man to be good" and to realize a little more "the good life" as described by Aristotle. In more concrete terms the Pope says it is the question of "how can a juridical body of norms be established that serves as an ordering of freedom, of human dignity and human rights." Here, the Pope calls to mind a non-believer, the thinker Jürgen Habermas, declaring to agree with him in identifying the two criteria that make legitimate the State's juridical body of fundamental norms (that is, its constitution): (1) "the equal participation of all citizens" and (2) "the reasonable manner in which political disputes are resolved."

---

19. Ibid., nn. 28–29; the other quotations in this paragraph also come from here.

20. Ibid., *Lecture at the University of Rome "La Sapienza,"* 17th January 2008, from which also the other quotations of this paragraph come.

Such "reasonable manners" required in the overcoming of the inevitable (and sometimes even necessary) conflicts that characterize the life of a democratic State are not reducible to a mere "fight for arithmetical majorities," but—Benedict XVI says, using the same words of Habermas—it is rather characterized by a "process of argumentation sensitive to the truth."

The Pope does not deny the difficulty of a concrete transformation of this model into political practice: the kind of mentality that describes "political parties as responsible of political will" is usually intended to reach the highest possible consensus, even satisfying disparate interests of individuals and groups very distant from the authentic good of the city. Benedict XVI is a realist, and—at the same time—he is able to recognize the "meaningful" fact that even an intellectual like Habermas, one of the thinkers most representative of contemporary lay philosophy, "speaks of sensibility to the truth as a necessary element in the process of political argument, thereby reintroducing the concept of truth into philosophical and political debate." But this necessarily means that in the search for true justice, true freedom, just cohabitation, "we have to listen to claims other than those of parties and interest groups." In particular, we have to listen to those forms of wisdom and to those disciplines (i.e., philosophy and theology) whose "permanent purpose" consists in "safeguarding sensibility to the truth." However, it is necessary to conceive the same disciplines according to their authentic nature and vocation: the Pope, calling to mind the great example of Aquinas, maintains that they can be neither confused nor totally separated from each other.[21]

21. It is worthy, concluding my contribution, to quote this entire passage from the lecture never pronounced by Benedict XVI at the University La Sapienza in Rome: "I would say that Saint Thomas's idea concerning the relationship between philosophy and theology could be expressed using the formula that the Council of Chalcedon adopted for Christology: philosophy and theology must be interrelated 'without confusion and without separation.' 'Without confusion' means that each of the two must preserve its own identity. Philosophy must truly remain a quest conducted by reason with freedom and responsibility; it must recognize its limits and likewise its greatness and immensity. Theology must continue to draw upon a treasury of knowledge that it did not invent, that always surpasses it, the depths of which can never be fully plumbed through reflection, and which for that reason constantly gives rise to new thinking. Balancing 'without confusion,' there is always 'without separation': philosophy does not start again from zero with every thinking subject in total isolation, but takes its place within the great dialogue of historical wisdom, which it continually accepts and develops in a manner both critical and docile. It must not exclude what religions, and the Christian faith in particular, have received and have given to humanity as signposts for the journey. Various things said by theologians in the course of history, or even adopted in practice by ecclesiastical authorities, have been shown by history to be false, and today make us feel ashamed. Yet at the same time it has to be acknowledged that

What are the most threatening challenges that human society has now to face and what are the directions given by Church social doctrine? This is the last topic that I would like to consider and here the Pope seems to derive from its "treasure" "things new and old." First of all, there are the "great challenges that endanger vast portions of the human family: war and terrorism, hunger and thirst, some terrible epidemics."[22] In numerous occasions the Pope has proposed the position assumed by the church and her social doctrine on each of these topics, formulating "principles of reflections, criteria of judgment and the directives for action."[23] During the early years of his pontificate, Benedict XVI focused his attention not only on the epistemic status of the Church social doctrine, but also on an aspect—capable of reformulating the Church social doctrine—that is probably one of the most original features of his thought.

Since the beginning of his pontificate the Pope has dedicated a consistent part of his studies to analyzing the plurality of cultures and religions, their specific differences, their peculiarities and correlatively their relationship with common human nature—the unity and universality that constitute human beings. Hegemonic culture tends to stress the first aspect, considering the plurality of cultures and the specific difference between each culture as something inevitable. As long as such a way of thinking exercises an undisputed dominion, the strife among civilizations—nowadays at the center of the interest of public opinion—can become a real danger says the Pope. How is it possible to face such a danger? Is there anything capable of "keeping the world united?"[24] Is there anything common to the *proprium* of each culture, which emerges through the differences and particularities of individual human beings or peoples? Is there anything that eventually would enable us to talk about a

---

the history of the saints, the history of the humanism that has grown out of the Christian faith, demonstrates the truth of this faith in its essential nucleus, thereby giving it a claim upon public reason. Of course, much of the content of theology and faith can only be appropriated within the context of faith, and therefore cannot be demanded of those to whom this faith remains inaccessible. Yet at the same time it is true that the message of the Christian faith is never solely a 'comprehensive religious doctrine' in Rawls' sense, but is a purifying force for reason, helping it to be more fully itself. On the basis of its origin, the Christian message should always be an encouragement towards truth, and thus a force against the pressure exerted by power and interests" (Benedict XVI, *Lecture at the University of Rome "La Sapienza"*).

22. Benedict XVI, *Address to the Participants in the Convention.*

23. Card. R. Martino, President of the Pontifical Councils for Justice and Peace and for Migrants and Travelers, *Address on the Laity in Singapore*, 25th June 2006.

24. Cf. Ratzinger, *Ciò che tiene unito il mondo*, 41–57.

common good and which could provide the basis for a real inter-religious and intercultural dialogue?

In his address to the members of the general assembly of the United Nations Organization, Benedict XVI, recalling the *Universal Declaration of Human Rights*, noticed that "this document was the outcome of a convergence of different religious and cultural traditions, all of them motivated by the common desire to place the human person at the heart of institutions, laws and the workings of society, and to consider the human person essential for the world of culture, religion and science." Below he considers that

> it is evident, though, that the rights recognized and expounded in the *Declaration* apply to everyone by virtue of the common origin of the person, who remains the high-point of God's creative design for the world and for history. They are based on the natural law inscribed on human hearts and present in different cultures and civilizations. Removing human rights from this context would mean restricting their range and yielding to a relativistic conception, according to which the meaning and interpretation of rights could vary and their universality would be denied in the name of different cultural, political, social, and even religious outlooks. This great variety of viewpoints must not be allowed to obscure the fact that not only rights are universal, but so too is the human person, the subject of those rights.[25]

## Bibliography

Benedict XVI. *Address to the Members of the General Assembly of the United Nations Organization*, 18th April 2008. Online: http://www.vatican.va/holy_father/benedict_xvi/speeches/2008/april/documents/hf_ben-xvi_spe_20080418_un-visit_en.html.

———. *Address to the Participants at the Ecclesial Convention of the Diocese of Rome*, 5th June 2006. Online: http://www.vatican.va/holy_father/benedict_xvi/speeches/2006/june/documents/hf_ben-xvi_spe_20060605_convegno-diocesano_en.html.

———. *Address to the Participants in the Convention*, Verona, 19th October 2006. Online: http://www.vatican.va/holy_father/benedict_xvi/speeches/2006/october/documents/hf_ben-xvi_spe_20061019_convegno-verona_en.html.

---

25. Benedict XVI, *Address to the Members of the General Assembly of the United Nations Organization*, 18th April 2008.

———. *Apostolic Journey to Austria, Eucharistic Celebration, Homily*, 8th September 2007. Online: http://www.vatican.va/holy_father/benedict_xvi/homilies/2007/documents/hf_ben-xvi_hom_20070908_mariazell_en.html.

———. *Apostolic Journey to Austria, Meeting with the Authorities and the Diplomatic Corps*, 7th September 2007. Online: http://www.vatican.va/holy_father/benedict_xvi/speeches/2007/september/documents/hf_ben-xvi_spe_20070907_hofburg-wien_en.html.

———. *Deus caritas est*. Encyclical letter, 25th December 2005.

———. *Lecture at the University of Rome "La Sapienza,"* 17th January 2008. Online: http://www.vatican.va/holy_father/benedict_xvi/speeches/2008/january/documents/hf_ben-xvi_spe_20080117_la-sapienza_en.html.

———. *Spe salvi*. Encyclical letter, 30th November 2007.

Chenu, Marie-Dominique. *La doctrine sociale de l'Eglise comme idéologie*. Paris: Cerf, 1979.

Colombo, Giuseppe. "Il compito della teologia nella elaborazione dell'insegnamento sociale della Chiesa." In *Aa.-Vv. Il magistero sociale della Chiesa. Principi e nuovi contenuti*, 23–34. Milan: Vita e Pensiero, 1989.

John Paul II. *Sollicitudo rei socialis*. Encyclical letter, 30th December 1987.

Pius XI. *Quadragesimo anno*. Encyclical letter, 15th May 1931.

Ratzinger, Joseph. "Ciò che tiene unito il mondo." In *Etica, religione e Stato liberale*, by J. Ratzinger and J. Habermas, 41–57. Brescia: Morcelliana, 2005.

———. *L'Europa di Benedetto nella crisi delle culture*. Siena: Cantagalli, 2005.

www.ingramcontent.com/pod-product-compliance
Lightning Source LLC
Chambersburg PA
CBHW031357230426
43670CB00006B/573